DESIGN AND MANAGEMENT OF INFORMATION SYSTEMS

DAVID H. LI
University of Washington

SCIENCE RESEARCH ASSOCIATES, INC.
Chicago, Palo Alto
Toronto, Henley-on-Thames, Sydney

A Subsidiary of IBM

Printed in the United States of America.
Library of Congress Catalog Card Number: 72-75327

Sponsoring Editor: Stephen Mitchell
Project Editor: Betty Drury
Designer: Naomi Takigawa

The text of this book was set in 10 point Press
Roman on a Magnetic Tape Selectric® Composer.
The display matter was set in Optima, Theme, and
Universe. Graphic Production of Redwood City,
California handled the composition. Printing and
binding was done by R. R. Donnelley & Sons Co.

PREFACE

Design and Management of Information Systems is intended for a beginning course in Information Systems Analysis and Design. It assumes some background in computer concepts and programming, and also presupposes familiarity with the fundamentals of business administration and accounting.

The underlying theme of this book is that the systems function is an integral part of management. Specifically, in the area of systems planning, the systems function is viewed as working *with* management; in the area of systems design, working *for* management; and in the area of systems management, working *as* management. This theme and its variations are elaborated upon in the three main parts of the text.

The book begins with an authoritative discussion of the field of systems work, followed by a treatise on management as a system and the role of information in the system.

In Part A, Systems Survey and Systems Planning, the work-with-management aspect of the systems function is examined. Chapter II presents a model for manager-analyst teamwork and some tests to determine the relevance of systems work; these are followed by a case study. (Each of the nine chapters in the three main parts ends with a relevant case study.) Documentation and the use of flowcharts and decision tables as communication devices are discussed in Chapter III, while the systems analyst's participation in feasibility studies and systems selection is covered in Chapter IV.

In Part B, Systems Design, the work-for-management aspect of the systems function is discussed. Chapter V treats project-priority determination and the project-management process, emphasizing the criteria relevant to, and the decision interaction with, management. Responsibility reporting and processing controls, which are input/output considerations of interest to management, are presented in Chapter VI, while program development and software make-or-buy alternatives are explored in Chapter VII.

In Part C, Systems Management, the work-as-management aspect of the systems function is covered. Chapter VIII identifies variables for successful systems implementation as well as techniques for effective post-implementation review. Organizational aspects of the systems function, both within and in relation to the entire organization, are discussed in Chapter IX; this is followed by performance standards and cost control of the systems function in Chapter X.

After taking a prospective look at the systems function in the 1970s, the book concludes with an authoritative discussion on systems education.

In all, this book presents twenty-two reading selections and nine case studies. These are culled from twenty-four different sources (of which nineteen are journals) published in four major English-speaking countries: Australia, Canada, the United Kingdom, and the United States. The international flavor of these selections underscores the broad interest in the systems function.

As editor, I wish to compliment each of the authors represented in the book for having made significant contributions to the literature in the systems field. I also take pleasure in acknowledging permission granted me to use materials copyrighted by the following persons and organizations (with names of journals shown in parentheses):

American Institute of Certified Public Accountants (*Journal of Accountancy* and *Management Services*)
American Management Association
Arthur Andersen & Co. (*Arthur Andersen Chronicle*)
Association for Computing Machinery (*Communications of ACM* and *Computing Surveys*)
The Australian Computer Society (*The Australian Computer Journal*)
Berkeley Enterprises, Inc. (*Computers and Automation*)
The British Computer Society (*The Computer Bulletin* and *The Computer Journal*)
Ned Chapin, Esq.
Foundation for the School of Business, Indiana University (*Business Horizons*)
Haskins & Sells
Hayden Publishing Company (*Computer Decisions*)
Institute of Chartered Accountants of England and Wales (*Accountancy*)
Michigan State University, Graduate School of Business Administration (*MSU Business Topics*)
National Association of Accountants (*Management Accounting*)
The National Computing Centre Ltd.
Peat, Marwick, Mitchell & Co. (*Management Controls*)
The President and Fellows of Harvard College (*Harvard Business Review*)
Price Waterhouse & Co. (*Price Waterhouse Review*)
The Society of Industrial Accountants of Canada (*Cost and Management*)
Touche Ross & Co. (*Tempo*)

Finally, it is my sincere hope that this volume, by bringing together some of the best writings in the systems field, provides the reader with a better appreciation of the broad dimension and rich potential of the systems function, as well as with a new awareness that the systems function is an integral part of management.

David H. Li
Seattle, Washington

CONTENTS

I. SYSTEMS CONCEPT AND THE FIELD OF SYSTEMS WORK

This selection provides an overview of the systems function, which has the objective of providing the right amount of the right information to the right control point at the right time. Systems responsibility and systems work are discussed and illustrated in two areas: the control information area and the computer data-processing area.

THE SYSTEMS FIELD—A DISCUSSION | 1
SYSTEMS ANALYSIS / DESIGN WORKING PARTY

INTRODUCTION

A good deal has been written about what Systems Analysis or Systems Design is or is not and several different conclusions have been reached. The work of the Techniques Committee itself was delayed because members' viewpoints differed quite radically. It is useful, therefore, to start from first principles in order to see how differences arose and how they have affected work in the techniques area.

A firm sets out with certain objectives and attempts to either maximize the return or minimize the losses consistent with achieving these. In order for this to be able to happen the management of the firm must

(a) Define the main and secondary objectives and their priorities.

(b) Design or plan an organization structure to achieve the objectives and priorities.

(c) Determine the means to be used to carry out each activity within the organization structure designed.

(d) Set control points wherever decision-making requirements exist, either within the organization structure itself or within individual activities. These are necessary for a number of reasons:

    1. The objectives or priorities may change.
    2. The structure, activities or means may be inherently unstable.
    3. A better structure may become apparent or better means available.

Reprinted with permission from *Systems Analysis Report.* © 1967 The National Computing Centre Limited, Manchester, England.

(e) Determine the quality (in terms of quantity, character and timing) of information necessary for making the requisite decisions at each control point.

(f) Set the minimum requirements in terms of decision-making material (including men) necessary for each decision required at each control point. This will be based on assessment of the availability and cost of decision-making material as opposed to the losses from a failure to achieve objectives which might arise from a wrong or poor quality decision at that point.

(g) Implement the organization.

(h) Monitor and control the organization.

The systems function may be concerned with problems arising out of (d) and (e) above, when it will have the objective of establishing the system whereby the right amount of the right information reaches the right control point at the right time so that information conditions exist which will allow the most effective decision to be made. Alternatively the systems function may concern itself with setting up a part of the organization, a working system, which contributes directly to the organization's main or secondary objectives (for example establishing a means of preparing and dispatching invoices so that cash may be collected, or maintaining employee records).

It must be made clear here that we are talking in the broadest systems sense and that all possible means available to make the system run must be considered. Human power, for example, is one means, general accounting and office machines another, and the computer a third.

THE CONTROL INFORMATION AREA

A control information system is concerned with the methods by which information that is necessary for the co-ordinated achievement of an organization's objectives is made available to all the relevant parts of the organization. The character of the information passing around the system is determined by the decision requirements of the various control points. The information itself may be derived from inside or outside the organization from sources which are likely to be highly dynamic. The system must therefore be able to react to changes in information as well as to changes in organization and objectives.

To achieve the objectives the activities required have been defined and located within an organization structure. Within the structure are sets of control points. Decisions are continually being taken at the control points based on the information available at the time of the decision. Any particular control point may be a man, a group of men or an automatic device.

The quality of information available at a control point at the time of decision is therefore all important and is fundamental to the achievement of the organization's objectives in the most efficient manner.

The procedures to be gone through in arriving at a working control information system are the same as those described in the introduction to this selection pertaining to the setting up of an organization. It is useful, therefore, to examine the procedures in this light although it must be borne in mind that the steps described are not discrete nor are they necessarily performed in the sequence laid down. In practice development will take place through and across the steps in many different sequences. However, every step must be carried out.

It is understood that the resultant system should be such as to achieve its objectives and priorities so as to maximize returns or minimize losses in achieving the objectives of the organization as a whole. Thus economic justification of the system being set up or proposed must be made continually. This will of necessity entail the evaluation of alternative systems and alternative means of working.

It is necessary to

(a) Define the objectives of the control information system and their priorities.

In order to do this it is essential to understand the organization structure within which the system must work and know the quality of information (in terms of quantity, type, timing and location) required at each control point. This necessitates discussion with the management controlling the organization to determine requirements and investigation into the possibility of providing the information specified.

Within an existing organization it is usual to analyze the current system in order to ascertain the information that it provides and to determine where, if at all, the existing systems structure may be retained. This involves fact gathering and sifting, isolating the relevant units of information and determining and evaluating information sources. A useful by-product of this work even if the system structure is retained basically in its existing form is that redundant information can be eliminated and further useful information may be generated.

In theory it is not necessary for the objectives and priorities of the organization to be known. In practice, if these objectives and priorities are not known and understood, then it is not possible to discuss with management meaningfully the usefulness of information or to suggest intelligently additional information, or alternative information where that specified initially is costly or difficult to obtain.

(b) Design or plan a systems structure to achieve the objectives and priorities.

This involves isolating the various information sources (activities) necessary to provide the required quality of information, determining the processing which must be carried out to achieve the desired information and describing the paths which must be followed for this information to arrive, as required, at the relevant control points.

(c) Determine the means to be used to carry out each activity within the system structure designed.

An illustration of the number of means available can be given by listing some of these against the various aspects of an information system.

1. Information collection and conversion—instrument, questionnaire, recording, document reading.
2. Information transmission—telephone, post, document, radio, land line.
3. Information storage—mental, paper, magnetic tape, recording.
4. Information retrieval—manual, machine, scanning, indexing.
5. Information processing—mental, clerical, desk machine, card equipment, computer.
6. Information presentation—visual, audible, signals.

The computer and its array of peripheral and ancillary equipment is obviously a very important means, but any information system is likely to use a combination of many of the above means in its processing and communications activities.

(d) Set control points for each activity within the systems structure.

The control points determined here will be specifically those of the systems structure and may be independent of the control points of the organization structure. The control points themselves may create a secondary system structure by generating further processing of information for their own use and requiring feedback in the communications activities.

(e) Determine the quality of information necessary for making the requisite decisions at each control point.

Strictly this refers to control points within the systems structure only. However, because organization management may not be aware of the possibility and practicability of obtaining the optimum information for control points within the organization structure, some work will generally be necessary in the organization area also.

(f) Set the minimum requirements in terms of decision-making material necessary for each decision required at each control point.

The same situation arises here as in (e). Management may need guidance on the potential of means available to it, other than men, for carrying out decision functions.

(g) Implement the system.

Here the detailed work of implementation of a working system passes into another function—perhaps organization and methods, perhaps electronic data processing. At all the stages of work in establishing a control information system close co-ordination must be maintained with the various means sections available to carry out the system. In this way the right means for each activity should have been chosen and changes required by the inability of a selected means to carry out its activity in the manner required will be minimized.

During implementation close control must be maintained to ensure that the working system set up is actually that required.

(h) Monitor and control the system.

The control points set within the system structure should be such as to enable it to be controlled to its required purpose. However, organizations change and a continual monitoring must be carried out to see that the system meets current organization requirements. If changes in the system structure or information in it are necessary then control must be applied to ensure that these changes are carried out.

THE COMPUTER DATA PROCESSING AREA

This area covers the development and establishment of the computer and associated peripheral activities within an organization so as to achieve certain of the organization's main and secondary objectives. The objectives may be the production of pay tickets, invoices, data for an overlying control information system and so on.

In contrast to the control information area a great deal of experience has been gained of computer data processing on many varied applications and it is possible therefore to describe this area in terms of the work that has to be carried out. However, because of the very many individual developments that are taking place, the part of the area defined as a systems responsibility varies widely from place to place. The members of the committee themselves represented a number of views on this matter and the following description is an attempt to describe work steps which must be taken rather than an agreed account of systems responsibilities in the computer data processing area.

A chart is given on the following page showing a breakdown of tasks to be carried out and relationships between the systems man and other parts of both the computer data processing area and the organization which must be established as the tasks are carried out.

For the purpose of this discussion the tasks are shown as being sequential but, in practice, cycling will take place and documentation (which is not specifically shown) will run through all tasks.

The tasks to be carried out are then

(a) Feasibility

Requests for a study to determine the feasibility of using a computer to achieve certain of the organization's objectives usually derive from other activities (including the control information area). Alternatively possible

DATA PROCESSING SYSTEMS DEVELOPMENT

NOTES: 1 The chart shows the involvement of various functions within an organization in the stages of systems development.

2 The time axis only indicates sequence in time and does not reflect actual time taken.

Key:
- Action / Objectives / Definition
- Evaluation & approval
- Partial participation

TIME / INVOLVEMENT	FEASIBILITY	SYSTEM DESIGN	PROCEDURE DETAIL	IMPLEMENTATION	MAINTENANCE AND DEVELOPMENT
SENIOR MANAGEMENT	Feasibility		Agreement		
DATA PROCESSING MANAGEMENT	Feasibility / Job assignment				Live running
USER	Feasibility / Job assignment	Investigation / Outline system	Detail system / Agreement	Change over plan / Systems Testing / Implementation / Parallel runs	
SYSTEMS ANALYSIS	Feasibility / Job assignment	Investigation / Outline system	Present / Detail system	Change over plan / Systems testing / Implementation / Parallel runs	System monitor / Live running
PROGRAMMING			Agreement	Programming / Systems testing / Parallel runs	Live running
OPERATIONS			Agreement	Change over plan / Trials / Systems testing / Implementation / Parallel runs	Live running

applications may be suggested to potential user departments by the computer data processing activity itself.

The feasibility study will cover economic and technical factors of the use of computers and will result in a recommendation to management of the relevant user department to carry on or not into more detailed work. The study may be concerned with one application on an existing installation or may be to determine whether to buy equipment or not and be based on several applications.

If the decision is to go ahead with an application then economic and technical feasibility should be under review at all stages of detailed development.

(b) Job assignment

This will be a matter determined between the computer data processing and user departments and amongst other things defined will be

1. Departments and procedures concerned
2. Scope and limitations of the project
3. Broad specifications of the resources to be used
4. Lines of communication (especially detailing responsibilities within the user departments, to provide information and assistance to the computer department)
5. Target dates for completion of the various stages at work

(c) Investigation

Investigation involves collecting all facts within the departments concerned, by seeing the system in operation and by interviewing its operating staff. These facts are then organized into a recognizable framework as a basis for future development.

An understanding of the existing system may be an essential first step in the investigation together with an appreciation of the effect and value of possible systems changes.

From the investigation phase a complete picture of the job and its requirements should be obtained, along with sufficient understanding to suggest improvements.

(d) Outline system

The outline systems stage, which should to a large extent overlap investigation, will produce a precise specification of the results the system must obtain. From this it is possible to specify inputs to the system (which either exists already or must be created) and the records to be maintained within the system.

The outline system must, of necessity, be documented to a standard format.

(e) Agreement

The systems function includes responsibility for ensuring the agreement of users, the data processing manager and the programming/operating team; ensuring, in other words, that all proposals are complete and technically sound from all viewpoints. The point at which the outline system is agreed is a major landmark towards complete implementation. It is therefore vital that this agreement arises from genuine involvement.

(f) Detail system

The completed detail system provides all the information required by the various departments and the programming section including

1. Clerical procedures
2. Changeover procedures
3. Documentation specifications
4. Data preparation and ancillary equipment detail and procedures
5. Input, output and file layouts
6. Processing requirements both on and off the machine
7. Coding systems, etc.

From this it will be seen that a comprehensive definition for programming may be presented and calculations of machine utilization figures made.

(g) Presentation

Completion of the systems function for a particular application is recognized by the acceptance and formal agreement of the complete systems specification. The prime responsibility for translating the specification into working computer programs now passes to the programming section. The importance of formal agreement of the system at this point cannot be over-stressed because alterations after programming has started are likely to prove very costly.

(h) Changeover plan

During completion of the systems specification phase a plan for a changeover is drawn up and then expanded into detail as described in the following sections.

(i) Systems testing

This entails validation of the complete system, including

1. Document origin and flow
2. Data preparation procedures
3. Data validation procedures
4. Internal and external communications
5. Ancillary equipment operation
6. Computer programs and procedures
7. Timing
8. Control and audit

The systems function must plan all such testing and lay down criteria by which the effectiveness of the new system may be judged.

(j) Implementation

The task in this area includes the compilation of any changeover manuals and recommendations on the training of staff. In parallel with this is the compilation of the new system's procedures manuals and operating instructions, for staff within both the computer department and other departments involved with the system.

Deliveries of new equipment, stationery, etc., required before the new system can be implemented, must be arranged. Wherever possible, new stationery should be introduced within the old system, prior to creation of or conversion to new files. Formal notices warning the company, its customers, and its suppliers of the commencement of the new system have to be circulated. Arrangements must be made for the redeployment of staff affected by the change and for the disposal of obsolete equipment.

(k) Parallel running

An exhaustive test of the system can, in practice, be achieved only by running live data within the planned processing time scale. Some computer running should be undertaken under very close control as the final stage in system implementation and testing.

The actual changeover may be made either in phases (running in parallel with a limited quantity of data) or by direct conversion from the old to the new system. It is the responsibility of the systems function to make recommendations on and, after their acceptance, implement and control this stage of operations.

(l) System monitoring

The final responsibility once the system is operational is to check that it is working as expected and to the greatest possible advantage. Volumes, timing and procedures have to be checked, error rates carefully monitored and any significant divergence from estimated volumes investigated. All output should be checked against requirements.

Should examination of the system prove that the full benefits originally specified have been achieved, day-to-day running of the new system may now become the responsibility of the operations section of the computer department. Any major amendments undertaken from this point onwards must be considered as new and separate projects.

This article provides an overview of the systems concept by first viewing the management process as a system with three major components: a strategic decision-making subsystem, a management control cycle, and an operating subsystem. The author then discusses the integration of these components, and the data-processing and information-provision functions, into a management system

2 | THE MANAGEMENT SYSTEM VIEWED IN PERSPECTIVE
LARRY N. KILLOUGH

Over the years many notions have been advanced regarding the management process, management system, and related planning, control and information components. To be most useful, this material should be visualized within an integrated framework emphasizing the various necessary relationships. It would appear that with such a structure in mind specific components could then be examined and conclusions drawn while maintaining consistency with other necessary elements.

The purpose of this paper is to provide an operational framework by examining, and pulling together, the integrative aspects of the management system, logical relationships of the framework, and finally the inter-dependency of planning, operations, data-processing, information and control components within the basic management system.

THE MANAGEMENT PROCESS

Management's unique contribution consists of the formulation of goals, and the gathering and control of their means of accomplishment. This includes modification of goals, where necessary in light of an increased awareness, to utilize most effectively and efficiently an entity's resources. In providing such a contribution, management personnel must be engaged in various functions and indeed must be operative at various levels within the organization. It is recognized that all managers participate in planning and control, that there are various levels of management, and that some management personnel are largely restricted to functional areas.

The problem then becomes one of developing a framework that gives recognition to the different management levels, to their sequential and non-sequential aspects, and finally to the traditional functional segments. Systems analysis is now utilized to view the firm in terms of some input, processor, and output for purposes of help in discerning a meaningful management structure.

Reprinted from *Cost and Management* (Canada), May–June 1971, pp. 23–27, by permission of the publisher, The Society of Industrial Accountants of Canada. Larry N. Killough is an Assistant Professor of Accounting at Virginia Polytechnic Institute.

CORPORATE SYSTEM

Conceptually a corporate system can be broken down into successively small components until all relevant parts are revealed. In this manner, and allowing for the degree of ignorance that must prevail at any given time, something approaching complete knowledge about the system should then be available.

Basic Components. The corporate system might initially be viewed somewhat as shown in Exhibit 1. Next, recognizing that a corporation must rely on objectives, plans, controls and operations (on a non-continuous basis and either formally or informally), an initial decomposition of the above structure might take the form reflected in Exhibit 2.

Three major sub-components result from this initial separation of the corporate structure: (1) a strategic decision-making system, (2) management control cycle, and (3) operating system.[1]

Strategic Planning. The schematic representation indicates that through strategic decisions, objectives for the corporation are formulated and indeed these basic objectives are altered only through the strategic decision making process.

In this hierarchical structure, strategic planning is assumed to involve only a few top level management personnel who are entrusted with the responsibility for considering significant alternatives as they may arise. Planning of this nature is not considered to be formally structured in terms of either goals or time periods, but is simply intended to provide a basis for all other activities of the

Exhibit 1
Corporate system

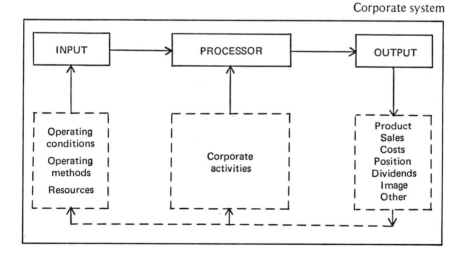

1. For an extensive discussion and justification for the individual components see Robert N. Anthony, *Planning and Control Systems: A Framework for Analysis* (Boston: Harvard University, 1965), pp. 1–93.

Exhibit 2
Decomposition of the corporate system

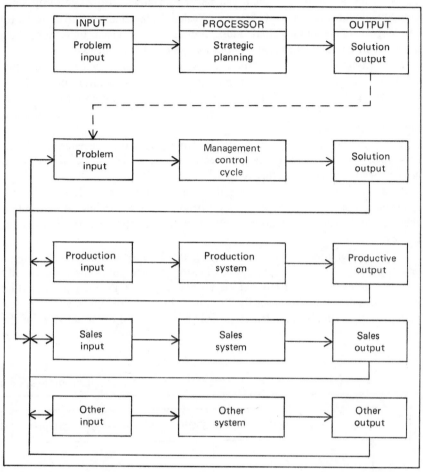

enterprise. Accordingly, strategic planning is considered non-continuous and is concerned only with problems that would tend to change the basic nature of the entity's objectives.

Management Control. By means of the management control cycle, the enterprise is guided to predetermined objectives established by management in the strategic planning process.

The estimates used in strategic planning are intended to show the expected results of the plan. They are neutral and impersonal. By contrast, the management control process, and the data used in it, are intended to influence managers to take actions that will lead to desired results.

In contrasting management control with strategic planning, it should be pointed out that the two overlap only in that strategic planning provides basic guidelines and directional dimensions for the continuous planning that takes place in the management control cycle. This latter planning, largely administrative rather than creative, then provides a basis for implementation of control within all ongoing activities of the enterprise.

Operating Control.   Operating control provides the mechanism to see that individual jobs are carried out within the framework of previously defined criteria. Moreover, just as management control operates within confines dictated by strategic planning, operating control utilizes further refinements of those same guidelines to establish control over individual activities. The major distinction to be made between management and operating control is that: (1) management control focuses on individuals, whereas operating control concentrates on tasks, and (2) these tasks are so well defined that little judgment should be required, while management control is likely to be predicated in large part on the judgmental factor.

LOGICAL RELATIONSHIPS OF FRAMEWORK

Exhibit 3 presents the various assumptions used regarding general flow of planning and control within the entity. The management system set, (A + B + C), is believed to be representative of earlier discussions in the paper. The information processing system set, (D), provides a conceptual means for

Exhibit 3
Major planning and control sets in the management system

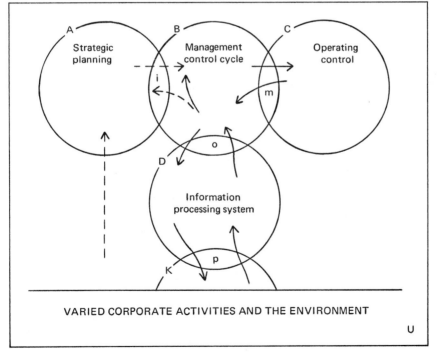

integrating management planning and control with overall corporate activities, represented by (K).

Directional arrows indicate the general flow of planning, control and integrative information. Broken lines are suggestive of a non-continuous flow as opposed to the continuous flow represented by solid lines. The framework is nevertheless deficient in failing to provide insight into the nature of the interaction of planning, operations, data-processing, information and control components within the basic management system. To provide this insight into the operational nature of the framework, these aspects are next considered.

INTERDEPENDENCY OF FLOWS WITHIN THE MANAGEMENT SYSTEM

Exhibit 4 outlines the other essential functions and the nature of their interdependency in providing an operational management system. The cycle begins with some process within the operating system—firm or component thereof—generating activities which result in data along with a need for their

Exhibit 4
Structural interdependency of management system

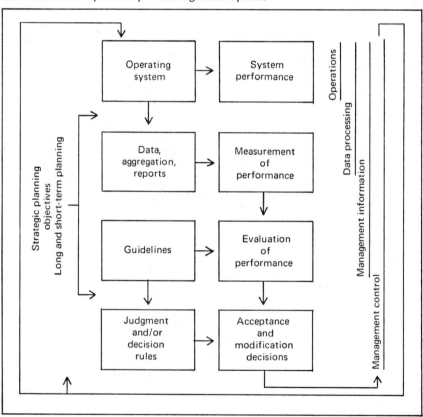

subsequent accumulation and aggregation for purposes of providing performance measurement. The essential nature of both operating and data processing sub-systems is identified in this flow of activities and data.

In deriving structurally consistent criteria from initial and continuous planning, a useful means of evaluating performance was provided—comparison of actual performance against the criteria. Thus, the two above-mentioned sub-systems are then combined with an additional component, criteria and performance evaluation, to provide a basis for the firm's management information framework.

Finally, assuming that provision is made within the firm to act upon information supplied to management, either by means of judgment or resort to decision rules, a final link in the management system has been provided—that of control. Thus, the schematic of Exhibit 4 reflects measurement, evaluation, decisions and feedback as minimum essentials to an effective and efficient management framework consisting of strategic planning, management control and operating control.

SUMMARY AND CONCLUSIONS

Three major sets were discernible in an analysis of the corporate structure: (1) an initial planning system, (2) management control cycle, and (3) operating control. Through strategic planning, objectives for the corporation were believed to be formulated. By means of the management control cycle, the enterprise was guided to those predetermined objectives. Finally, plans subsequently formalized in the management control cycle were viewed as being carried out by individual segment control through the derivation of guidelines and application of objective decisions to specific activities.

As a last item, insight was provided into the nature of the interaction of planning, operations, data-processing, information and control components within the basic management framework. In this regard planning, measurement, evaluation, decision-making, and feedback were reflected as minimum process essentials to an operational management system.

PART A

SYSTEMS SURVEY
AND SYSTEMS PLANNING

After discussing the integration of the systems concept with systems work, this article stresses the need for cooperation between the manager and the systems analyst when designing information systems. This cooperation is then illustrated at several different levels.

MANAGER-ANALYST TEAMWORK IN MIS | 3

WILLIAM R. KING and DAVID I. CLELAND

Modern management information systems are supposed to help the manager make better decisions. Few, however, are true *management* systems; they have been shaped by improvements in existing data processing functions, and do not significantly increase the decision-making effectiveness of managers. The 20/20 hindsight which we all possess in abundance reveals that this is the natural result of leaving information systems design to technicians. The manager has abdicated control over the design and implementation of the organizational MIS because systems design and the intricacies of such technicalities as data files are beyond his expertise. He has charged the computer specialists with these tasks, and the results are clear. Most of these systems are not truly helpful in decision making.

Computer systems analysts generally are unaware of the myriad complexities of management decisions. They cannot know all the subjectivities and intangibles. Therefore, the systems they design do not account for subtleties, and are often no more helpful to the manager than the stacks of hand-produced reports he previously had at hand. The speed with which computerized systems make data available is useful, but systems clearly have not made for a revolution in management as many thought they would.

Information systems circles are not unaware of this situation. A McKinsey and Company report reveals that "...many otherwise effective top managements are in trouble with their computer efforts because they have abdicated control to staff specialists." A recent survey "...indicates that technicians, not management, are setting goals for the computers."[1]

From *Business Horizons*, April, 1971, pp. 59–68; used by permission. William R. King is a Professor and David I. Cleland is an Associate Professor at the University of Pittsburgh.

1. John Diebold, "Bad Decisions on Computer Use," *Harvard Business Review*, January–February 1969.

The solution to the dilemma is clear. Since neither the manager nor the analyst alone can design and implement a true management information system, they must work cooperatively. Each must make his own unique contribution, and anything short of complete cooperation will probably result in a systems design that is either ineffective or inefficient.

THE VEHICLE FOR INTERACTION

If the manager-analyst cooperative effort in MIS design is such an obvious necessity, why has it not occurred naturally? Part of the reason lies in the failure to adopt a vehicle for cooperation. Managers and analysts think in different terms, and attempts at sustained cooperation usually conclude with each returning to familiar ground to independently attack his pressing problems. Thus, the analyst ends up designing the MIS, since that is his primary charge, and the manager largely ignores its development, since his primary job is decision making.

But a vehicle for cooperative manager-analyst MIS design does exist. It is the decision model, which has been used for some time by management scientists and operations researchers.

The objective of this article is to outline a process of manager-analyst interaction. This process concerns cooperation in the explication of models for decision problems and decision areas. If the manager and analyst work together to develop models in the manner to be described and if they ask the right questions, management effectiveness will be improved through MIS, which is the product of the design process, and the increased understanding and learning which comes from the process itself.

THE ROLES OF MODELS IN MIS DESIGN:
MANAGER-MACHINE SYSTEM INTERFACES

Two extreme positions on the role of models in an MIS will define the problems involved. First, the data processing expert says that models, aside from simple model accounting procedures, have a minor role or none at all in an MIS. Their role is in using MIS-generated information to analyze decisions. He might argue that most complex strategic decisions cannot be solved with formal mathematical models; rather, they must be dealt with on the basis of the judgment, experience, and intuition of an informed manager. The providing of information to the manager is the task of the MIS.

The other extreme is the position of the management scientist, who holds that mathematical models are an intrinsic part of any modern MIS. He argues that all decisions cannot be left to managers, since decisions which involve many alternatives and in which the objective is rather clear can be more efficiently solved by a computerized model. For example, the manager of an oil refinery would find it impossible to consider each of the myriad of alternative production plans without the aid of linear programming models.

The resolution of these extreme positions is simple. If one accepts the premise of a decision-oriented MIS, both of these positions are correct! *A modern sophisticated MIS should allow for all varieties of model utilization from the most formal to the most subjective and informal.* The simple MIS flow diagram of Exhibit 1 describes this. A data source provides information to a data base, a storehouse of data. The data are then used in predictive models and optimization models before action is taken. Predictive models are used to predict future events; optimization models evaluate and select a best course of action on the basis of predictions. Thus, a formal predictive model might result in sales forecasts, while a linear programming refinery model which produces the best production plan is an optimization model.

Many of the problems with MIS design and operations rest on communications difficulties concerning the man-machine system interface in the information-decision process. To illustrate, consider some of the possible interfaces as described by the numbered locations in the exhibit. In the case of each possible interface, the machine system is presumed to occupy those activities to the left of the interface, and the manager is presumed to deal with those to the right. For instance, if the man-machine system interface of a particular MIS is at the point labeled 1, the MIS is simply an information collection system; all of the data and all of the models used in the decision process, if any, are "stored" in the mind of the manager.

At the interface designated as 2, the data base is a part of the machine system, but all of the real decision-making mechanisms are handled by the manager; he is simply provided with reports which summarize and aggregate data. In situation 3, the manager also is provided with the output of predictive models, such as sales forecasts and forecasts of GNP. In situation 4, the manager is provided with the recommended courses of action as determined by

Exhibit 1
Information-decision process

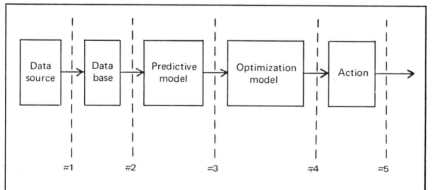

SOURCE: Adapted from Richard O. Mason, Jr., "Basic Concepts for Designing Management Information Systems," AIS Research Paper No. 8, Graduate School of Administration, UCLA, October, 1969.

optimization models. He might, for instance, be provided with the new product opportunity which is selected as best according to some criterion from among a set of available opportunities. He could then evaluate this recommendation in the light of his knowledge of the model and of those things which the model omits. In the last situation, 5, we have automated decision making, since the machine system even goes so far as to perform the action.

There are two important aspects of the various interfaces in Exhibit 1. First, one should recognize that it is common practice to use the term "management information system" to describe systems which have their sole or major interface at 2, 3, 4, and sometimes even 5. (Seldom does anyone use the term to describe situation 1.) Thus, two people may find themselves agreeing on MIS procedures, only to find that they are each using different MIS definitions, depending on their own concept of the interface.

The second important aspect is that any modern information system should include all of these interfaces. It should allow for the collection of information for unique, high-level, subjective decisions such as those involving the identification of who will be the "real" governmental decision maker for a weapons system contract. In such a case, the manager would be provided with basic information insofar as possible, but the decision would revolve about his contact, experience, and knowledge of governmental organizations and operations.

At the other extreme, a modern MIS should include a capability for automated routine decision making. For instance, a computerized model for monitoring stock levels and placing orders where stock levels have reached prescribed levels is operational in many companies.

DETERMINATION OF NECESSARY INFORMATION

The most critical question involved in designing a management information system is the determination of what information is necessary to enable the manager to effectively make decisions. The requirements cannot efficiently be identified by concentrating on the information which is available in the organization, since much of it is superfluous and redundant. Much information needed for good decision making is unavailable.

While this may seem incongruous at first, it becomes more believable when one recognizes that most of the models actually used for decision making in an organization are implicit rather than explicit. Most large organizations have formalized and computerized models for operational control: inventory reports, production schedules, cost analyses, and the like are prepared using simple formalized models. However, the way in which these simple models and data are synthesized in the important decision-making models of the organization are usually imprecisely defined. Most of these strategic models are buried in the minds of the managers who make these high-level decisions.

The effective use of models in MIS design revolves about a manager-analyst interactive process which has a goal of model explication or verbalization. If the manager's mental models can at least be verbalized, they can be used in the MIS design process to define information requirements. They need not be reduced to mathematical form, or even made completely explicit to be used in this way, so long as they can be communicated.

Four primary features of models permit them to be used to define information requirements: the model's predictive variables, its criterion, its solution, and the sensitivity information associated with the solution. We will consider each of these aspects using an illustrative situation which also demonstrates some of the operational aspects of the manager-analyst interactive process.

Predictive Variables. To understand how a model's predictor variables prescribe some of the information requirements, one must recognize that every problem situation may be described in terms of various models. Every manager would probably develop a slightly different model to describe a given problem. Successful managers in similar situations probably have models that have a great deal in common, but since the model is an abstraction which describes the salient properties of a problem situation, it is clear that value judgments determine the most appropriate model.

A hypothetical manager-analyst discussion is related to the various models that might be applied to the problem of selecting market areas for expansion of the sales territory for a product. The analyst might begin by asking the manager how he values a potential area in terms of his past experience with the product, similar products, and similar marketing situations. Suppose the manager responds by saying that, because of market survey results and the product's price, he knows that the product appeals to the affluent. Therefore, he says, "We should try to sell it in the most affluent markets where it will obviously do best." The analyst concludes that perhaps expansion markets could be selected on the basis of the mean annual income of the market population or on some buying power index.

Then the manager says, "Well, it isn't quite that simple, since the competition which we face in an area is important too. We feel that it's more difficult to enter an area in which a number of competitors are already entrenched than it is to enter an area where only a few competitors are selling their products."

"Perhaps," thinks the analyst, "we can quantitatively assess this factor by simply using the number of competitors in the market or the market share of the largest competitor." While he is thinking, the manager says, "We have another problem. Whenever we've gone into an area like San Antonio, which has a large foreign-born or non-English-speaking population, we've had difficulties. We think it is because they are just more conservative, don't generally react as well to new products, and are difficult to communicate with through advertising."

In this dialogue, we see that a number of different models have been suggested through manager-analyst interaction. The process would probably go on for some time, but we can view these three alternative models as described in Exhibit 2. The first is a simple one in which product success could be predicted by the market population's affluence. The analyst complemented this with a possible quantitative measure of the predictor variable—median annual income.

Exhibit 2
The criterion for product success in three models

Model	Predictor	Measurement
1	Population affluence	Median annual income
2	Population affluence	Median annual income
	Competition	Number of competitors *or* market share of largest competitor
3	Population affluence	Median annual income
	Competition	Number of competitors *or* market share of largest competitor
	Population background or language capability	Percent foreign-born / Percent English-speaking

In the second model, the manager includes competition as a predictor, and the analyst suggests ways in which this factor might be measured. The third model also includes either population background or language capability, or both.

The manager could have gone on to suggest other more comprehensive models and, as is usually the case, he probably would have gone so far that the model finally selected as best would not have been the one which was most comprehensive. Usually, in such a process, factors will be considered and then dropped as not sufficiently significant to warrant inclusion. The analyst in the hypothetical dialogue was performing two of his essential functions: interacting with the manager in order to help him enumerate the salient factors, and trying to suggest quantifiable measures of the factors.

Hence, one of the basic ways in which a model prescribes information requirements is in terms of the specification of the predictors and the measures which will be used to assess them. If the model described as 2 in Exhibit 2 is finally selected to describe the decision problem, the predictor variables prescribe that the information system must produce information on mean annual incomes, market shares, and the number of competitors in each market.

The Model's Criterion. Another important aspect of the model—the criterion—also prescribes information. In the three models of Exhibit 2, the implicit criterion involves the choice of markets to maximize product success. Of course, this aspect must also be operationalized; it might, for instance, be measured in terms of sales revenue. Thus, the criterion would be to choose those markets which are expected to produce the greatest sales. Alternatives are the market share measure or some measure which balances revenues with the significant costs of selling, say sales revenue dollars per promotional dollar. The criterion in these latter cases would be to choose as expansion markets those which can be expected to produce the greatest market share or the largest ratio of sales revenues to promotional expenses.

In each instance, the manager is considering various quantities to serve as a basis for his decision. He and the analyst jointly determine if a particular quantity is useful and can be measured and predicted. In doing so, they generate alternative models through a process of considering various criteria.

The Model's Solution.   If an optimization model is developed for a decision process, its solution may prescribe important information requirements, or it may constrain those already developed using the predictor variables and the criterion. For instance, the solution may be in the form of a simple rule, which specifies that a potential area is to be considered more like past good areas than like past bad areas if a quantity which is to be calculated from the potential area's characteristics (income, number of competitors, and so on) is numerically greater than a prescribed cost ratio.

Sensitivity Information.   Models prescribe information requirements in a fourth way—in terms of sensitivity information. This information simply tells the manager how sensitive the solution is to changes in various input quantities. For example, if the mean annual income in an area is expected to increase by $100 next year, how would the solution to the model change? Or if our estimate of the number of competitors in an area is inaccurate, how does this change the answer that the model has given us? Such information is a natural by-product of analytic models. As such, it is a new variety of information for the manager to use and should be formally incorporated into the MIS.

IMPLICATIONS OF MODEL-BASED MIS DESIGN

The model-based MIS design process does not increase the importance of models in decision making; models are used by all of us in each decision that we make. The process does, of course, increase the importance of explicating and verbalizing the mental models that managers use. The manager and analyst work together to verbalize the manager's model so that it can be used as a basis for prescribing MIS information requirements.

Another important implication has to do with the concept of evaluating information, which has been much discussed but rarely implemented by computer analysts. This concept becomes less significant, since the real problem is one of evaluating alternative models. In effect, this design process evaluates alternative models in terms of their accuracy, utility, and the cost of developing and maintaining them. Once this has been done, the best model prescribes the required information through its predictor variables, criterion, solution, and sensitivity information. Thus, the need for an explicit cost-value analysis of individual elements of information (a process which has proved to be more difficult than analysts imagined it to be) is avoided.

More important, perhaps, is the effect of new information, such as that contained in the solution and its associated sensitivity information, on the management decision-making process. Such information enables the manager to question both the usefulness of the model and the need for additional or different information. For instance, a manager who finds that the action tentatively chosen is very sensitive to the accuracy of a particular piece of information may well decide that it is better to allow time to make a more accurate assessment of the element of information. He is thereby led to question the model and his own decision process in a way that would not otherwise be possible.

A MODEL FOR MANAGER-ANALYST MIS DESIGN

The concept of manager-analyst cooperative MIS design is not new. However, if this cooperation is to be raised above the level of maintained contact or infrequent interaction, the concept must be operationalized. This may be done by defining the process more precisely and by assigning responsibilities for the various phases of the model-based MIS design process.

Exhibit 3 is a model of an MIS design process which attempts to provide a basis for manager-analyst shared and interrelated responsibilities. In the exhibit, each activity is designated as "M," "A," or "M, A" to indicate that the particular task is the prime responsibility of the manager or the analyst, or is to be shared. In the upper left, the manager and analyst work together to verbalize the model in much the way described in the market selection illustration. Then the analyst is given the task of finding measures for the factors which have been enunciated. The entire process is a series of feed-back loops, since the analyst must return to the manager for review and evaluation of his work at the completion of each of the three tasks assigned primarily to him. In each loop, the manager and analyst also jointly consider revision of previous steps.

If the two agree on the model's general form and the measures to be used, the analyst tries to construct explicit predictive or optimization models which can be used in the situation. Of course, in many instances it is impossible to develop adequate models of this nature; if so, the process simply continues on to the right.

Once some model—informal, predictive, or optimization—is agreed upon, the manager decides and takes some action. The analyst is then given an opportunity

Exhibit 3
Manager-analyst MIS design process

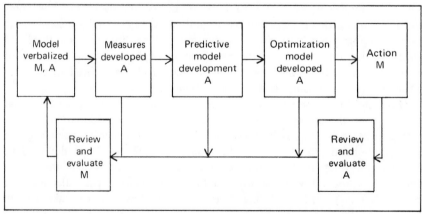

to review and evaluate the results. Together, they then determine whether a complete rerun of the process is necessary.

The model that is finally developed determines the information requirements for this particular decision problem or area in the organization through its predictive variables, criterion, solution, and sensitivity information. The analyst then goes on to another area or problem, and the manager is left to manage the area; hopefully, he has both a better understanding of his problem and adequate information to solve it.

SUMMARY

The process of creating the MIS is as important as the end product. The model-based MIS design process is one that emphasizes both the design process and the product; too many other approaches to design focus almost exclusively on the end product. The model-based process is most likely to provide the manager with the right information on an economic basis. Also, it virtually ensures that he will come to a better understanding of his job and the decisions which it entails. If the model-based design leads solely to better decisions through better understanding, rather than through better information, it more than justifies itself.

This article considers the information system as a series of operating elements that support different ongoing processes of the business. Attention is then directed to nine questions, the answers to which are important to management in running a business; five tests are included to determine the relevance of systems under development.

4 | A MANAGER'S PERSPECTIVE OF MANAGEMENT INFORMATION SYSTEMS

WARD A. FREDERICKS

A plethora of seminars, speeches, articles, and scholarly books extolling the virtues of MIS (management information systems) has descended upon the business community. On-line, real-time, data base, and teleprocessing have become part of the "compleat" manager's vocabulary, albeit with less understanding of meaning than usual. In fact, management has accepted the reality of the concept of MIS with open arms, trusting that the types of key decisions which have to be made daily will somehow become easier when the promised data appear in precisely organized formats.

Major companies have mounted massive efforts aimed at designing MIS with results ranging from disaster to partial success. It is still appropriate to say that well-designed and operating MIS are much easier to find in the pages of technical and management journals than in real life.

In order to look at the concept and the application of MIS, an appropriate starting point is to look at management and its most fundamental actions and processes to see what role systems can play in aiding managers in the attainment of their objectives.

The term top management as used in this article will cover those members of management whose perspective must include the operation of the entire company—typically the president and executive vice-president in centralized companies, and division general managers in decentralized companies.

Textbooks list planning, controlling, organizing, and so on, as the major functions of management. In an ongoing business enterprise, however, top management makes key decisions relating to certain aspects of the business which determine the size, character, and long-term viability of the organization. These decisions are made in every company, regardless of size, and represent the most difficult part of the management process. They set the tone for the entire enterprise. To simplify the perspective in these key decisions and actions, a five-way categorization would be: (1) decisions and actions which affect pricing, (2) decisions and actions which affect volume, (3) decisions and actions which

From *MSU Business Topics*, Spring 1971, pp. 7–12. Reprinted with permission of the publisher, Division of Research, Graduate School of Business Administration, Michigan State University. Ward A. Fredericks is Vice-President of Management Services, Massey-Ferguson, Inc.

affect overhead or structural cost, (4) decisions and actions which affect product (or service) cost, and (5) decisions and actions which affect asset turnover.

In every business enterprise it is the interaction of the decisions made in each of the above categories which determines the viability and profitability of the organization. Any MIS effort, then, should address, both in cause and effect terms, the impact of having systems which can influence the outcome of these various decisions and actions.

PROFITABILITY: A COMPLEX RESULT

In order to put proper emphasis upon the complex interaction of the five main areas for management action just listed, let us investigate the "anatomy of a profit." Profit is certainly one of the major objectives of business enterprise, although not the only objective in today's complex society. Continued existence of the enterprise is dependent upon the generation of acceptable profit, however, and therefore management thrust must be directed toward this result.

Management action aimed at producing profit in an ongoing business enterprise may be looked at in terms of the four parts to the profit equation below:

1. $(P \times V) - PC - SC = PROFIT$

2. $\dfrac{Profit}{Assets} = $ Return on Investment

Simply stated, price times volume equals gross revenue for the enterprise, from which is subtracted product cost and structural cost (or overhead). Profit-oriented management action must be aimed at impacting one or more of the variables in the equation to have a favorable effect on the result. Return on investment of the enterprise is a function of profit, certainly, but turnover of assets involved in the business plays a major role in determining the resultant rate of return.

It is prudent to begin an analysis with simple truths in order to follow the flow of logic to the desired end. In terms of the actions of management and the impact of various kinds of decisions on profitability and return on assets employed, the "truths" exposed above are certainly simple and both mathematically and judgmentally provable to the most practical manager.

Where does the impact of various elements of the MIS come into the picture? Basically, operating systems in any company form the basis for the information system, and these operating systems impact the profit equation by their very existence.

SYSTEMS IMPACT ON THE PROCESS OF THE BUSINESS

Perhaps the easiest way to visualize the inter-relationships between the business, operating data processing systems, and the overall MIS is to visualize the total enterprise as being made up of intertwined key processes. Then it can be seen that the planning, control, and administration of these key processes constitutes the overall management of the company.

The major interacting processes which together make up the entity called the company include:

1. The financial analysis and control process.
2. The market research—product definition—product interduction process.
3. The sales planning—forecasting—and monitoring process.
4. The purchasing—provisioning—manufacturing—and finished product distribution process.

Each one of the four processes needs to be managed at strategic, tactical, and operational levels. In order to properly manage each process, an information system must exist which provides data to the manager which is a symbolic representation of the process itself. The information system needs to provide the planning, control, and administrative data necessary to constantly evaluate and take appropriate action upon the process to bring it under control. Therefore, in each area or department of the business, management must go through a disciplined thought process in order to: (1) define the process (or processes) for which the function is responsible; (2) define the information necessary to plan, control, and administer the process; (3) design the operating and/or information systems which will provide operational assistance and reports necessary to plan, control, and administer the process; (4) determine the level of cost which the present and proposed techniques will require to carry out the process; and (5) determine what changes in the method or technique of handling the process are required to minimize costs or allow for greater volume at minimum expenditure.

Let us take the process of acquiring raw materials, transforming them into finished product, and distributing the product, as an example. Let us examine it at operational, tactical, and strategic levels, and then look at the implications. Exhibit 1 summarizes the aspects of the process.

It is evident that in the development and implementation of information systems in a company, when we view the problem as one supporting the planning, control, and administrative functions of a major process, we must define the operational, tactical, and strategic requirements and considerations which permit management of that process on a continuous basis under constantly changing circumstances.

Conversely, when we are looking at the strategic, tactical, and operational management needs of the corporation, we have to take into consideration and formalize the planning, control, and administrative systems necessary to manage the major processes.

It is obvious that with this approach we are no longer talking about the MIS, as if it were some mythical beast like the unicorn; we are talking about an interlocking, coordinated set of management systems designed to optimize the planning, control, and administration of specific processes operationally, tactically, and strategically. Modularity is essential in our approaches to management concepts and to system design.

Exhibit 1

Aspects of the business logistics process

Functions	Operational Level	Tactical Level	Strategic Level
Planning	a) Plan the receiving and progress chasing schedule for next day's schedule of material deliveries. b) Plan releases on suppliers to be processed next day. c) Plan machine shop schedule for next day. d) Plan next day's assembly schedule. e) Plan inspection, packing, and shipping schedule for next day. f) Plan minimum/maximum in-process inventories (short lead items).	a) Forecast of sales in detail of each specific product within lead time of material acquisition. b) Translation into future build program. c) Determination of sourcing pattern. d) Planning of inventory levels of raw material, work in process, and finished goods. e) Planning of purchasing quantities and orders on suppliers. f) Planning and scheduling of utilization of existing facilities and available labor. g) Planning of requirements for cash to finance any seasonal needs.	a) Determine future product line requirements and strategies. b) Estimate long range demand for existing and planned products by demand region. c) Determine production and warehousing facilities requirements. d) Plan management, administrative, labor, and other resources required for planned growth. e) Determine capital requirements and financial conditions for successful growth.

Exhibit 1—Continued

Functions	Operational Level	Tactical Level	Strategic Level
Control	Control all activities (processes) against documented plan prepared yesterday; report and take appropriate action on variances.	Monitoring of accuracy of all forecasts up to cut-off point determined by lead time of materials and components. Continuous feedback in response to market changes and production achievement, modifying tactical plan on a continuous basis.	Control against predicted performance and to adjust strategic plans on a continuous basis in response to: economic trend changes, inflationary changes, political situations, industry and competition, technological developments, and current performance accomplishment.
Administration	Prepare and communicate all operational control documentation and capture for future analysis and extrapolation of historical performance. (Receiving documentation, machining orders and instructions, scrap reports, assembly tallies, packing instructions, shipping documentation, production volume data, and so forth.)	Maintenance and communication of all tactical planning and feedback information. Acquisition, maintenance, and extrapolation of historical data.	Maintain continuously updated planning data base containing feedback from the tactical control system and monitoring of external environment.

A SENSE OF STRATEGY: MIS

Management information systems don't just happen; they have to be uniquely constructed to fit the enterprise they are to serve.

We have already seen that the management perspective of MIS implies that there are operational elements as well as tactical and strategic planning elements in the hierarchy of systems which together make up an MIS.

From a strategic standpoint, development of an MIS must start with development of operational systems which have immediate benefits to the enterprise in terms of reducing overhead costs or some other major variable in the profit equation.

Information to be used in MIS originates at the operating levels within the company, and in the marketplace. In order to develop an MIS one does not set out to design one, but one should set out to design specific operational and control systems required for the on-going management of individual processes and functions in the company. Further, each operational and control system in a given functional area consisting of a series of specific applications needs to be evaluated and brought into being only after identifying the business goals of the system and performing initial cost/benefit analysis prior to expenditures on design and installation.

In terms of a basic strategy of systems development, one of the key management goals in a manufacturing company is the control of cost of goods sold. In a situation where material is the dominant element of the total cost of finished goods, a key system to be developed would be a manufacturing and logistical control system primarily oriented toward optimizing work in process and raw material inventories, and toward optimization of assets used in the production process, machine tools, toolage, and so forth. Justification of such a system would lie in increased untilization of assets, reduction of inventories in relation to throughput, and, in general, increased throughput through the factories for a given level of investment.

Similarly, in the marketing area as far as control of the flow of finished goods from factory door to retail is concerned, information on order status through the distribution system leads to better information on product mix and volume. Relating production mix to demand mix makes lower inventories in the distribution pipeline possible for any given level of sales activity. This again leads to conservation of assets employed in realizing a given level of revenue.

We find that if we define and implement an information system designed to control the process which has to be carried out (such as purchasing, production control, machining, assembly line scheduling, wholegoods warehousing, wholegoods distribution, and so forth), the data which have to be maintained to do so almost automatically include information needed to control costs—to account for the operation, and to develop historical data for statistical and forecasting purposes. It is really right at the basic level of operational control data that a computer-aided MIS is anchored, because it is at that level that facts for planning, extrapolation, and monitoring of progress have to be captured.

These examples are given in an attempt to illustrate the point that the foundation of an MIS is in the information and operating systems designed to control and support operations in the manufacturing, distribution, marketing, financial, and logistics areas.

BACK TO THE BASICS

We began this analysis with a discussion of the basic tools open to the manager and of the arena in which he could take actions to increase profits. Where then, does the construction of an MIS aid him in the manipulation of the variables which determine the result of his efforts? Let's look again at the variables and indicate where the elements of an MIS impact each and what abilities the manager has with operating management systems which he would otherwise forego.

Structural Costs (Overheads).   Perhaps the most difficult group of decisions made by top management revolve around the ongoing costs of administering the company. Early EDP (electronic data processing) applications typically address segments of this expense in terms of mechanizing payroll, accounting, and billing. The key decision factors in mechanizing these areas are those which relate to the relative simplicity of accomplishing the EDP application and the high level of predictability that savings in overhead will, in fact, occur as a result of the mechanization effort. Order processing, warranty claim processing, purchase order preparation, and work in process inventory status are all applications which form the most basic parts of an overall MIS, and which, if properly conceived and executed, should provide for a reduction in overhead cost at expected levels of volume.

Many technical writers bemoan the fact that companies tackle the administrative and accounting applications first rather than some abstruse decision-making types of functions. Business logic and the realities of commercial life strongly suggest that these applications are, in fact, the most appropriate bases upon which to build an MIS effort.

Price and Volume.   It is in the marketing and sales area of price and volume that creativity in systems design can pay off for the knowledgeable businessman. The customer of any company is looking for a supplier and a product which minimizes his total cost of doing business. Development of systems which make it easier to do business with your company than with competitors can provide opportunity to maximize price without attendant loss of volume. Providing the customer with an inventory control system and maintaining his inventory records allows for reductions in his costs while giving sales management useful information on product movement.

Price and product cost analyses with the kind of detail possible by use of EDP systems may suggest different pricing approaches where basic models of the product are sold at low margin while typical add-ons carry higher profit. In addition, the relatively fixed nature of the cost of mechanically handling administration activities may make it possible to go after incremental volume at less than fully absorbed price when circumstances are appropriate.

Product Cost. While product cost may be reduced by better scheduling of manpower and assets utilized in the company, many other opportunities also exist to employ EDP-generated intelligence to minimize costs. Product-by-product cost/price analysis will invariably show up specific products where inflation or other factors have seriously deteriorated margins. Decisions can then be made on pricing action or product phase out. Purchasing systems which analyze bought-out materials by commodity type, vendor, frequency of usage, commonality of usage, or multiple vendors in various geographic locations are relatively straightforward systems applications which typically yield profitable results. These applications will often provide summarized data which establish different make/buy situations than had been previously recognized.

Asset Turnover. The critical elements which lead to improved asset turnover are summarized in the ability to tightly and precisely schedule usage of assets, and in the ability to react to changes in need for assets quickly enough to avoid acquisition of unnecessary dollars of inventory. Sales analysis and forecasting systems can provide intelligence on shifts in needs for inventory and production. Combined with appropriate production control and material provisioning systems, lead times to react to market changes may be reduced by months. The ability to react to change should, in fact, be the overriding objective in design of material and production control systems, since an overly precise result which cannot be changed quickly in the face of market shifts will straitjacket management instead of providing the flexibility necessary to maximize results.

THE MANAGEMENT QUESTIONS

We have seen that an MIS is not one system but a series of interrelated operating elements which support different ongoing processes of the business. How then does operating top management select and determine priorities of effort in the systems area, and how does the management know when the efforts it is sponsoring are paying off?

Basically, there is a set of questions to which management needs to know the answers in order to effectively run the business. The questions are simple, their answers straightforward, and their interrelationships obvious. They are:

Q. What are we selling?—Product and dollars.
Q. Where are we selling it?—Geography and product mix.
Q. What will we be selling and where?—Forecast—units and dollars.
Q. What do we own?—Company inventories—product and dollars and age.
Q. Where is it?—Locations of inventory.
Q. What are we producing for sale?—Production schedules.
Q. When will it be ready for sale?—Future product availability.
Q. What will it cost us?—Product cost.
Q. What should we be producing and selling tomorrow?

Any MIS which is truly responsive to the needs of top management should provide the answers to these questions—accurately and quickly. The system will be composed of a number of sub-systems which address certain aspects of one or more questions—and which are used by operating personnel as an inherent part of their activities. The answers to the questions will provide management with data indicating whether action needs to be taken in the area of price, volume, structural cost, product cost, or asset turnover—and should indicate the basic area for action. And it should be paying for itself, in reduction of structural costs or product costs; the MIS benefit should be a product of the "gestalt" equation where $2 + 2 = 5$.

If the EDP systems in a company can answer the questions posed above then they represent truly an MIS.

It is managements' responsibility to ask "why not?" if the systems efforts in their company do not appear to produce the desired end results. If systems in a company do not provide answers to the key questions, then management hasn't been providing enough input to the systems development process and the technicians have been practicing their own brand of footwork. One can consider the projects currently underway in any systems group and determine if they meet all the tests of relevance contained below:

1. Will existence of the system being designed help to answer one or more of the nine key top management questions about the business?

2. Has the system been cost-justified by the operating area which is to use it?

3. Are the systems people working with (and for) the staff of the operating area of the business which is the sponsor of the effort?

4. Are there explicit time targets for the systems people to meet in order to finish the project?

5. Does overall systems management know and recognize where this systems effort will fit into the total information system needs of the company?

If systems efforts in a company can meet the tests of relevance, chances are good that an overall MIS is coming into being. If not, management is not being served, and whatever is to be produced by the systems effort will not aid in making the kinds of decisions necessary to produce profits.

It remains up to management to produce an MIS which will produce profits instead of costs for the company. The final product of management is, after all, profits.

The Company. John Lysaght (Australia) Limited is a manufacturer of steel products. The company is primarily engaged in producing steel sheet and coil for use in the following industries:

Automobile manufacture;
packing and containers;
consumer durables;
furniture and office equipment;
building;
machinery;
electrical equipment.

The head office of the Company is located in Sydney.

The major manufacturing plant is located at Port Kembla, a second minor plant at Newcastle. Service Centres, which do a limited amount of final processing, are located in each State.

Sales offices are spread throughout Australia, in each capital city and a few other selected cities.

Product is distributed in three different ways, direct to customer, through merchant distributors and through the Service Centres where final processing is carried out. In the case of roofing and walling material, the basic steel coil is sold from the manufacturing division to a Service Centre which then sells the final product to a distributor.

In 1966, when the Feasibility Study was carried out, the total sales tonnage was 724,000. In 1969 this had risen to 950,000 tons.

The total number of employees throughout all divisions of the Company is around 6,000.

The Picture in 1965. Lysaghts had been making use of data processing equipment since 1947, first with unit recording equipment and later with a small computer.

At one stage three small installations existed within the Company but by 1965 this had been reduced to two, one at Newcastle and the other at Port Kembla. The former consisted of a calculator, tabulating machines and ancillary unit record equipment. The latter installation housed an 8K 1401 computer and its ancillary unit record equipment. All applications were based on card systems—no disks or tapes.

Existing systems were the traditional accounting applications to be found in most data processing installations at the time. Staff Payroll, Works Payroll (a

---

From L. A. Webster, "The Development of an Information System for a Manufacturing Company, 1. The Feasibility Study," *The Australian Computer Journal*, May 1970; used by permission. At the time this selection was written, L. A. Webster was associated with John Lysaght (Australia) Limited

good system which has stood the test of time), Invoicing, Debtors [Accounts Receivable], Stores Inventory, and Product Inventory were on the list, together with some other minor accounting applications.

Computer usage was also fairly "normal" for that period of time in Australia. The Port Kembla installation, for example, operated one full shift plus some overtime at busy periods. The meter on the 1401 clocked up about 150 hours per month.

LAUNCHING THE FEASIBILITY STUDY

Senior management members of the company realized that the full potential of data processing equipment was not being realized. They realized that opportunities must exist within a company of this size, but that the opportunities which would yield the greatest ultimate benefit could only be unearthed by a detailed study. They also realized that such a study, to be effective, must be a full-time activity and should cover all areas and aspects of the company's operations.

The Team.   The Feasibility Study Team was formed in July, 1965. The Team consisted of four people who were relieved of their normal duties for the full period of the Study—about twelve months.

All members of the team were Company employees, service ranging from two years to twenty-eight years. All had experience in data processing, from three to eleven years. It is fairly obvious that experience in data processing and a good knowledge of Company operations would be an advantage, but the attitude of personnel is also important.

The people carrying out a feasibility study must be flexible in their thinking because the successful use of computers in most cases requires a break with the tradition associated with manual methods. The computer hitherto closed doors. Everything is possible until proved impossible (or maybe too costly!).

Subsequent events have suggested that the composition of the Study Team could have been varied to advantage. Representation of operating departments may have eased the introduction of computer-based systems at a later date. If the Team remained together throughout the Study it is quite possible that one person with E.D.P. experience would be adequate. In our case, since the Team split into two pairs for lengthy periods, we would have probably required a minimum of two such people.

The Study Brief.   The broadest possible scope was given to the Study Team. This was definitely one of the major contributing factors towards the success of the exercise. No doors were closed, and no activities were considered to be outside of the scope of the Study. For this reason, no formal brief as such was set up, but instead the Team was asked to report on any aspects of Company operations which deserved comment, whether related to data processing or not. In the specific area of data processing they were instructed to report on the following aspects:

(a) The extent to which the company's business information requirements in the future should be met by A.D.P. systems, and the use of A.D.P. equipment for business decision-making, planning and control.

(b) The best methods of catering for the unique requirements of the separate physical establishments within the company, whether there should be one or more computer installations, and what use should be made of data transmission equipment.

(c) The use of process control computers and automatic recording devices and their place in the total scheme.

(d) The prospects of external integration with suppliers, customers and bankers.

(e) Hardware configurations and software to achieve these ends.

(f) An appropriate organization structure, and

(g) Suggested timed steps with planned applications to achieve the eventual total integrated system.

Timing and Cost of the Study.   It was proposed that the entire Study should be completed within twelve months and that this time should be divided as follows:

1st stage—six months:

Investigation of the company's needs, inspection of other Australian companies' developments, study of overseas information, initial formulation of basic concepts in approach to Company's problems without arriving at firm proposals.

2nd stage—three months:

Overseas visits to A.D.P. installations, equipment suppliers, and consultants, to compare local basic concepts with developments in other countries.

3rd stage—three months:

Sifting of knowledge and experience gained, reappraisal of approach to Company's needs, formulation of a plan for progressive implementation of a system, and reporting.

Although the eventual allocation of time was varied slightly the general principles were adhered to.

The total cost of the Study, including salaries and all local and overseas travelling expenses, was estimated to be in the vicinity of $60,000.

MANAGEMENT CONFERENCES

The Study Team, when they came together for the first time, looked at the rather formidable task which lay ahead of them. It is very easy to talk about carrying out a feasibility study but where do we begin and how should we go about it?

The members of the Team very quickly decided that they would not get very far on their own. They had been given the time and the opportunity to get away from their normal duties and carry out the investigation but it was an investigation on behalf of the managers at various levels within the company. It would be these managers, or their successors, who would "require" the "business information" referred to in the brief given to the Team.

It was obvious that these managers must become involved in the Study. They would be able to make a maximum contribution only if they had a reasonable understanding of the uses, facilities, advantages and disadvantages of computer equipment and systems.

With the permission of the Managing Director a two-day conference was arranged, to be run six times on consecutive week-ends, and attended by just over one hundred senior company personnel from directors down to middle management level. These sessions were held during August and September, 1965.

Aims of the Conference.   The communication advising personnel that the conference would be held set out the aims of the conference as follows:

To obtain acceptance by management at all levels of the need to conduct the Feasibility Study, to discuss with them their contribution to its effective conclusion; to broaden their understanding of the uses of computers and associated equipment, and to discuss the role of modern management information techniques.

Format of the Conference.   The conference was held on a Friday and Saturday at the company's Training Centre.

A director of the company attended and participated in each session. He briefly opened the session by indicating to those attending the importance of the conference and of the Feasibility Study itself.

The Manager, Administration and Finance, who was responsible for initiating the Study, then explained why it was necessary at this particular time. He went on to introduce the Team members and describe how they would operate. The Study program was outlined and the need for management participation was emphasized.

The remainder of the first day was given over to participation in a computer version of the "Management Game," which was supplied by IBM (Australia), from 10:30 a.m. until 9:30 p.m. The personnel who attended the conference were divided into three syndicates who were "running" three different companies in competition. This program is readily available from the computer company and we had very little difficulty in setting up and running the "game."

The decision was made to devote almost 50% of the conference time to this exercise because it enabled the participants to become directly involved in a computer controlled process. It gave a vivid portrayal of the potential of a computer, particularly the speed with which data could be absorbed and information generated.

Without exception, all of the conferees enjoyed this part of the session and many millions of dollars were "made" and "lost." Throughout the day, the members of the Study Team acted as runners for the syndicates and maintained graphs of the performance of the rival "companies." In the evening, when the game was concluded, a review session was held and the graphs were displayed while each syndicate reported on their performance to their "Board of Directors."

To wind up the first day, the participants met together informally to discuss the day's activities and the success or otherwise of the respective "companies."

On the second day, the Study Team members gave a series of talks covering Management Information Systems, Computer Equipment and the concept of Total or Integrated Systems. After the talks, a final discussion period was held and the Study Team answered any questions from the group relating to the Study, to computers, and information systems in general. Conferees also discussed among themselves how they would best assist in making the Study a success.

Success of the Conferences.   The conference sessions were an outstanding success. In the immediate sense it provided an opportunity for the Study Team members to meet in advance the management people they were to interview later during the course of the Study. This alone made the exercise worthwhile. Acceptance of the Team in all areas of the company, as the Study progressed, was excellent.

The conference achieved its aims because the managers were well prepared when the Team visited them to seek information and ideas. It obviously whetted the appetites of those who attended and aroused their interest in computers, so much so that they were later to grow impatient because it took so long to satisfy all of their demands. At the time of writing many requests still remain unfulfilled.

A tribute must be paid to the Training Department which performed a magnificent job in organizing the sessions. Not a hitch occurred during the six sessions.

THE STUDY ITSELF

The first phase of the Study was carried out between September, 1965 and April, 1966.

Development of a Program.   During the six weeks while the conference sessions were being held the Study Team set about developing a program so that all areas of the company could be adequately covered by four people in six months.

A PERT diagram was prepared in order that the meager manpower resources could be deployed effectively. Already two of the available twelve months had been given over to the conference sessions.

One very useful suggestion had emanated from the panel discussion at one of these sessions. This was that the Team should make one quick pass around the major centers of company activity. This "exploratory phase" was undertaken to:

(a) Determine a broad picture of all present and future requirements on a company-wide basis and relate these requirements to each other;

(b) Establish priorities among the activities to be studied in detail; and

(c) Decide on the allocation of time and resources to the detailed study of major areas and activities.

At first glance it would appear that more time was being frittered away but this proved to be a very successful maneuver and the Team is indebted to the conference group which made this suggestion.

A period of four weeks was devoted to this exploratory phase and the first Progress Report was issued at that time.

The Detailed Study.   This phase extended from early November, 1965, until April, 1966.

There were three major divisions of the company to be studied in depth and a further Progress Report was issued at the completion of each stage.

During this period a lot of territory was covered around Australia and the Study Team worked in two pairs in order to complete the fact gathering mission on time. Much of the data collected proved to be very useful at a later stage when application development commenced.

As stated earlier the Study Team had been given a very wide brief and the Progress Reports covered matters which the Team believed were deserving of immediate attention. In most cases these bore no relation to the use of computers. A number of worthwhile improvements in company methods of operation were brought about as a result of these recommendations.

Up until this stage the Team, in accordance with the original brief, had reached no firm conclusions and made no recommendations about the future use of computer equipment within the company.

OVERSEAS MISSION

Two members of the Study Team were sent overseas to investigate developments in the use of computers and other associated equipment. Quite a number of the companies visited were in the same business as our own and we planned to look at their general organization and methods of administration.

Since Australia is so isolated from Europe and America a trip such as this is an expensive affair and we were determined to make it as profitable as possible. Many hours of personal research were carried out and the aid of equipment suppliers was enlisted in trying to determine the best places to visit.

In some respects the results were disappointing. As a warning to others it should be pointed out that articles in overseas publications can often paint a falsely glamorous picture. One should read between the lines to ascertain what is being done rather than what some theorist has proposed should be done. One installation which was to be one of the highlights of the trip turned out to be particularly disappointing.

Despite the fact that our aims were made quite clear to equipment suppliers we also felt that some of them let us down quite badly. Local suppliers had information about installations overseas which used their equipment but were unable to supply us with details of applications and achievements. We were quite convinced that they sent us to the wrong places in many instances. Though this sometimes became evident while we were away, time did not permit us to make amends by further visits. During a more recent trip a very interesting installation could have been missed for the same reason. On this latter occasion time was available to correct the situation.

One also has to be careful about the relative scale of activities. Although our own company is fairly large by Australian standards, some American companies in the same line of business are so large that comparisons are useless. One company, for example, had a seven storey building which housed nothing but computers and computer staff. This is reminiscent of the old story about the operator at the U. S. Bureau of Census and Statistics who, when asked what his job was, replied "I sort on column 1."

Taking this scale into account it is obvious that Australia could be quite proud of its achievements in the data processing field. However, being in an environment where the greater resources ensured that there would be more knowledge and experience available certainly helped to broaden one's outlook!

A small, portable dictating machine was taken overseas and reports on the visits to the various companies were taped during or immediately after each visit. No more than two days was spent with any company and in most cases the duration of the visit was one day only. So much had to be observed and absorbed in a small space of time that this practice was found to be essential. It is not always convenient or polite to take down notes during discussions and plant tours. The human memory is not very reliable and, under such circumstances, very quickly becomes a muddled mess of facts and figures.

The tapes were mailed back home as they were completed and all but the last few reports had been typed and distributed to interested parties by the time the two team members arrived back in Australia.

THE FINAL REPORT

During the detailed study, voluminous notes were taken. These were assembled together and charts were prepared showing the broad information flow within the company.

From these it was possible to determine those areas where data processing could be used to provide information needs. The next step was to establish priorities.

As is inevitable in seeking out areas for the application of computer systems, volume of activity is a self-determining factor. The major manufacturing division of the company singled itself out for special attention.

Which functional area, however, should receive highest priority in the plan for development? Traditionally, the use of computers had been directed towards accounting applications. The Study Team recommended, however, that priority should be given to the processing of customers' orders and the manufacturing of products to fulfill those orders. The three main factors supporting this recommendation were:

1. Selling and manufacturing were the mainstream activities in the company.

2. The receipt and processing of customers' orders formed the base of the information triangle within the company. All other activities were offshoots from this mainstream flow.

3. Unless the base data being gathered is accurate it is not much use developing sophisticated applications in other areas, such as accounting.

A detailed report was issued by the Feasibility Study Team to formally complete the Study. It may be interesting to indicate that the report was written three months after the initial steps were taken to implement the recommendations.

The overseas trip was completed in June, 1966, eleven months after the Study was launched. The management of the company was anxious to quickly gain a return for the money invested, and the Team was instructed to submit its recommendations immediately. Fortunately, the Team had reached the conclusions set out above and was able to take this unexpected request in its stride. It was very gratifying to know that the events surrounding the Study had aroused so much interest.

Ignoring this fact for the moment, and returning to the report itself, its contents were as follows:

A. An introduction which set out the reasons for the Study and described the planning activity.

B. A recapitulation of the observations made during the Study of company operations. Most of this information had been covered in the Progress Reports.

C. A summary of the reports on visits to overseas companies. The details recorded on each visit were re-arranged and presented under a series of subject headings such as:

   D. P. Organization within Companies
   Systems Approaches
   Equipment in Use
   Data Transmission
   Applications

D. Recommendations and proposal for implementation.

IMPLEMENTATION PROPOSALS

It was proposed that a top level Steering Committee be formed to set objectives, to be an active body initiating and directing action, to resolve contentious issues and to measure performance.

Two major projects were to be initiated, one to develop a system for the commercial processing of customers' orders and the other to develop a system for production recording in the major manufacturing division.

A third project involved extension of the data processing activities at the second but smaller manufacturing division. This project would operate in-dependently of the other two except where co-ordination was necessary.

Project Teams were to be formed, under a new project co-ordinator, each Team to be given a systems brief and a clear set of objectives. It was proposed that the objectives should be set by the Steering Committee, a timetable be prepared by the Project Team and ratified by the Steering Committee.

Project Teams.   It is considered that a little more detail about the setting up of the first two project teams is warranted.

All members of the Project Teams were recruited from within the company. The Team members themselves represented a cross-section of experience from as many functions as possible—Sales, Technical, Accounting, Production and Data Processing.

The Steering Committee was established, under the Chairmanship of the Managing Director, with representatives from each division of the company. The Steering Committee chose the two Project Team Leaders and set down objectives.

The Team Leaders chosen were selected from the function which was most involved in the particular project. The order processing project was Sales oriented and the Manager of a State Sales Office was chosen as leader. A Production Superintendent was chosen to lead the second project Team.

This selection of Project Team Leaders was to prove a major contributing factor in the ultimate success of systems implementation. These two men were ideally equipped to represent their disciplines, and, as implementation progressed, were able to confidently represent the systems team they were managing.

THE PROJECTS

Commercial Order Processing.   The original plan envisaged that this project would cover:

1. Order Entry
2. Raw Material Providing
3. Dispatch
4. Invoicing
5. Debtors

The second project lay between (2) and (3).

This first project was intended to cover the processing of a customer's order from the time of receipt, using master files to build up individual order records, providing documentation as required, calculating raw material requirements and issuing the actual raw material orders. It would then pick up when production was complete and carry out the remaining "commercial" operations up to the point where money was received from the customer to conclude the transactions.

Production Recording.   The second project was to receive order records from project 1 and its systems would commence with the receipt of raw materials.

The four main applications to be covered were:

1. Tracking of material through the plant and maintaining inventories at the various stock locations.
2. Scheduling of production units.
3. Preparation of performance reports covering the operation of plant units or facilities.
4. Reporting on the status of customers' orders as they move through the plant.

The Feasibility Study Team, from its observations overseas, favored the development of an on-line system, using terminals on the plant floor, but it was left to the Project Team to prepare a final recommendation of this aspect.

QUESTIONS

1 Does the Study Team have top-management endorsement?

2 How do management conferences contribute to user participation?

3 Are recommendations made by the Study Team consistent with the five tests of relevance offered in the article by Ward A. Fredericks (Selection 4)?

4 Is the Study Team successful in completing its assignment?

After discussing the history of and the standard symbols for flowcharting, this paper demonstrates the differences between a system chart and a flow diagram. Guidelines for preparing flowcharts are also presented.

FLOWCHARTING WITH THE ANSI STANDARD | 5
NED CHAPIN

HISTORICAL DEVELOPMENT

Flowcharting is a means of graphically stating ways of solving information-handling problems. Flowcharting, as people use the term in working with computers, must be distinguished from other graphic aids. The emphasis in this paper is on stating information-handling problems where the information handling is done at least in major part with the aid of the automatic computer.

The intellectual father of flowcharting is John von Neumann. He and his associates at Princeton University's Institute for Advanced Study were the first to use graphic aids systematically for this purpose and publish their use.[1] Even though the details of the flowcharting as the standard specifies it today differ considerably from what they advocated, the spirit, the philosophy, and the rationale remain much as they presented them.

During the 1960s a committee attempted to develop a standard for flowcharting. Working through the Business Equipment Manufacturers Association and the American Standards Association,[2] with the committee members drawn from computer vendors and a few major computer users, the committee after the usual compromises drew up a proposed standard and circulated it for reaction. With revisions, it was approved in 1963 and published as an American Standard. The Association for Computing Machinery and other

---

Excerpted and reprinted with permission from parts of chapters 2, 3, and 4 of Ned Chapin's *Flowcharts,* a book published by Auerbach Publishers Inc., of Princeton, N. J. in 1971; and from pages 119 through 143 of Ned Chapin's "Flowcharting With the ANSI Standard: A Tutorial," an article published in the Association for Computing Machinery's *Computing Surveys,* Vol. 2, No. 2, for June 1970; and all copyrighted by Ned Chapin.

1. H. H. Goldstine and John von Neumann, *Planning and Coding Problems for an Electronic Computing Instrument* (Princeton, N. J.: Van Nostrand, 1947 and 1948).

2. As of 1969, the American National Standards Institute (ANSI).

groups published this standard in their periodicals, giving it considerable publicity. This standardization effort in the United States paralleled a similar effort conducted for the International Standards Organization (ISO).

Subsequently, in 1965 and again in 1966, 1968, and 1970, the American Standard was revised. The 1970 revision extended the standard to match more closely the ISO standard. The standard as it is presented in this paper is the ANSI 1970 revision.

ANSI STANDARD

Outlines

The ANSI standard consists, in the first place, of a series of graphic outlines or boxes, which the standard terms "symbols." The standard advances these flowchart outlines in three groups: the basic, the additional, and the specialized. Complete flowcharts can be drawn using only the basic and the additional outlines. The use of the specialized outlines is optional. If they are used, however, they should be used in a manner consistent with the standard.

For the outlines in each group, the standard specifies the shape, but not the size. The shape is specified in two ways: by the ratio of the width to the height and by the general geometric configuration. This means that the user of the standard is free to draw outlines of any size to fit his own convenience.

Basic Outlines

The basic outlines specified in the standard are the input-output, the process, the flowline, and the annotation outlines. These are illustrated in Exhibit 1.

The input-output outline indicates an input or output operation, or input or output data. It is defined for use irrespective of media, format, equipment, and timing. Some specialized outlines may be substituted for this outline.

The process outline is the general purpose outline. It is the *de facto* default outline for use when no other outline is specified by the standard. The process outline indicates data transformation, data movement, and logic operations. Some specialized outlines may be substituted for this outline.

The flowline outline is an arrow of any length which connects successive other outlines to indicate the sequence of operations or data (the "direction of

Exhibit 1
Basic outlines

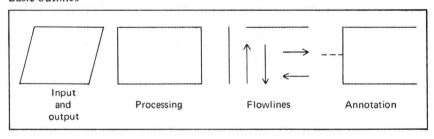

flow"). It is defined for use in an alternating fashion with the other outlines. As such, it also indicates the sequence in which the other outlines are to be read. To specify the direction of flow or reading, open arrowheads may be used on any flowline as shown in Exhibit 1.

The normal direction of flow is the normal direction of reading for people trained in the English language: from top to bottom and from left to right. Where the flow follows this normal pattern, no open arrowheads are needed to remind the reader. In the event of any significant deviation from this pattern, arrowheads are required to signal the deviation to the reader's attention. Whenever the direction of flow might be ambiguous to a reader, arrowheads should be used to provide clarification. Bidirectional flow may be indicated by dual arrows each with open arrowheads, or less preferably by open arrowheads in both directions on single flowlines.

The annotation outline provides a way to supply descriptive information, comments, and explanatory notes. Its dashed line indicates the outline to which this explanation or clarification applies.

Additional Outlines

The additional outlines are for the convenience of the reader, and not for the purpose of describing data-processing action. These symbols provide for handling the limitations of pages of various sizes, and make it more convenient to show connections in the sequences of flow. These outlines are shown in Exhibit 2.

The connector outline, a circle, must in practice be used at least in pairs. To that end, the standard advances two varieties, the inconnector or entry connector, and the outconnector or exit connector. An inconnector or entrance has a flowline leaving it but none entering it; an outconnector or exit has a flowline entering it but none leaving it. Each inconnector may have from zero through any number of outconnectors associated with it. However, each outconnector must have exactly one inconnector associated with it. One function of the connector outline is to enable a long sequence of outlines (a "flow") to be broken into pieces to fit conveniently on a page. The connector outline also provides ways of joining together covergent lines of flow that fan in to some particular point. And, it provides a way of identifying divergent lines of flow.

Exhibit 2
Additional outlines

| Inconnector entrance | Outconnector exit | Terminal | Parallel mode |

The terminal connector outline serves to indicate a beginning, an end, or a break in the usual line of flow. In the first two uses, it substitutes for an ordinary connector at the beginning and the end of major portions of a sequence of outlines (a "flow"), particularly when these portions are identified by a name, as, for example, for a closed subroutine. In its third use, it may represent a start, stop, halt, delay, pause, interrupt, or the like. For this use, it has both an entry and an exit flowline.

The parallel mode outline is a pair of horizontal lines with one or more vertical entry flowlines and one or more vertical exit flowlines. It is used to indicate the start or end of simultaneous operations.

Specialized Outlines

Groups.   The specialized outlines fall into three groups. One group permits specification of the data-carrying media (see Exhibit 3). Another permits specification of the peripheral equipment type (see Exhibit 4). A third permits specification of selected types of processing action (see Exhibit 5). In each case, where no specialized outline has been provided, the standard specifies that the basic outline covering the situation should be used. Thus, for any media or equipment, it should be the input-output outline. For any processing, it should be the process outline. The one exception is the communication link, for which the basic outline is the flowline.

Media Outlines.   The document outline is the most commonly used of all the specialized media outlines. This outline, a stylization of a torn piece of paper, represents data in the form of hard copy input or output of any type. For example, it may represent data taking the form of printing on paper produced by a high speed printer, or of marks on cards read by an optical reader, or of a graph produced by a data plotter, or of a page of typing produced on a terminal.

The magnetic tape outline is a circle with a horizontal rightward pointing line tangent to the bottom. This outline represents data in the medium of magnetic tape.

The punched-card outline represents data in the medium of a punched card of any style, size, or punching, such as Hollerith punched cards, binary punched cards, Binary Coded Decimal (BCD) punched cards, fifty-one column cards, and the like. Thus, a time card which only has on it printed numbers and never is punched with equivalent or even unrelated information does not qualify for representation with the punched-card outline (it takes a document outline instead). Two further specialized forms of the punched-card outline are described below.

The punched-tape outline represents data in the medium of any punched continuous material, such as paper tape, punched plastic tape, punched metal tape, etc. The requirements to be met are that the medium be indefinite in length and that the data be represented by punch patterns. The outline is a stylization of a partial fold of paper tape.

Equipment Outlines.   The display output outline is a stylization of a cathode-ray tube (CRT) with the face of the tube to the right and the neck of

Exhibit 3
Specialized outlines for media

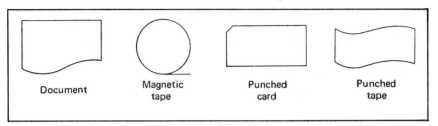

Exhibit 4
Specialized outlines for equipment

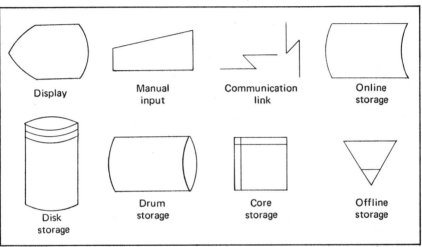

Exhibit 5
Specialized outlines for processing

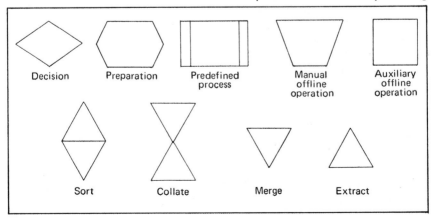

the tube to the left. This outline represents any kind of transitory data not in hard copy form, as for example CRT displays, console displays, and the like. But the standard also advances the display outline for intermediate output data used during the course of processing to control the processing. Common examples are the data produced on console printers and time-sharing terminals if the human user is expected to utilize immediately the data presented.

The manual input outline represents data acquired by human control of manually operated online equipment. Examples are data from the operation of keyboards, light pens, console switch settings, push-buttons, transaction recorders, tag readers, and the like, where the human operator provides the timing.

The communication link outline is represented by a zigzag flowline. This is appropriate because typically data communication done with the aid of equipment provides a flow of data from one place, or from one medium or equipment, to another. As such, even though the outline is equipment oriented, it is used as a specialized flowline. Where necessary, open arrowheads may be used to indicate the direction of flow, in the same manner described previously.

The on-line storage outline represents data held in any on-line intermediate and external storage device of any type, as for example magnetic disks, magnetic tapes, magnetic drums, magnetic cards, additional banks of magnetic core storage, microfilm, etc. For data on some of these devices, the standard provides more specialized outlines when more precise specification is desired, as described below. A more specialized outline for data on magnetic tape was noted above in the media group.

The disk storage outline represents data stored on a disk device of any type, especially a magnetic disk. The outline is a stylization of a cylinder standing on end. The outline is a further specialization of the on-line storage outline.

The drum storage outline represents data stored on a drum device, especially a magnetic drum. The outline is a stylization of a drum lying on its side. The outline is a further specialization of the on-line storage outline.

The core storage outline represents data stored in a magnetic core or similar high speed device that is *not* the primary internal storage for the computer. It might be, for example, an auxiliary on-line bulk core device, or a remote computer connected on-line with the computer doing the main processing. The outline is a stylization of two drive lines in a magnetic core array.

The off-line storage outline is an equilateral triangle with a small bar. This outline represents any data stored off-line regardless of the medium and regardless of the equipment used. In common practice, it is used for manually maintained data files.

Process Outlines.   The most common of the specialized process outlines is the decision outline. It indicates comparison which determines or selects among a variety of alternative flows (sequences or operations). As such, the number of flowlines leaving a decision outline must always be greater than one.

Sometimes the number of flowlines leaving a decision outline (the number of exits) exceeds three. In this case, the standard advances, as shown in Exhibit 6, several alternatives which are equally acceptable. One is the organizational chart

Exhibit 6
Outlines for large numbers of decisions

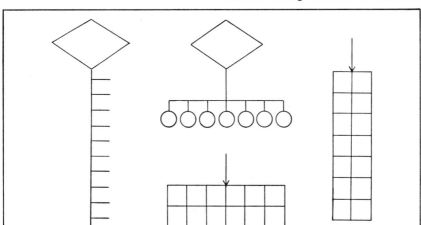

tree pattern of flowlines from a single flowline leaving a decision outline. Another alternative used in the same way is a vertical flowline which has a number of horizontal flowlines from it. To save space, formal outconnectors may be omitted from these two forms. Quite a different alternative is a "branching" table in the form of a series of pairs of rectangles, packed together in a double row or a double column. The upper or left portion replaces the decision outline; the lower or right portion replaces the usual outconnectors. The tables use their first pairs of boxes for explanation of the branching.

The preparation outline indicates operations on the program itself. They are usually control, initialization, cleanup, or overhead operations not concerned directly with producing the output data, but usually necessary to have done. Three examples are setting the limiting value as an iteration control, decrementing an index register, and setting the value of a program switch. By convention, when either a decision or a preparation outline could be used (such as for testing a switch), the common practice is to use the decision outline.

The predefined process outline indicates or identifies one or more operations which are specified in more detail elsewhere, as in a booklet or in a different flowchart (but not in another part of this same flowchart). Examples of a predefined process are a named closed subroutine or a routine from the operating system for the computer.

The manual operation outline indicates any off-line input or output producing operation which has its speed determined by the speed of the human operator, as for example entering data off-line by means of a keyboard as in a keyboard-to-magnetic-tape operation, or finding a folder in a file cabinet drawer.

The auxiliary operation outline indicates any off-line operation performed on equipment which operates at its own speed or a speed determined by something other than the speed of its human operator. Examples of auxiliary operations are card-sorting operations, punched-card interpreting operations, and the like. Auxiliary operations are performed by equipment, not by human beings.

The merge outline indicates the creation of one set of items from two or more sets having the same sort sequences. The outline may be used for both on-line and off-line operations.

The extract outline indicates the reverse of the merge. That is, it indicates the creation of two or more sets of items from and in the same sort sequence as the original set. The outline may be used for both on-line and off-line operations.

The sort outline indicates the sorting of a set of items into some sequence on the basis of some (usually specified) key. The outline may be used for both on-line and off-line operations.

The collate outline indicates a combination of merge and extract. Thus, this outline requires more than one entrance flowline and more than one exit flowline. This definition of collate used in the standard is not fully consistent with the usual definition of collate. The outline may be used for both on-line and off-line operations.

USE OF STANDARD

Situations

The ANSI standard flowchart symbols for information processing cover two major situations. One situation is for representing algorithms, especially those for execution by a computer. The other is for representing systems without indicating the character of the component algorithms. Some other situations are noted briefly later in this paper. The term "flowchart" as used in the standard may therefore refer to either of these situations. Hereafter in this paper a clear distinction is necessary between flowcharts of systems and flowcharts of algorithms. Hereafter, "flow diagram" designates a flowchart of an algorithm, and "system chart" designates a flowchart of a system.

Other terms are also current in the field for these two situations. Thus other terms sometimes used for flow diagram are block diagram, logic chart, and process chart, as well as flowchart. For system chart, other terms are run diagram, procedure chart, and flowchart.

The distinction between the flow diagram and the system chart is vital because the use of the standard differs considerably for these two. In the case of the system chart, the focus is upon the inputs and the outputs produced by the sequences of runs, programs, or procedures. In contrast, the focus in the flow diagram is upon the sequences of data transformations needed to produce an output data structure from an input data structure. The flow diagram tells "how." Whereas a system chart identifies programs, runs, or procedures by name and data structure by name, the flow diagram identifies individual operations on portions of data structures. The flow diagram is usually an elaboration of what is indicated by a single process outline in a system chart (see Exhibit 7).

Exhibit 7
Relationship between flow diagram and system chart

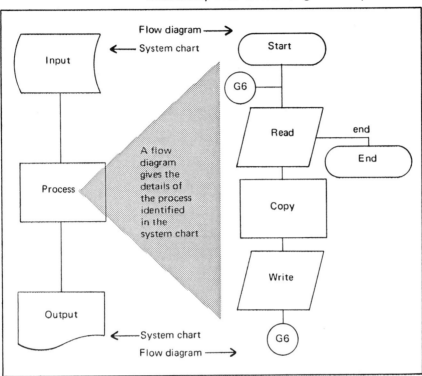

System Chart Conventions

Basic Format. The basic format of the system chart follows a sandwich rule—that is, it is composed of alternating layers of data identifications and process identifications. The data identifications are equivalent to the bread of the sandwich, and the process identifications are equivalent to the filling in the sandwich. Just as sandwiches may be of the Dagwood type, so the output produced from one process operation may serve as the input for a following process operation (a compound system chart). But a system chart must always begin with inputs (data identifications) and must always end with outputs (data identifications).

To see this sandwich rule in use, consider the creation of a system chart using only the basic outlines. Assume that the input available is a set of data about the ages of employees. Assume that the output desired is a single number, the average age of employees. Using the basic outlines, no attention is needed to the media or to the equipment. Hence, as shown in Exhibit 8, the system chart begins with an input-output outline for the input. Connected to that by a

Exhibit 8
A simple system chart using only the basic outlines

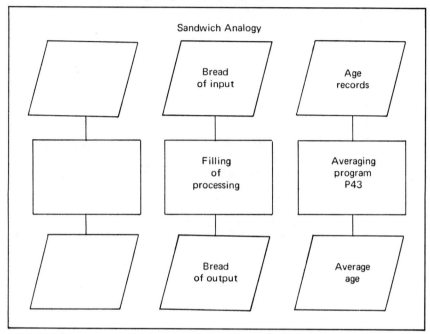

flowline is a process outline. Connected to that by a flowline and ending the system chart is an input-output outline for the output.

Identifications. The bare outlines shown in Exhibit 8 are meaningful to someone who has the identification of the input, the output, and the processing clearly in mind. But it has less communication value to others because, even though it tells that input is to be converted into output, it does not identify which particular input, what particular processing, or what particular output. To improve the communication value of the system chart, therefore, a common convention is to indicate within the outlines the identification of each input, each output, and each process.

For this purpose, the usual convention is to use the names normally assigned at that installation to the input and output. If the system chart is likely to be read by persons not conversant with those names, then the English-language equivalent in full may be written out within the outlines to provide the identification.

This same system chart is also present in the top part of Exhibit 9. But Exhibit 9 also illustrates more, since it shows a compound system chart rather than just a simple one. The average which was the output of the first processing operation in turn serves as input for another operation. Here the average age of employees is to be combined with previously calculated data on the average age of employees to produce a chart showing the trend of the average age of

Exhibit 9
Compound system chart
using only the basic outlines

Exhibit 10
Compound system chart
using the specialized outlines

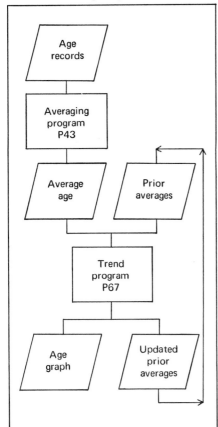

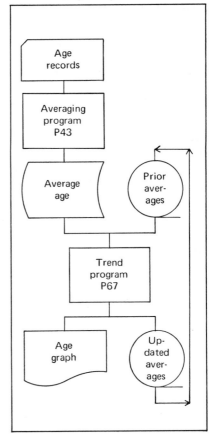

employees over the course of time. A preparation of this chart is a separate processing operation from a computation of the current average age. The other output of the trend program is the updated record of the prior averages.

Here, as before, clear identification of each of the inputs, outputs, and processings is provided, but no indication of the nature of the medium or equipment is provided in the choice of outlines. Note the Dagwood sandwich structure.

Specialized Outlines.   In order to improve the communication value of the system chart still more, specialized outlines may be used in place of the basic outlines already presented. Thus, Exhibit 10 presents a redrawing of Exhibit 9 using the specialized outlines. Exhibit 10 shows that the data on the age of employees is on cards, and that the output of the average age is put onto a magnetic disk or other external storage device where it serves as input to the trend program.

The other input to this trend program is from a magnetic tape, which has recorded on it the previously computed average ages. A magnetic tape also receives the output from this program so that it can be recycled to serve again as input if necessary.

The hard copy output from the second program is a time series graphic plot. Assuming that the stress is upon the hard copy aspects of this output, then the document outline is the appropriate specialized outline to use. If this plot, however, were displayed on a CRT, then a display outline would be the appropriate choice.

Use of Connectors.   If a compound system chart requires more space on the page to represent it than is available, then connectors may be used to break the chart into parts and to indicate the connection between the parts on the separate pages. This procedure is consistent with the standard but does not improve the communication value of the chart. An alternative procedure also consistent with the standard gives superior results.

To make the communication value of the system chart high, it is important to show all of the inputs and outputs for each part of the system. If one of these appears at one place as an output, and at another as an input, then it is only necessary to repeat the outline with the identical identification and appropriate cross-reference. This is illustrated in Exhibit 11. Notice that the disk output from the first run which serves as an input to the second run is shown twice. This is considerably more illuminating to someone who studies any part of the

Exhibit 11
Example of good practice in breaking a system chart

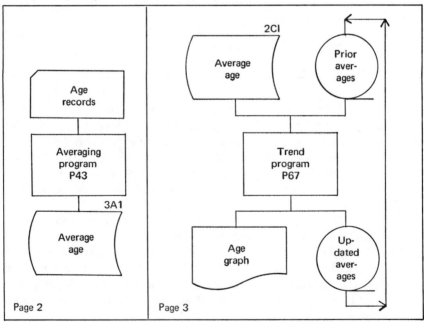

chart than would be the alternative of using a connector outline, illustrated in Exhibit 12, where two different ways of doing it are shown.

In summary, the most effective way to break a system chart into parts in order to fit it on limited size pieces of paper is to repeat the representation for selected inputs or outputs, identifying and cross-referencing them appropriately. In this way the material shown on each page is complete in itself.

Exhibit 12

Examples of poor practice in breaking a system chart

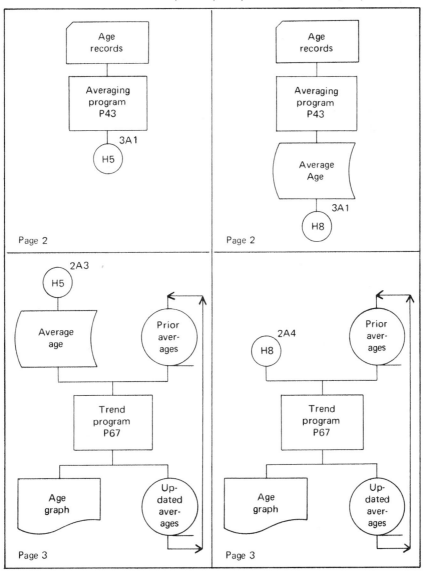

Annotation.   When breaking a system chart, a problem arises on identifying the source and use of data. The clearest convention is as shown in Exhibit 11, by the use of cross-references with an exact repetition of the data identification. This also serves well for multiple uses of an output as inputs to several process outlines.

To avoid the clutter of the annotation outlines yet provide the annotation, an alternative is to add a column of annotation to the right (or the left) of the system chart. This can provide information that is frequently helpful in interpreting the system chart; see Exhibit 13 for an example. The information most commonly shown in such annotation columns is the volume of the input and output, the timing of the availability of input or output, the control procedures,

Exhibit 13
Annotation column for system charts

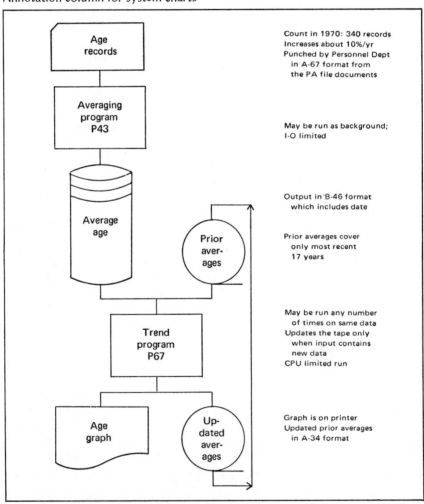

Age records	Count in 1970: 340 records Increases about 10%/yr Punched by Personnel Dept in A-67 format from the PA file documents
Averaging program P43	May be run as background; I-O limited
Average age	Output in B-46 format which includes date
Prior averages	Prior averages cover only most recent 17 years
Trend program P67	May be run any number of times on same data Updates the tape only when input contains new data CPU limited run
Age graph / Updated averages	Graph is on printer Updated prior averages in A-34 format

the equipment configurations required, the personnel complements, and the geographic locations. These items are normally not conveniently shown in the system chart itself because they clutter it up too much, and are not of concern to all readers. The use of this column alternative is an elaboration of the standard.

Guidelines for System Charts.   In preparing system charts, the following guidelines have been found helpful from experience. A first guideline is to choose the wording within the outlines (the data and process identification names) to fit the needs of the readers of the system chart. A chart using something approaching the English language, as illustrated in Exhibit 13, can be widely understood. A chart which uses only specialized names can be fully understood only by those who know the specialized names. Thus, the system chart shown in Exhibit 14 is less easily understood than the same system chart shown in Exhibit 13.

Exhibit 14

Examples of specialized wording within the outlines of a system chart

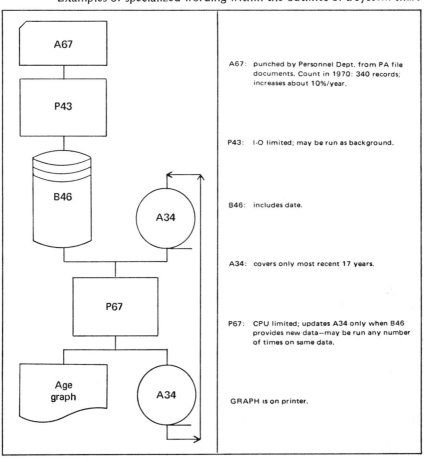

A67: punched by Personnel Dept. from PA file documents. Count in 1970: 340 records; increases about 10%/year.

P43: I-O limited; may be run as background.

B46: includes date.

A34: covers only most recent 17 years.

P67: CPU limited; updates A34 only when B46 provides new data—may be run any number of times on same data.

GRAPH is on printer.

A second guideline is to use the data and process identification names consistently and to keep them brief. If the same name appears more than once anywhere in the system chart, it should always identify the same thing.

A third guideline is to use a relatively small size for the outline. It improves the communication value of the chart because it enables a more compact layout, which allows the reader's eye to take in more at one glance.

A fourth guideline is to leave blank space around major unconvergent flows. This visually sets them off, and makes their role in the system more easily comprehended.

A fifth guideline is to collect incoming flowlines and outgoing flowlines so that the flowlines actually entering and leaving a processing outline are kept to the minimum. This is illustrated in Exhibit 13.

A sixth guideline is to minimize crossing flowlines. Crossing flowlines can be eliminated by repeating input or output outlines with appropriate cross-references as to source or destination.

A seventh guideline is to use the specialized outlines wherever possible (compare Exhibits 9 and 10). Their use improves the communication value of the system chart. They are only slightly more difficult to draw.

An eighth guideline is to use cross-referencing and annotation generously, but not to excess. The more the system chart can tell the reader quickly and easily, the more valuable it is. Ways of providing cross-referencing and annotation are mentioned above.

A ninth guideline is to give particular attention to the processing that affects data prior to the time that the data become input to a computer program or run. These are most often manual operations and auxiliary operations. Failure to specify them in full is one of the most common shortcomings of system charts. (Example: How did the data get punched into the cards in the system shown in Exhibit 14?)

A tenth guideline is to begin with what is known and well understood. Prepare the system chart describing that. Then extend the system chart in each direction. That is, for each of the inputs shown, find the processing that produces it and what its input is. Then, regarding those inputs as outputs, continue the procedure for each of those inputs. The same can be done in the other flow direction for the outputs. In this way the system chart can be extended to cover the entire system, as well as covering this system's tie-in with other systems. Typically, particular attention is needed to the manual and auxiliary processing of data in the system.

An eleventh guideline is to make no violation of the standard, and to shun deviations.

Flow Diagram Conventions

Functions.   The flow diagram describes the algorithm for transforming input data structures into output data structures. As such, the primary emphasis is upon depicting the sequence of operations that tell how data are transformed. The secondary emphasis is upon identifying the portions of the data structures affected and the operations performed. Questions of media or equipment typically become trivial.

Since commonly the operations to transform data structures consist of long sequences of actions, the character of the flow diagram differs considerably from that of the system chart. In the system chart, a sandwich rule describes its basic structure. No such convenient rule serves in the case of the flow diagram. Since it is in effect an elaboration and extension of what is usually shown as a single outline on a system chart, the flow diagram requires many more outlines and a much more extensive presentation of details than does the system chart.

The general character, therefore, of a flow diagram is of a sequence of alternating flowline and process outlines. Somewhere in the early portion of this sequence will usually appear one or more input-output outlines to indicate the input of a data structure. Near the end of the sequence will usually appear one or more input-output outlines to indicate the output of a data structure.

Because of their greater length, the flow diagram must be broken into parts, as a practical matter. For this reason, connector usage and cross-referencing become important considerations in the creating and reading of flow diagrams.

Basic Format.   Flow diagrams may be drawn with the basic and additional outlines described previously. For example, consider the program to find the average age of the employees shown in the system chart in Exhibit 13. Using the basic and the additional outlines, the flow diagram can be stated as shown in Exhibit 15.

Some comments are in order on this example. First, the beginning and the end of the flow are marked with the termination outline. This is unlike the case of the system chart, where the start or the end of anything was an input-output outline.

Second, the sequence shown follows the common pattern of read-transform-write. Since that transformation cannot usually take place until the input data have been read, the input operation precedes the process operation. Both precede the output operation.

Third, a very common feature of algorithms prepared for implementation on a computer is the use of iteration. This commonly appears in a flow diagram as a loop of flow, as shown in Exhibit 15. Note that, in order to indicate a section of flow contrary to the normal rule, a long flowline together with open arrowheads has been used.

Specialized Outline.   To improve the communication value of a flow diagram, the usual practice is to use the specialized process outlines wherever possible. The specialized process outlines available for this purpose are the decision, preparation, predefined process, merge, extract, sort, and collate outlines. The manual and auxiliary operation outlines are not usually applicable because the flow diagram commonly represents only processing operations carried on within a computer.

Exhibit 15
A flow diagram with identifications

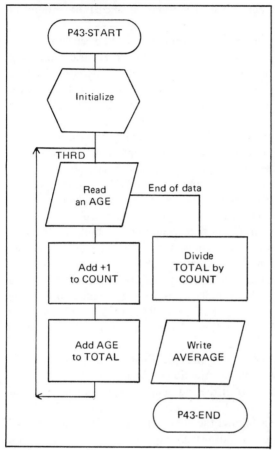

Using these outlines, Exhibit 15 can be redrawn as shown in Exhibit 16. Here the decision outline provides an explicit end-of-input-data test. The striped preparation outline refers to the short flow sequence called INITIAL.

Also available in the standard, as described previously, are specialized input-output outlines such as those to indicate media or equipment. As mentioned previously, the main attention in a flow diagram is not upon the media or the equipment but upon the logical character of the data transformations. Use of the specialized input-output outlines clutters the flow diagram with additional shapes which tend to distract from the main focus of attention. Further, with present-day operating systems, the equipment and media for input and output can be altered at any time for operator convenience, and hence are neither statically nor dynamically determined by the character of the data. For these reasons, the use of specialized input-output outlines in a flow diagram is not recommended.

Exhibit 16
A flow diagram using specialized outlines

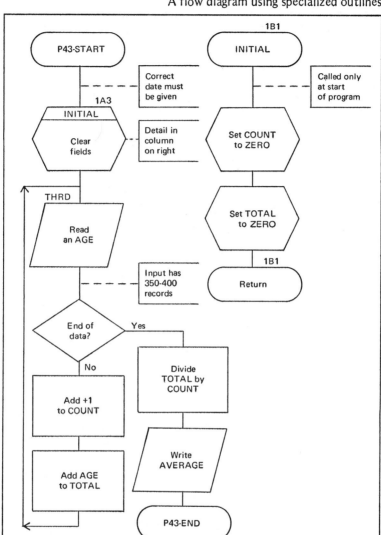

One outline that is illustrated is the annotation outline. This outline can be very helpful in the flow diagram to describe values and to provide explanation. Thus, in Exhibit 16, an annotation outline has been used to indicate, for the iterative loop, the expected number of times the loop will be executed. This information, it should be noted from Exhibit 15, is not available from the outlines or from the normal identification information supplied within the outline. Another use of annotation outlines is the warning about the need for the accurate date of the run, as shown in Exhibit 16.

Connectors and Cross-References. Connectors and cross-references are important in flow diagrams because of the common length of flow diagrams and because of convergent and divergent flows. Flow diagrams are almost always too large to represent on one sheet of paper. Usually they include alternative flow paths. Convergence points (fan in) and divergence points (fan out) must be presented and the flows clearly identified.

To make the communication value of a flow diagram high, it is desirable to have the flow pattern shown in as linear or straight-line a form as possible. The more cut up, chunky, bunched, or branched the flow pattern is, typically the more difficult it is for a person to comprehend. For this reason, the use of connector outlines and of cross-referencing normally helps give a smoother, more linear appearance to the flow.

Guidelines for Flow Diagrams.   A first guideline is to choose the wording or symbols within the outlines to fit the readers of the flow diagram. This depends in a major part upon the level of detail to be shown. The more summary (less detail) this is, the more difficult it is to find a satisfactory wording or symbols to use within the outlines. As a general rule, whatever is chosen should be terse in order to permit the use of small size outlines.

A second guideline is to be consistent in the level of detail shown in the flow diagram. If some parts of the flow diagram are in great detail and others are only sketchy, the statement of the algorithm is distorted. A consistent level of detail provides a sounder basis for making judgments about the algorithm and presents a better basis for making estimates of computer time, programming time, and conversion difficulties and for debugging than does a fluctuating level. Maintaining a consistent level of detail is simple only when the level of detail matches the implementing programming language. The difficulty comes with flow diagrams at summary and intermediate levels of detail.

A third guideline is to use identifying names consistently. Given the type and level of symbols for use within the outline, names for data and operations should be used uniformly and accurately. Exhibit 15 illustrates good practice, for example.

A fourth guideline is to use cross-reference liberally in the flow diagram. Cross-references to both the program and to locations in the flow diagram improve the communication value of the flow diagram.

A fifth guideline is to keep the flow diagram simple and clean. Clutter and lack of "white space" decreases the communication value of the flow diagram. For convenience and clarity, spacing the diagram so it can be typed is a real assistance.

A sixth guideline is to keep clearly separate the operations to be performed on program data structures from those to be performed on operand data structures. That is, operations on the program itself, such as switch settings, indexing, initialization of program control variables, and the like, should be shown in preparation outlines, separate from operations that transform input into output data. This guideline helps make a flow diagram more easily understood, and it improves debugging work.

A seventh guideline is to avoid using successive connector outlines. If more than one connector should properly appear in a series (as when multiple names are assigned to one entry point, or when the program calls for consecutive unconditional transfers of control), good practice is to collect the connectors to the left or above the line of flow.

An eighth guideline is to observe consistently the general flow pattern from top to bottom and from left to right. When this guideline is observed, arrowheads may be omitted from the flowlines that conform to the guideline. Clarity in a flow diagram is improved by arranging the main flow to conform as much as possible to the guideline. Minor and alternative flows may then deviate from normal, and by this deviation can be identified as not part of the main flow.

A ninth guideline is to draw entrances at upper left and exits at lower right. Entry and exit connectors are most noticeable if they are in a consistent position.

A tenth guideline is to draw flowlines so that they enter and exit at the visual centers of the outlines. The outlines usually possess either vertical or horizontal symmetry, typically about their center points. If therefore entrance and exit flowlines be drawn vertically and horizontally so that they appear to point toward or emerge from the center point of the symbol, the visual appearance of the flow diagram is improved.

An eleventh guideline is to use connectors and cross-references to avoid excessive crossing flowlines.

A twelfth guideline is to draw only one entrance flowline per outline symbol. This is especially important in summary and intermediate levels of flow diagram.

A thirteenth guideline is to draw, with four exceptions, only one exit flowline for each outline. One exception is the decision outline which by definition must have multiple exits. The second is the input-output outline when an end-of-file or end-of-data condition may result in a failure to read input data. The notation within the outline should specify clearly the basis for the choice of the exit. The other exceptions are the extract and collate outlines in system charts.

A fourteenth guideline is to identify clearly all multiple exits. This is an extension of the previous guideline.

A fifteenth guideline is to make no violation of the standard, and to shun deviations.

CONCLUSION

Both the system chart and the flow diagram provide important tools for the analyst and the programmer in preparing and in documenting work for implementation on a computer. Carefully prepared, flowcharts can enhance the rigor with which the analyst and programmer think through the systems, programs, and associated procedures. This greater rigor in turn typically reduces the cost of debugging. But the major contribution of the system chart and the flow diagram are to communicate some essential aspects of information processing work from one human being to another. The quality of this communication is enhanced by a consistent use of the standard.

The construction of decision tables is presented in this article by means of a series of interrelated illustrations. Also included are the requirements for using decision tables, a discussion of their advantages, and a comparison with the use of flowcharts.

6 | DECISION TABLES
JAMES I. MORGAN

This article discusses the concept, structure, and synthesis of decision tables and describes some of the ways in which they can be used in management.

DEFINITION

A decision table may be either an *action* or a *result* table. Basically, an action table is a compact representation of a procedure or system in which alternative courses of action are specified for various combinations of conditions. The table states what action (decision) should be taken for a given combination of conditions. This action (which actually may be several actions) is a decision rule which basically states that if such and such happens then this and this should be done. This type of decision table may be viewed as an organized set of decision rules designed to tell what to do for given circumstances. The doing might be done by a person as part of some system or procedure or by a computer as part of a routine. The table can even specify which person is supposed to execute the action.

The result type of table is similar except that numerical results are specified for given combinations of conditions and/or actions. The result might be a cost, mileage, or physical property. This type of table is often helpful in evaluating which decision or action is better in which circumstances.

In its simpler forms the decision table is not new. One of the best known, and least popular, examples is the table from which we compute our income tax. This table gives the tax, or a rule for calculating it, for certain conditions of income and exemptions. A price schedule which relates unit price to quantity ordered is another frequently used decision table. Many other common examples might be cited of tables in which a result or action is given for certain conditions.

A more general form of decision table has come into use within the last few years. The impetus for its development has been the need for designing, communicating, and understanding complex control systems that have been programmed for electronic computers. Although especially advantageous for explaining decision procedures for computer systems, decision tables are by no means limited to computer uses.

Reprinted by permission of *Management Services*, January–February 1965, pp. 13–18. Copyright 1965 by the American Institute of CPAs. James I. Morgan is a staff member of the Dow Chemical Company.

INVENTORY CONTROL

As an example of this new form of decision table, let us look at an inventory control situation. We have a case where inventory replenishment is made on the basis of the relationship of available inventory to a specified reorder point. We use the decision procedure:

> If inventory is less than or equal to the reorder point, then order a replenishment. Otherwise, don't order.

The procedure can be expressed more succintly:

> If inventory ≤ reorder point, then order. Otherwise, don't order.

Basically, we have a decision situation based upon one condition (the inventory level). Two alternative courses of action (order or don't order) and two decision rules (based on a "yes" or "no" answer to the condition relationship) are available. The action taken depends upon the condition. The condition states a relationship. The action states a command.

An alternative way of expressing our decision procedure is given by Exhibit 1. This is a simple decision table. It is not necessarily more desirable than the narrative description given above. Its desirability would increase, however, if we were to add more conditions and actions.

The table has four principal parts as shown

Condition stub	Condition entries
Action stub	Action entries

Exhibit 1
Inventory decision table

CONDITION	Rule 1	Rule 2
1 Inventory less than or equal reorder point	YES	NO
ACTION		
1 Order	X	
2 Don't Order		X

We separated the four parts by double lines in our illustration. The table defines and separates the conditions and the actions. In practice, it would not be necessary to use the headings for each stub. Each row is a condition or action. Each column is a decision rule or course of action. In decision table terminology, a decision rule is a vertical combination of conditions and actions. The condition entries are yes or no. (In more complicated tables, there may not be a condition entry in each square. If so, the condition is not significant and is therefore ignored.) An action entry is a check whenever the action is to be executed. If all the condition entries in a column are satisfied, then the actions checked are effected.

Let's complicate our situation slightly. Suppose that we will order only under two combinations of conditions: (1) if the inventory is less than or equal to the reorder point and the production plant is currently making the item, (2) if the inventory is less than a special critical point which is less than the reorder point. We now have three conditions: inventory in relation to the reorder point, inventory in relation to the critical point, and the existence of current production. As before, we have two actions, order and don't order.

Our decision table might look like Exhibit 2. Some simplifications have been made to avoid unnecessary writing. We now have four decision rules. There is no required reason for putting the rules in the order given. The given Rule 4 could have been Rule 1, and so forth. In practice, it is preferable to put the most common situation first. For instance, if the inventory were more likely to be above the reorder point, then the given Rule 4 would be made Rule 1. Thus, in checking which rule to execute we would come to this rule, and if it were applicable we would not need to try the other rules.

In this particular case, the order of the conditions or the actions is not of major importance as far as simplifying the table is concerned. In general, it is preferable to put the most sensitive condition first.

Exhibit 2
Additional conditions

		1	2	3	4
1	Inventory ≦ Reorder Point	Y	Y	Y	N
2	Current Production Run	Y	N	N	
3	Inventory ≦ Critical Point		Y	N	
1	Order	X	X		
2	Don't Order			X	X

TESTING ALL CIRCUMSTANCES

Of prime importance is whether or not we have evaluated all the possible rules. To check, we need to know how many conceivable rules there are.

We have three conditions which can have either a yes or a no state. The conceivable number of rules is thus 2^3 or 8. (A general formula is 2^c, where c is the number of conditions.) If we were to evaluate all eight eventualities we would get Exhibit 3.

We note that whenever we have a no answer to the first condition, we have the same action. Hence, the first condition is the significant one. If the inventory is greater than the reorder point, it doesn't make any difference whether there is a current production run or how the inventory compares to the critical point. Thus, we really need only one rule. Hence Rules 5 to 8 in Exhibit 3 can be replaced by Rule 4 of the previous table. Similarly, if the inventory is less than or equal to the reorder point and there is a production run, then the critical point comparison is immaterial, and Rules 1 and 2 can be combined. Thus the eight conceivable rules have been reduced to four.

If we apply some logic, we note also that Rules 5 and 7 cover impossible circumstances. Since the critical level is less than the reorder point, the inventory cannot be above the reorder point and less than the critical point.

This evaluating of all conceivable circumstances is important in many cases. It is a check to see that a possible situation is not overlooked and that there is a course of action for each situation. (The action might be to call the boss or to go out of business, but it must be specified in the table.) One of the key advantages of constructing decision tables is that omissions, inconsistencies, and unforeseen circumstances can be discovered.

If the number of conditions were large, it might be difficult to evaluate all possible circumstances. For instance, if there were ten conditions, there could be

Exhibit 3
All possible rules

	1	2	3	4	5	6	7	8
1 Inventory ≤ Reorder Point	Y	Y	Y	Y	N	N	N	N
2 Current Production Run	Y	Y	N	N	Y	Y	N	N
3 Inventory ≤ Critical Point	Y	N	Y	N	Y	N	Y	N
1 Order	X	X	X					
2 Don't Order				X	X	X	X	X

1,024 possibilities. Generally, however, it is possible to find situations where a given answer to one condition will specify a course of action that is not influenced by the answers to the other conditions. Also, as in our example, there may be combinations of conditions which may be illogical because of physical, mathematical, or other impossibilities.

Identifying all conceivable conditions is a major job in constructing a table—and also in designing a system. Generally, it is not practical to include all possible conditions. There are almost always cases with infinitesimally small probabilities of occurrence. However, while it is desirable to keep the number of conditions to a minimum, care must be taken to include all conditions that will significantly affect the decision made.

OTHER FORMS

The decision table of the example might also have been written in the form of Exhibit 4. This table tells us that if one of the two combinations of conditions holds, we order. Otherwise, we don't.

The example could also be written as Exhibit 5. Here we have included relationships in our condition entries and commands in our action entries. If all the entries were relationships or commands, then we would have an extended entry table as contrasted to the limited entry table given previously. A limited entry table has only yes, no, and execute entries. We have a mixed entry table here because there are relationships and commands and also yes or no and execution statements for entries.

The particular form used depends upon the preference of the table developer. Ease of understanding should be a major consideration. Except for a few fundamentals, the rules for constructing decision tables are not too explicit. The

Exhibit 4
Simplified form

		1	2	3
1	Inventory $\leq$ Reorder Point	Y	Y	ELSE
2	Current Production Run	Y	N	
3	Inventory $\leq$ Critical Point		Y	
1	Order	X	X	
2	Don't Order			X

Exhibit 5
Mixed entry table

		1	2	3
1	Inventory	≤ Reorder Point	≤ Reorder Point	ELSE
2	Production Run		Yes	No	
3	Inventory			≤ Critical Point	
1	Action		Order	Order	Don't Order

skill of the developer, the situation which the table describes, and the use to which the table is put are factors that influence the table's structure. The important thing is that the table be easily read.

A MORE COMPLICATED EXAMPLE

So far we have discussed only relatively simple situations. If there were other conditions that influenced our course of action, then they should be included. Some additional conditions might be these:

1. Were there sales in the last month?
2. Does the sales department feel the product will continue selling?
3. Is the item highly profitable?

Inclusion of these conditions might give the decision procedure illustrated by Exhibit 6.

RELATIONAL SYMBOLISM

The conditional statements are relationships. As a result, a decision table can be simplified by using symbols representing relationships. An example is the symbol ≤ to stand for *less than or equal.* Other commonly used symbols are:

$$= \quad \text{equal}$$
$$\neq \quad \text{is not equal}$$
$$\geq \quad \text{greater than or equal}$$
$$> \quad \text{strictly greater than}$$
$$< \quad \text{strictly less than}$$

Exhibit 6
Additional conditions

	1	2	3	4	5	6	7
1 Inventory ≤ Reorder Point	N	Y	Y	Y	Y	Y	Y
2 Sales in last month		N	Y	Y	Y	Y	Y
3 Inventory ≤ Critical Point			N	N	N	N	Y
4 Current production run			N	N	N	Y	
5 Sales future optimistic			N	Y	Y		
6 Profitable item				N	Y		
1 Order					X	X	X
2 Don't Order	X	X	X	X			

Further simplification can be achieved by use of the set-theoretic symbols ∩ and ∪, which stand for *intersection* and *union,* respectively. The former indicates that both events must happen. The latter indicates that one or the other must happen. For example, with current production run ∩ profitable item, a yes answer indicates that there is a current production run and the item is profitable. With current production run ∪ profitable item, a yes indicates that either there is a current production run or the item is profitable. Both events may be true, but at least one of them must be true before the yes answer is valid. Using these symbols, we can shorten the table of Exhibit 6 to get Exhibit 7.

Exhibit 7
Use of symbolism

	1	2	3	4
1 (Inventory > Reorder Point) ∪ No sales in last month	Y	N	N	N
2 Inventory ≤ Critical Point		Y	N	N
3 Current production ∪ (Sales future optimistic ∩ Profitable item)			Y	N
1 Order		X	X	
2 Don't Order	X			X

FURTHER APPLICATIONS

This inventory control example is just one of many uses to which decision tables have been and could be put. Exhibit 8 is an example of a table used in the handling of customer orders. Here we have combined the order handling with our previous inventory replenishment example. Such a combination would be used with a transaction inventory control system. Other examples include take-home pay determination, handling of airline reservations, listing insurance rate schedules, listing product specifications for given customer requirements, listing of quantities to buy of different materials at various prices, determining transportation cost schedules, credit rating determinations, maintenance procedures, medical diagnoses, and so on.

Strategies for games of chance can be set up as decision tables. As an exercise, the bridge player might set up his own strategy, or Goren's, as a decision table. He would soon be impressed with the need for defining the significant conditions and also would be able to discover the situations about which the experts are "silent." Such an exercise would undoubtedly improve his bridge game just as the development of decision tables in business situations often helps to improve business operations.

FUNDAMENTAL REQUIREMENT

The use of decision tables depends upon some kind of logical procedure for arriving at the actions or results. In many cases, the actions or results may be based on definitions, laws, mathematical formulas, or experiences. In other cases, they may be based on policies or subjective reasoning. For some situations, they may be based upon some "best" procedure determined by an

Exhibit 8

Procedure for handling customer orders

Order size less than truck load	Y	Y	Y	Y	Y	N	N	N	N	N	N	N	N	N
Inventory at nearest warehouse	Y	N	N	N	N									
Inventory in transit		Y	Y	N	N									
Inventory at nearest plant						Y	N	N	N	N	N	N	N	N
Production run scheduled							Y	Y	Y	Y	N	N	N	N
Can be made by requested date							Y	N	N	N				
Customer will wait		Y	N				Y	N	N	N				
Inventory at another plant								Y	Y	N	Y	Y	N	
Customer will order truck load				N	Y									
Can be shipped by requested date								Y	N		Y	N		
Ship from warehouse	X													
Ship from w.h. when available		X												
Ship from plant						X								
Schedule production											X			
Ship from plant when available							X				X			
Ship from other plant								X				X		
Refuse order			X	X					X	X			X	X
Investigate stocking item			X	X							X	X	X	X
Continue with rest of table					X									
Go to Exhibit 6	X	X				X	X	X			X			

objective analysis. Unless such a procedure can be determined, a decision table cannot be developed.

Decision tables are but one way of expressing a system or procedure. We could take the table of Exhibit 6 or Exhibit 7 and express it in words. It might, however, take a page of writing to express it adequately. Even then some ambiguity might be present. A decision table has the advantage over the narrative in its conciseness and its precision. The table allows easier visualization of relationships and alternatives. Furthermore, with the table, it is easier to see that we have covered all eventualities.

Other means of expression are flow and block diagrams. These have been used extensively by computer programmers. Exhibit 9 is an example. Depending upon the use and the person's familiarity with them, these diagrams may or may not be easier to read and use than decision tables. They are harder to draw neatly and are not as compact. They are generally harder to modify than decision tables. With a decision table, it is easier to trace results for a given set of conditions.

For a complicated system, it is generally helpful to have both flow diagrams and decision tables. One can often be a valuable check on the other. With more complicated systems, more than one decision table may be required. The tables

Exhibit 9
Flow diagram

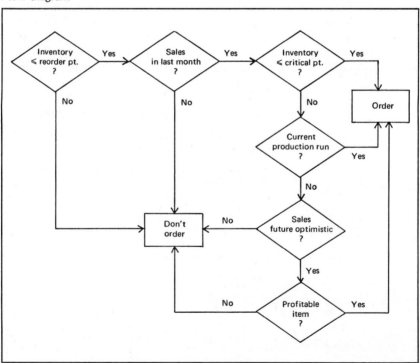

are connected by use of "Go to . . . " executions. With complex systems, flow diagrams can help to show the interconnections among decision tables. The flow diagrams can give the generalizations, leaving the details to the decision tables.

ADVANTAGES

A main value of decision tables is their use as a communication tool. An analyst or engineer can design a system, express it as a table (or tables), and then use the same table to explain the system to a computer programmer, an inventory scheduler, a manager, or another analyst. A decision table gives them all a common language that is precise and less likely to be misinterpreted.

To the analyst, decision tables are extremely valuable in helping to think through a problem. They aid in defining relationships and actions. They are an easy and concise way to present a solution to a problem and to document and implement a system.

For the programmer, tables are an aid in coding computer programs with a minimum of misunderstanding and further analytical work. Some high-level computer languages are under development which will have special instructions for handling decision tables.

To managers and users, tables are effective means of understanding, checking, and modifying a proposed system. For the users, tables are an explicit, easy-to-use tool.

To date, the use of decision tables has been in areas where there are a relatively small number of well-defined possible combinations of conditions and where logical decision procedures can be determined. Within these areas, decision tables have been an important tool in making more effective decisions. In some cases they have been a factor in "automating" decision procedures. Further use will depend upon man's ability to interrelate logic with the need for choosing alternative courses of action. For the manager who is concerned about being put out of a job by a computer system based on decision tables, it should come as some solace to learn that business appears to be growing more complex at a faster rate than man's ability to comprehend it by decision tables or other means.

Recently, the management of one company in the concrete block industry decided to study the possibility of complementing their rule-of-thumb decision-making with automated techniques. This article is the result of that study. In undertaking this investigation, it was hypothesized that computer technology and the related quantitative techniques were practical and applicable to management in the concrete block industry.

The company produces concrete blocks for use in the building industry. There are over 150 different types produced, and for each size, shape and color block there is a different raw material input mix which basically consists of cement, sand, silica, color, admix, and pumice. The different mixes are fed into one of three machines, which are set to produce different molds. The block is then heated, and cubed (stacked) on pallets and stored in the yard or shipped to a job.

Currently, production is decided upon at the beginning of each week based on orders needed for that week. A count of what is in stores is kept and is updated on a monthly basis. Every three months a physical inventory is taken. However, with this system, it is difficult to keep an accurate count of what is outstanding, owed, or in inventory.

Forecasts are made from previous history. The forecast for a particular month is made by looking at the figure for the corresponding month in the previous year and adding a growth factor. This method would always project upward and not take into consideration cycles and trends.

In the area of production, standards are set by the home office and in some areas weekly comparisons are made of actual vs. standard. The comparisons are made manually and are lengthy and time consuming, and in some cases meaningless when performed on a weekly or monthly basis.

THE PRODUCTION CONTROL CYCLE

The basic production control cycle can be broken down into the following steps:

Step 1. Production Planning. Production planning activities are undertaken to develop sales/marketing and production goals and policies.

Step 2. Order Entry. Order entry refers to system activities relating to the determination and entry of production orders needed to cover specific customer orders as well as to implement established inventory policies and decisions.

From Ralph E. Struzziero, "Computer Application by a Concrete Block Manufacturer," *Management Accounting,* May 1971, pp. 34–38; used by permission. Ralph E. Struzziero is a staff accountant with the Portland, Maine office of Peat, Marwick, Mitchell & Co., certified public accountants.

Exhibit 1
Production control cycle

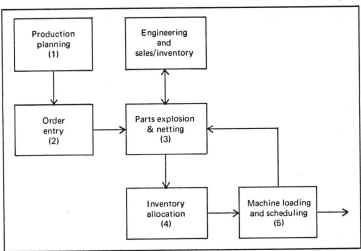

Step 3. Parts Explosion and Netting. Parts explosion and netting refers to system activities related to the determination of the net quantities of materials which must be manufactured or purchased to cover factory orders.

Step 4. Inventory Allocation. Inventory allocation refers to the allocation of on-hand inventories to cover open make-orders and parts releases needed to cover shipments to customers or to transfer to special accounts.

Step 5. Machine Loading and Scheduling. Machine loading and scheduling encompasses all activities relating to the projection of machine and labor loads, the set-back scheduling of production and, when practical, the determination of detail schedules specifying the time each job is to be processed by each factory resource.

The steps followed in the production control cycle are illustrated in Exhibit 1. The arrows indicate the sequence in which the steps are performed.

DECISION MAKING

Decisions must be made at each step of the production cycle. In the product mix and resource planning area, typical decisions must be made to determine the "best" mixes of products to be manufactured in order to minimize product mix cost.

The decisions that must be made in the order entry activity are essentially "inventory" oriented. Specific questions which must be answered are:

1. Which items should be sold "off-the-shelf"? Which items should be made to order?

2. What should the safety stock levels be? Should safety stock levels be established for finished goods and at what levels?

3. What allowances should be made for rejection of manufactured and/or purchased products; for breakage in subsequent processing? (Culls are equivalent to breakage.)

4. What should the economic order quantities be?

To answer these questions, it is necessary to forecast demand and make/purchase lead times for each item and to forecast variances of the forecasts. It is also necessary to take account of the possible effect of contemplated changes in the firm's inventory policies on the buying habits of customers, the effect which a change in the stock level of one item may have on the lead times and safety stock of other items, and on total costs of holding inventories.

In product explosion and netting, the problems are primarily computational. The basic decision required is how to allocate unreserved inventory to exploded production and purchase orders?

The inventory allocation activity controls the issuance of on-hand inventory to cover open manufacturing orders, shipments of items to customers and transfers to special inventory accounts. These problems can be very complex, particularly when a given item is a component of two or more different higher assemblies.

In production scheduling, the basic objective is to recognize impending scheduling difficulties (that is, impending overloads and/or underload conditions) in time to ward off the trouble. Because the techniques for warding off scheduling difficulties frequently call for the exercise of special knowledge (e.g., alternate ways of methodizing a product's manufacture, of the availability of extra capacity at a vendor's plant or other divisions of the firm, availability of overtime hours or extra shift operations, etc.), the selection of the techniques to be used will normally be made by the production managers and supervisors who are privy to this knowledge.

DATA FILES

The data base for production control consists of both the engineering data files and the sales/inventory activity data files. Engineering data covers bills of material, operations routing and methods sheets, while the sales/inventory data includes transactions files and open order files. Several of the more critical engineering and sales/inventory data files are described below.

ENGINEERING DATA FILES

The Bill of Material File.   The bill of material file generally contains a record of each manufactured item. Its purpose is to indicate the quantities of materials which are directly consumed in making one unit of the item. The components are limited to the next-lower assembly level.

Operations Routing and Rate File.   This file normally contains a record for each manufactured item. The record lists each successive operation required to make the item plus information used to estimate the time and cost to perform the operations. The time to perform the operation is usually independent of small variations in the total quantity; therefore, it can be treated as a fixed time similar to the set-up and tear-down times on manufacturing operations. It is also convenient to include purchased items in the operations routing and rate file.

SALES / INVENTORY FILES

Inventory Balance File.   The purpose of the inventory balance file is to indicate current inventory status of each type of block. There are three main inventory balances. They are:

1. The on order balance (accounted for and not made).
2. The on hand balance (on hand and accounted for).
3. The unreserved balance (on hand and unaccounted for).

These balances are related by the following inventory equation:

$$\text{Unreserved balance} = \text{On order} + \text{On hand} - \text{Reserved}$$

The unreserved balance is normally built up as a result of a make (or purchase) order to produce "buffer" stock. In such a case the ordered quantity of the end-item is added both to the on order and unreserved balance.

Other Inventory Balances.   Additional balances may be derived from the preceding equation. One of these has already been mentioned; namely, the "reserved" balance. Another is the "available unreserved" balance. This last balance is defined by the following inventory equation:

$$\text{Available unreserved balance}$$
$$= \text{Unreserved} - \text{On order}$$
$$= \text{On hand} - \text{Reserved}$$

The available unreserved balance is the amount of stock in the current on hand balance which is not needed to cover an existing on order demand. This balance can be either positive or negative.

Other useful inventory balances are the "back-requisition" balance, the "allocated" balance, and the "special account" balance:

1. The "back-requisition" balance is the quantity which has been promised to cover an in-process order.

2. The "allocated balance" is the quantity which is in the process of being reserved for that purpose.

3. The "special account" balance is the quantity which has been physically reserved in a special account. This account may be set up to protect a customer, to create and/or maintain emergency stocks to fill "off-the-shelf" orders or for any special purpose.

The inventory balance file contains the current balances for each type of block. It will also frequently contain a safety-stock or re-order point, the economic order quantity, and storage location of each type of block.

Production/Purchase Status File.   The production/purchase status file is used:

1. To determine the current manufacturing status of open and in-process orders.
2. To compare the orders' progress against the specified delivery dates and to pinpoint late orders for corrective action.
3. To supply necessary input data for factory scheduling.
4. To unload machine and labor-load projections.

The Factory Schedule.   The factory schedule indicates when and on which facilities the operations are to be performed. It also provides information used to monitor and expedite production. This file generates the following information:

1. The operation's starting time
2. The operation's ending time
3. Facility-type and specific facility which performs the operation
4. The time the operation is scheduled to wait in queue
5. Preceding facility idle time
6. The operation's slack time
7. Next operation to follow on the same facility

Additional data carried includes total and average delay to all operations processed by each facility-type, total idleness of all facilities of each type, and scheduled down periods for maintenance and change of shift.

Inventory Transaction File.   The inventory transaction file describes the circumstances of each change in the inventory balance file. For example, if an order is written for a type of block, an entry in the inventory transaction file records the order quantity, date, order number, the end-time and end-item order number for which the part is required and the next higher assembly order number. Similarly, when the part is received in stores, there would be another entry to indicate the quantity to be transferred from the on order to the on hand balance, date of the receipt, and the quantity and the details of the make/purchase order which authorized the producing of the blocks.

Open Order File.   This file is a list of all make orders which have not yet been released to the factory as well as orders to cover blocks required for shipment to customers or transfer to special inventory accounts. It also contains quantities for all components (and/or raw materials) needed to cover the open make orders included in the file. The file is used to supply necessary input data for allocating inventory and for creating the necessary packing lists.

PRODUCTION ANALYSIS

Each day, a standard for production is set by the production manager for each of the three machines at the facility. This standard is set in 8 inch equivalents so that output can be measured. (Eight inch equivalents are determined by the length of the block; i.e., a 12 inch block would be 1.5 equivalents.) Using the standard and the actual figures the computer can generate a report on a daily, weekly or monthly basis to measure production efficiency.

The following computer program generates a report on a daily or weekly basis for use in analyzing the production efficiency of the three machines used in making the blocks. The programs are run at the end of each week. At the end of each four-week period, a cumulative report is available with pertinent production information for each of the three machines. Exhibit 2 is a typical Monthly-Weekly Production Analysis Report.

MATERIAL COST AND CONSUMPTION

For each size and type block produced there are different mixtures of raw materials used. Each of these raw materials has a unit cost. Given the unit cost, amount of each raw material used, and quantity of each block produced, the report breaks down the raw materials unit cost for each type block and compares this figure to a standard. This comparison is made on a daily basis and is then accumulated for a week end total.

Exhibit 3 shows the daily material consumption for the blocks produced on each day. This report is now calculated on a weekly and monthly basis. It could, using a computer, be produced on a daily basis and thus give the manager more current information on which to base his decisions. It would then be possible to calculate material cost and consumption on a weekly basis, as shown in Exhibit 4. The total cost is calculated and measured against 8 inch equivalents produced to get an average equivalent material cost.

OUTSTANDING ORDERS

This program maintains a list of all orders that have a balance due to deliver or a balance or pallets owed to the company. For each outstanding account, the program lists company name, location, type of block ordered, quantity ordered, date shipped, quantity shipped on that date, balance to ship, pallets shipped, pallets returned, and 8 inch equivalents shipped. Data is kept on a running cumulative basis until both the block balance to be shipped and the pallets outstanding are zero.

NEEDED PRODUCTION

This program takes information calculated on the Outstanding Orders program and calculates the surplus of blocks unaccounted for that are held in inventory or the balance below that which is needed to fill existing orders.

Exhibit 2
Block production analysis

	Standard Goal	Total Production	Production Gain/(Loss)	Gain/(Loss) $.08/Block	Production Efficiency	Production Hours	Average Machine Speed
Machine No. 1	100,000	80,000	-20,000	$1,600.00	80%	300	267
Machine No. 2	50,000	60,000	10,000	800.00	120%	160	375
Machine No. 3	50,000	50,000	0	.00	100%	120	417
Total (net) gain (loss)	200,000	190,000	-10,000	$ -800.00	95%	580	327

Total culls   1,000 x .15 = $150.00   or   .5 (standard)   .5 (actual)
Total seconds   2,000 x .05 = $100.00   or   .5 (standard)   1.0 (actual)
Total yard culls   1,000 x .15 = $150.00   or   .5 (standard)   .5 (actual)

Cumulative report January 1 to December 31

Standard production	Actual production	Culls	Seconds		Yard Culls
2,400,000	2,190,000	11,000	17,000		11,000

Total monthly production hours		Total monthly production	Blocks per man hour
5,580		2,190,000	392

Exhibit 3

Daily material consumption report

Month January 1970

Type: -800-high
Plant: -Medford

Date	Size	8-Equiv.	Cement	Silica	Sand	Grit	Masslite	Pumice	Color	Ad-mix
20	08-02-12	5000	10	10	0	10	10	10	10	10
21	04-04-04	2500	5	5	5	5	5	5	5	5
21	04-04-04	2500	5	5	5	5	5	5	5	5
21	04-04-04	2500	5	5	5	5	5	5	5	5
22	12-02-12	3000	4	4	4	4	4	4	4	4

Item	Cement	Silica	Sand	Grit	Masslite	Pumice	Color	Ad-mix
Quantity	29	29	29	29	29	29	29	29
Unit cost	$ 1.09	$ 14.00	$ 2.30	$ 3.20	$ 9.20	$ 10.48	$ .15	$.01
Total cost	$31.61	$406.00	$66.70	$92.80	$66.80	$303.92	$4.35	$.29

	Unit Cost
Aggregate	$25.33
Cement—Silica—Ad-mix	$15.10
Total	$40.43
Standard	$70.00

Exhibit 4

Weekly material consumption and cost report

Material	Cement	Silica	Sand	Grit	Masslite	Pumice	Color	Ad-mix	Grecian Pumice
Tonnage consumed	20	20	20	20	20	20	20	20	20
Unit	bags	tons	tons	tons	tons	tons	lbs.	ozs.	tons
Unit cost	$ 1.09	$ 14.00	$ 2.30	$ 3.20	$ 9.20	$ 10.48	$ .15	$.01	$ 12.00
Total dollar cost	$21.80	$280.00	$46.00	$64.00	$184.00	$209.60	$3.00	$.20	$240.00

Total cost—material consumer $1,048.60
Total equivalents produced 10,000
Average equivalent material cost is $ 10.48

Exhibit 5

Block balance to date

Type	Qty. On Order	Qty. On Hand	Qty. Produced	Qty. Shipped	Trans. In	Trans. Out	Trans. Bal.	Bal. On Hand	Tot. Bal. to Ship	Surplus
38112	6600	10000	5000	2640	500	700	-200	12160	1980	10180
3818	10800	20000	3000	0	1000	800	200	23200	10800	12400
3816	7200	15000	4000	0	700	700	0	19000	0	19000
3814	1800	12000	2000	900	400	300	100	13200	0	13200
3813	3840	11000	1000	0	700	800	-100	11900	3840	8060
3812	36000	50000	7000	0	600	500	100	57100	25200	31900
38212	4400	14000	5000	0	1000	1000	0	19000	3960	15040
3828	3600	17000	6000	720	300	200	100	22380	360	22020
3826	1920	16000	4000	0	700	900	-200	19800	0	19800
3824	6000	15000	3000	3000	800	800	0	15000	2400	12600
3823	1440	20000	2000	720	400	400	0	21280	0	21280
3822	12000	30000	8000	0	1000	1200	-200	37800	10800	27000

Exhibit 5 lists the date, type of block, quantity on order, quantity on hand, quantity produced, quantity shipped, transfers in (inter-company shipments to the installation), transfers out, transfer balance, balance on hand, total balance ordered but not shipped, and surplus. This program is linked by subroutine linkage to the orders program. Once the orders program has been generated, needed values are sent to this program so that a block balance can be calculated based on the day's activities.

FINISHED GOODS INVENTORY

The Finished Goods Inventory uses information from the Needed Production program as well as the Outstanding Orders program in order to provide a closing inventory for each type block at the end of the day. Specifically, the program generates the following data: block type, quantity on hand, quantity produced, transfers in, transfers out, day's sales, breakage, write-offs, closing inventory, cost, and the dollar value of the closing inventory based on production costs.

SALES FORECASTING

A forecast of expected sales for the upcoming twelve months is provided. This forecast draws on information reflecting past production, current trends, and expected trends. Two types of forecasting models are used to forecast sales. The first is based upon exponential smoothing of past production and recent influences in trend. Emphasis is put on the most recent data and abnormal tendencies in sales will produce a high forecast error. The second forecast model is adapted to seasonal or cyclic trends. This forecasting is strongly influenced by last period sales and is adjusted by an appropriate base series to correct for cyclic trends.

ECONOMIC ORDER QUANTITY

In order to satisfy demand for off-the-shelf service a stock is usually replenished by a non-routine make order. When the stock of a particular item falls beneath a predetermined safety stock level, an EOQ is placed to replenish the stock. This program can determine for various type blocks at what point a re-order should be initiated and how many blocks of that size should be re-ordered.

ACCOUNTS RECEIVABLE

The "orders" program also produces an accounts receivable report, Exhibit 6, based on existing shipments. This report tells management at a glance the status of any outstanding account.

Exhibit 6
Accounts receivable to date

Company Name	Type	Total Accounts Payable	Total Amount Paid	Last Date Paid	Balance to Pay
Jones Bros.	3816	$ 15,000.00	$ 0.00	00/00/00	$ 15,000.00
Johnson Bros.	38112	9,500.00	500.00	01/25/70	9,000.00
Woodson Inc.	3826	10,500.00	0.00	00/00/00	10,500.00
Smith Company	38212	4,500.00	0.00	00/00/00	4,500.00
ABC Corporation	3818	8,000.00	400.00	01/28/70	7,600.00
XYZ Company	3828	56,250.00	600.00	01/17/70	55,650.00
Moss Bros.	3814	14,000.00	0.00	00/00/00	14,000.00
Misiaszek Bros.	3824	32,500.00	10,000.00	01/25/70	22,500.00
Misiaszek Bros.	3824	32,500.00	5,000.00	02/05/70	17,500.00
Lewis Corp.	3813	19,500.00	0.00	00/00/00	19,500.00
Firestone Inc.	3823	4,320.00	0.00	00/00/00	4,320.00
Goodyear Inc.	3812	24,000.00	15,000.00	01/25/70	9,000.00
Walton Bros.	3822	6,600.00	0.00	00/00/00	6,600.00
Totals		$204,670.00	$31,500.00		$173,170.00

CONCLUSION

The goal of this study was not to make a complete analysis of the company's problems but, rather, to answer the question: Is the use of computer technology and the related quantitative techniques practical and applicable to management in the concrete block industry? The answer must be, as it is in most industries today, definitely yes. All phases of the company's production control cycle from production planning to machine loading and scheduling can be subjected to automated techniques. The use of computer technology and quantitative techniques is practical and applicable to management in the concrete block industry.

QUESTIONS

1 How would you prepare a system chart relating to Production Analysis?

2 How would you prepare a system chart relating to Materials Consumption?

3 How would you prepare a system chart relating to Finished Goods Inventory?

IV. SYSTEMS PLANNING: FEASIBILITY STUDY AND SYSTEM SELECTION

The nature of feasibility studies and the framework for making them are the subject of this selection. The use of the present-value method in making economic feasibility studies is also illustrated.

7 | FEASIBILITY STUDIES FOR THE SELECTION OF COMPUTER SYSTEMS AND APPLICATIONS

JOHN E. COOKE and TED KUCHTA

WHY FEASIBILITY STUDIES ARE IMPORTANT

Patterns of Development of Computer Use. Before considering feasibility studies for the selection of computer systems and applications, it is first necessary to review the pattern of computer use which is emerging in business and the resulting problems which are confronting management. The typical pattern of development is shown in Exhibit 1.

The automation of record keeping forms the first stage. Where the planning of the computer installation and the preparation of the programs have been properly done, the benefits are tangible. Direct and immediate cost reductions usually occur, along with other benefits. The fact that virtually all firms of any significant size now use a computer for basic record keeping is an indication of the acceptance of this type of use.

The second stage involves the computer in the operations of the firm. Programs are written, often based on the mathematical models of operations research, which result in an improved or cheaper product or service. Such examples as order entry, inventory control, assembly line balancing or product design may be cited. The development of means for the communication of data over long distances directly between elements of a computer system has meant that the operations of a firm can be much better integrated and controlled. The greater sophistication of most of these applications requires more professional and scientific staff for their development. Not only is the cost of developing the programs higher, but the pay-off occurs at a later date, and with less certainty, than for the computerization of record keeping. Despite this, many large firms

Reprinted from *Cost and Management* (Canada), September–October 1970, pp. 11–19, by permission of the publisher, The Society of Industrial Accountants of Canada. John E. Cooke is Professor and Head of the Department of Finance and Quantitative Methods, University of Saskatchewan; Ted Kuchta is Director of Information Services, Federated Cooperatives Limited.

Exhibit 1

Stages of computer use

Stage	Function Involved	Benefits	Pay-off
1	Record Keeping	Reduced clerical cost Reduced marginal cost of increased volume Improved speed Improved accuracy	Immediate upon introduction of effective, working system
2	Operations	Improved service Improved product design Improved production scheduling Improved production control Reduced inventory Reduced cost of product	One to three years after intro- duction of system
3	Strategic Planning	Improved information Improved prediction Improved decisions by top management	Five to ten years after intro- duction of system

now make extensive use of computers for applications relating to the planning and control of their day-to-day operations.

Some firms, mainly the largest corporations, are looking ahead to the use of computers to aid in strategic planning. Sophisticated systems for the storage and retrieval of information needed by top management are being developed. Complex simulations of the whole firm, and even its environment, are increasingly being attempted, and serve to aid top management in making predictions about the future. Not only is the cost of such systems very high, but the pay-off, which is bound to be uncertain, only occurs several years after the expenditures have been incurred. However, as the complexity and cost of possible new applications increases, along with uncertainty about the outcome, so the potential pay-off increases considerably.

These changing patterns of use have been partly caused by changes in the cost and performance of computer systems themselves. Considerable improvements in design, manufacturing, reliability and the software of computer systems have occurred. As a result, the cost of a computer system to perform a given amount of computing has been reduced. Because of this, and the greater sophistication of new applications, the ratio of the cost of computer staff to the cost of computer hardware has been considerably increased. The 1968 report of McKinsey and Company[1] estimates that for every $100 spent on hardware, companies now spend $187 on staff. A few years ago the two figures would have

1. McKinsey & Company, Inc., *Unlocking the Computer's Profit Potential: A Research Report to Management* (New York: McKinsey & Company, Inc. 1968).

been more comparable. Thus, faced with demands each year to make substantial increases in the funds allotted for computer staff, the management of many firms are becoming concerned about mounting costs and apparently diminishing returns.

Problems Confronting Management.   The period of blind enchantment is over and managers are concerned. What are they concerned about and what are the causes of the problems? The 1968 McKinsey report, together with its predecessor of 1963, provides a good survey. Both reports suggest wide differences in return on the dollar invested for computer systems and services, even between comparable firms. The returns range from excellent to catastrophic.

There are certain problems which are common to all firms using computers. Paramount among these is the shortage and cost of well-trained technical experts. The rapid expansion of computer use, the greater sophistication of new applications, and the shortage of good courses of instruction for analysts and programmers have combined to produce a "people problem."

A second common problem concerns feasibility studies themselves. Any new system or application should be assessed on the following three counts:

1. technical feasibility—"Can we do it?"
2. economic feasibility—"Is it worth doing?"
3. operational feasibility—"Will it be used?"

As will be shown later, the methods of assessing economic feasibility are comparatively primitive and unreliable. In addition, it is often difficult to measure the true return on the investment even after it has occurred.

Plainly, the management of a firm where the computer system is economically unsatisfactory faces major problems. With the advantage of hindsight, the actual problems are often obvious. The following list is typical of problems cited by such management:

1. The wrong system was selected in the first place.
2. The implementation phase took longer and cost more than was predicted.
3. The resulting savings in staff cost did not materialize.
4. The operating managers won't use the information provided.
5. The new application never did work properly.
6. The new application works well but it costs more than the old method did
7. The new application is all right, but I wish we had done this instead.
8. Turnover among computer staff is far too high.

All too often, the causes of such problems are assumed to be the incompetence of the computer staff or the intrinsic uselessness of computers. As Diebold argues,[2] the problems are frequently the fault of top management itself,

---

2. J. Diebold, "Bad Decisions on Computer Use," *Harvard Business Review,* January–February 1969, pp. 14–28.

which has not understood computers or become involved with the planning and thus cannot communicate with the experts.

A THEORETICAL FRAMEWORK FOR FEASIBILITY STUDIES

Of the three types of feasibility, technical feasibility is a matter of expert judgment; operational feasibility is partly a question of human relations and company politics; economic feasibility is a complex problem, and the most amenable to rigorous analytical techniques. The following sections consider how the economics of a possible application should be assessed and how uncertainty can be reduced.

The Present-Value Method for Cost-Benefit Analysis. Whether we are talking about the economic feasibility of a proposed computer system or the feasibility of a specific application for a system, the basic principle is the same. An initial investment is made, which is subsequently recovered in the form of reduced costs or increased benefits. Let us consider a hypothetical application.

A mechanical system of inventory control can be replaced by a computerized system, which would be acceptable to the operating managers. It is necessary to perform calculations to determine the economic feasibility of this proposal. First we must calculate all costs of the existing system for the four-year period over which we have assumed the program will be in operation. These will form the base for evaluating the savings from the computerized system. These costs might be as follows:

Mechanized System	Year 1	Year 2	Year 3	Year 4
Staff	$16,000	$18,000	$21,000	$26,000
Machines	$ 5,000	$ 5,000	$ 8,000	$ 8,000
Supplies	$ 3,000	$ 4,000	$ 5,000	$ 6,000
Total	$24,000	$27,000	$34,000	$40,000

Next we calculate the investment cost of producing the program and the cost of performing the same service, plus perhaps some additional reports and the use of more sophisticated decision rules for reordering. (Note that although the actual computer already is owned by the company, its use may be charged to this application on a pro-rata basis.)

Computerized System	Year 0	Year 1	Year 2	Year 3	Year 4
	(Investment)				
Staff	$50,000	$ 6,000	$ 7,000	$ 8,000	$ 9,000
Machines	$15,000	$10,000	$10,500	$11,000	$11,500
Supplies	$ 3,000	$ 2,000	$ 2,500	$ 3,000	$ 3,500
Total	$68,000	$18,000	$20,000	$22,000	$24,000

We can now summarize the position with regard to costs as follows:

	Year 0	Year 1	Year 2	Year 3	Year 4
Mechanized System		$24,000	$27,000	$34,000	$40,000
Computerized System	$68,000	$18,000	$20,000	$22,000	$24,000
Cost Savings	-$68,000	$ 6,000	$ 7,000	$12,000	$16,000

Also, tangible benefits in the form of reduced inventory levels may be reliably estimated and added to the cost reductions, as shown below.

	Year 0	Year 1	Year 2	Year 3	Year 4
Cost reductions	-$68,000	$ 6,000	$ 7,000	$12,000	$16,000
Inventory benefits		$ 7,500	$ 8,000	$ 8,500	$ 9,000
Net savings	-$68,000	$13,500	$15,000	$20,500	$25,000

Thus, for an investment of $68,000 in year 0, we receive savings of $13,500 in year 1, $15,000 in year 2, $20,500 in year 3, and $25,000 in year 4. The simplest calculation that can now be made is to add together the savings, which amount to $74,000. Since this exceeds the investment amount of $68,000, we might conclude that the application is justified. However, this fails to take into account the fact that the firm would have to borrow the money for the investment at say 8 per cent (or forego investment possibilities if it already has sufficient spare capital). The correct method is to calculate the present value of this investment possibility, thus discounting savings in the future. Present values are as follows:

Number of Years after Investment	Savings Obtained	Present Value per Dollar	Total Present Value
2	$13,500	$1/(1+.08)^2 = .857$	$11,570
3	$15,000	$1/(1+.08)^3 = .794$	$11,910
4	$20,500	$1/(1+.08)^4 = .735$	$15,070
5	$25,000	$1/(1+.08)^5 = .681$	$17,000
Total	$74,000		$55,550

Thus the net present value (the difference between the present value of the returns on the investment and the investment itself), is -$12,450 and the investment should not be made. However, it should be noted that the number of years during which the application will be used is a vital figure. If a five-year period is selected, with net savings of $30,000 in the fifth year, then the net present value becomes +$6,450, and the investment is profitable.*

The present-value method should be used to calculate the economic feasibility of any proposed computer application. Also, by selecting the project with the highest net present value, it can be used to choose between two profitable alternatives when only one can be selected. To justify an expansion of computer facilities or staff, several applications can be combined to prove the economic feasibility of the proposed expansion. Despite its simplicity and theoretical correctness, the method is not widely used or understood.

Coping with Uncertainty. One of the reasons economic feasibility is often not calculated is that there is uncertainty associated with all of the estimated numbers used in the analysis. The uncertainty of development costs or machine-time costs exists even if an experienced computer manager with a well-trained staff estimates these figures. Other numbers which critically affect the analysis, such as a projected increase in volume, the effect of cutting down billing time, or the value of a new form of sales analysis, cannot be accurately determined. In the past, undesirable applications have been accepted because wildly exaggerated figures for these sorts of savings have been accepted or developed by computer staff who may be enthusiastic about a project. Obviously, quantitative estimates of such numbers should be made by the operating managers who know most about the topic in question.

PRACTICAL APPROACHES TO FEASIBILITY STUDY

Having illustrated the use of the present-value method as a theoretical base for feasibility studies, we can proceed to some of the practical details.

Computer processing within a typical firm is rarely static. Present-day computer systems are increasingly being designed on a modular basis, and the planned development of computer use frequently calls for the gradual addition of extra components to cope with the extension of existing applications and the introduction of new ones.

Change and expansion become necessary for many reasons, such as technical improvements or innovations, the increasing sophistication of operating managers with regard to computer use, or changes in the structure or size of a corporation.

Some of these changes may be predicted and included as part of the plan for computer development. Others may not, and the plan must therefore be flexible enough to cope with unexpected changes. Whatever the nature of the change, it should be justified by some form of feasibility study.

---

* Editor's note: The present value of this $30,000 savings during the fifth year is $18,900 ($30,000 X .630); the total present value for the five-year period then becomes $74,450 ($55,550 + $18,900), which is $6,450 higher than the investment of $68,000.

Major System Changes. A major change requires a major feasibility study. The change may be justified by several reasons, some of which are discussed by Amdahl:

1. Maintenance—Older equipment under extensive use needs more maintenance, and this may become a significant expense.

2. Capacity—Although the capacity of existing equipment can be increased by additional memory or channels, it may eventually be overloaded and a change to a larger machine is necessary.

3. Performance dollar—Technical improvements may mean that the performance/dollar of a newer machine is better by a factor of as high as ten.

4. Peripherals—Changing applications may need new peripherals such as terminals or optical character readers. These may fit more readily into a newer system.

5. Fashion—Fear of appearing antiquated may provoke the investigation of a change. Poor publicity or difficulty in attracting computer staff may result from an outmoded installation.

6. Third-party leasing—Firms are coming into existence which lease computer systems at a lower rate than the manufacturers.[3]

Any or all of these reasons might make a firm decide to expend money for a feasibility study to determine the justification of a major system change. The steps to be followed are basically the same whether the company is contemplating a change or the installation of a computer system for the first time. A thorough investigation of all possible applications and all possible systems should be made.

Approval for Expansion—The Annual Review. Continuing analysis of the "profitability" of the computer center is often not done. Follow-up to test the validity of the original estimates may not be made, and feasibility studies for new individual applications are often not requested.

In some cases the annual rate of growth of total computer expense is arbitrarily restricted to a figure of, say, 10 percent. This figure may be in line with other increases, and is restricted in an attempt to defeat what is seen as "empire building." Yet, by this strategy, the firm may well be missing out on new applications which may have a very high return.

If the firm has followed the wise policy of involving its managers in the developments and educating them about the possibilities of computer use, they will be continually seeing new ways in which the computer can help them. Effective feasibility studies will determine whether the investment in each application is justified.

---

3. L. Amdahl, "Computer Obsolescence," *Datamation*, January 1969, pp 27–28.

If a detailed annual review of all computer applications is made, then less desirable applications may be dropped or changed. By showing that new applications or new extensions to the system are feasible, the computer manager will justify his claim for expansion. The responsibility for requiring this type of a review rests with top management.

CONCLUSION

While there is no foolproof way of ensuring the success of computer development the following principles serve to reduce the chance of failure:

1. Identify the key objectives and likely progression of the company.

2. Set up a high-level steering committee and recognize thereby the high cost and potential of computers.

3. Involve the operating managers in the computer development and ensure that they benefit from and contribute to it.

4. List all potential applications, looking particularly for applications in areas of high company expenditure or revenue.

5. Consider each application as a potential investment and assess its profit potential by present-value analysis.

6. Draw up long-range plans for the successive implementation of different applications.

7. Review progress and profitability regularly.

8. Appraise each project and the estimates of it after completion.

9. Be prepared to revise the plan.

This article presents an approach to determining system configuration. The use of systems measurement tools to monitor current utilization and to project future workload is discussed.

8 | TACKLE SYSTEM SELECTION SYSTEMATICALLY
JOHN W. SUTHERLAND

Investments in data processing systems are taking an increasingly large slice out of company budgets. Computers are more and more at the core of organizational activities. Winding up with an inefficient or ineffective system, then, can have very serious and wide-ranging consequences. Yet system selection decisions very seldom appear to be taken with the care and discipline they so obviously deserve.

Configurator and performance evaluation programs play an important role in the system selection process. But they are by no means all of it. In fact, in the broadest sense, they merely automate the mechanical mathematical exercises which must be gone through. It remains for the decision-maker himself to supply the logic and "intelligence" at all points.

In the system selection process, unless the job which a system is to do is accurately defined, there is no point in going any further. With data processing systems, workload projection involves a great deal more than collecting requirement estimates from all users and then just adding them up. In fact, there are four rather complex tasks which must be done before accurate requirements can be arrived at; these are shown as Exhibit 1.

If these four tasks are done properly, the workload projection should reflect what the real-world situation will actually be. The system selected to meet these requirements then will have minimum overcapacity.

Users within the organization often cannot accurately predict their workloads without considerable help. A common error, for example, is to identify the number of man-hours currently being spent on tasks and divide this by some factor reflecting the probable speed advantage of the machine. As one financial executive told us: "If a manager's department was spending 15,000 man-hours per month on billing operations, and he was told that the system coming in was supposed to be 500 times faster than a man, he projected a need for about 30 hours of machine time per month. Such estimates were consistently too low, largely because the automated system permitted us to do more elaborate things than we did by hand. (Now, for example, we give customers year-to-date totals by category of expense.) So, soon after the system arrived, it began to fall behind."

In another firm, this time a plastic manufacturer in the Midwest, the situation was just the opposite: it wound up with a system that was too large by a factor of about 40 percent. The reason is interesting: "We deal with a lot of companies

Reprinted from *Computer Decisions*, April 1971. © 1971, Hayden Publishing Company; used by permission. John W. Sutherland is Senior Editor of *Computer Decisions*.

Exhibit 1
Organizing the future workload

Task	Purpose
1. Collect estimates of the applications to be run by all potential users within the organization.	To arrive at a first gross estimate of the processing and data-handling operations the system will have to perform.
2. Correlate and cross-check all individual applications.	To eliminate any areas of redundancy or overlap among the applications, see where data may be shared, and minimize the aggregate workload.
3. Establishing a job arrival schedule which shows when each of the applications will arrive for processing by the system.	To establish a projected job stream which has the lowest permissible peak loading factor by distributing job arrivals as evenly as possible.
4. Establish a desired output schedule which indicates what turnaround times can be tolerated for these applications.	To establish a schedule of required turnaround times which maximizes the permissible interval between job arrival and return.

that know exactly what they want in a product. We're a job shop producing highly specialized stuff, and this takes a lot of talking back and forth. So we got the idea that we could do this with teleprocessing. We'd put terminals at our prime customer locations and let them feed coded revisions or status information right into the plant. So we leased a system that could handle teleprocessing loads. But then it turned out that everybody was still using the telephone—they liked to talk back and forth and nothing was so simple that there weren't side problems to thrash out. Thus, our customer representatives were still having their girls keypunch everything and then running it in batch-mode. The teleprocessing power was wasted."

It is extremely important, therefore, that the system staff get involved with the line managers in estimating their individual processing requirements right at the beginning. It is not just that the non-technicians mistranslate their real needs in going from the manual to the machine mode, but that whatever needs to emerge must be translated into terms which will directly reflect computer requirements. The system engineers must help managers phrase applications according to:

1. Major processing events for each application
2. Input/output services or system executive functions which the applications will require
3. Storage needed, both for applications and data
4. File descriptions showing approximate size, data type and access requirements

A set of models must be developed from this data to reflect the demands applications will make on system resources.

AIMING TOWARD A COMPROMISE

Now the really hard work begins, the problem of establishing input/output schedules for the applications programs and trying to reduce the raw workload to its lowest permissible limit. This is not a simple matter of statistical computations or of imposing requirements from the controller's office; it is a political problem. A compromise has to be struck between managers' insistence on quick service and attention and the rapidly increasing cost of computers as they become more powerful. Something has to give.

A widely used technique for arriving at complex compromises involves scheduling a series of seminars which are to be attended jointly by all potential users and the system staff. The purpose of these carefully controlled meetings is to try to get users to develop an evenly-distributed arrival rate for their applications, and to extend as far as possible their turnaround requirements. There is every incentive for the managers to cooperate because they will be charged on a pro rata basis for use of the data processing system. Those managers who insist on quick turnaround will be charged accordingly; those who agree to operate during less strained periods will be charged a reduced rate. Thus the way each manager schedules his jobs for input, and the intervals insisted on for completion of work, will directly affect his department's budget.

At the first of these meetings, individual managers submit the application models that the system staff helped develop. The system staff brings two things:

1. A model of the corporation showing the flow of work and the way the individual departments interact.

2. A highly simplified schematic of the various broad system designs which might be considered, along with their comparative price/performance characteristics.

When the seminar is re-convened, another problem is attacked: Is there any way in which processing requirements among the various departments could be telescoped and redundancies eliminated? Also, each manager must factually defend his needs as both necessary and unique, otherwise his share of the system will be quickly curtailed.

Subsequent seminars would examine the scheduling needs of each individual manager, the aim being to arrive at the lowest possible overall input and output peaks. At various stages in the process, the then-prevailing peaks would be examined and some rough idea of the cost of the system required given out (along with each department's pro rata expense share). The scheduling exercises are reiterated until marginal improvements become negligible.

Three very interesting and promising things are happening when a process like this is undertaken: First, the organization is quite properly being looked at as an integrated system in itself, not as a collection of independent departments. Second, managers find themselves defending their demands of a prospective system against their peers, not against some isolated staff of experts. Third, the problem of resolving possible conflicts among individual users and the problem of reaching a compromise between demands and costs is solved at the operational level, not imposed from above.

MAKING THE FIRST ROUGH CUTS AT SYSTEM DESIGN

At this point a projected workload profile has been established which predicts what processing and data loads the prospective system will have to handle at what points in time (from hour to hour, by days of the week, or within whatever intervals seem significant). In other words, the model of the input stream, application by application, provides the best estimate of what load the prospective system will have to handle within what time frames. The staff can now begin to set the broad specifications for what the new system should look like. This is done to restrict subsequent evaluation exercise to the fewest serious alternatives. System selection studies cost time and money and there is no point in testing configurations or components that are not real contenders.

The organization that is already using a system has a significant edge here. Whereas the company contemplating its first installation must start from scratch, the experienced user can take advantage of an analysis done on the way his current system is reacting to the current workload. An examination of his existing system can indicate bottlenecks. This points toward things to avoid in the new system.

IBM's Statistical Gathering System (SGS), for example, can monitor exactly what is going on in an operating System/360 installation and generate information on many factors. This measuring tool was developed for a NASA-Houston RTOS installation and is not generally available. It produced:

1. Applications program statistics:

    (a) discrete applications executed
    (b) cpu time used by each application
    (c) elapsed time for each (throughput)
    (d) control program services used by each

2. Operating system statistics:

    (a) control program functions executed
    (b) average time for each discrete service
    (c) cpu utilization by control services
    (d) frequency of use of each service program

3. Operations statistics:

    (a) overall cpu utilization
    (b) overall idle and input/output wait times
    (c) device utilization (by application program)

When such statistics on the current system's performance have been collected over a long enough period, it is possible to develop a rather detailed profile of the way the current configuration is reacting to the existing workload. An example is illustrated in Exhibits 2 and 3.

Exhibit 2 represents a composite average of the work input to the computer center during an average working day. The curve over the lower part represents the current requirements, and the curve above that shows the projected increase in workload expected by 1974. Note that the work input peaks about mid-morning.

Exhibit 2
Requests for system resources

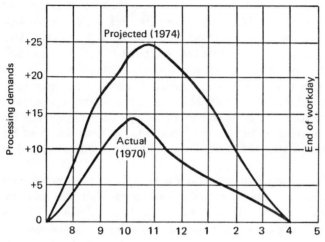

Exhibit 3
Responsiveness of system

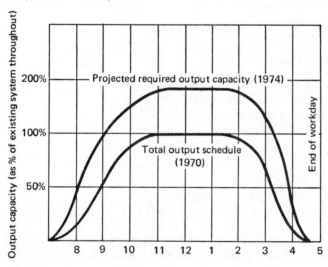

Exhibit 3 plots a composite figure based on statistical records of the capacity utilization of the present configuration. The installation reaches a saturation level for the system resources about 11 a.m. and finishes the required day's workload by about 4 p.m. The curve above this represents how a projected increase in workload capacity would be able to deal with the expected increase in work input shown in Exhibit 2. If the present configuration were to be used for the 1974 work, the system would have to work into the night in order to meet the demand.

Also, the statistical records should be detailed enough to point out specific problem areas which will have to be changed in the system up-date. For example, during certain periods or with certain applications, the system may be continuously process-bound. This would suggest that the new system should either have an expanded instruction set or perhaps have more raw processing power (higher internal speed). Other statistics might show that the system is input/output-bound at certain points. This might suggest to the analyst that more powerful channels are required in the new system, or that new types of storage devices should be considered.

At any rate, the statistical information helps the analyst zero in on areas to be given detailed analysis later on. Thus, the experienced user can considerably constrain the types of hardware or software components to be evaluated.

Even the new user can establish some generic system specifications, but not with the precision of the experienced user. For one thing, the novice can ask other organizations doing similar work what their configuration looks like and how it is performing.

The new user would also know what broad types of system software he is going to want to consider. If he has a commercial installation, Cobol or PL/1 or some other procedure-oriented language would be specified. Scientific installations might be more interested in Fortran. To relatively small users, an easy-to-use, fully-optioned and well-tested monitor system may be essential, whereas large users often write their own.

Finally, there is another broad system specification which may have to be considered: required system reliability. This is the company's estimate of the average down-time it thinks it can live with both for the system as a whole and for individual components. Reliability involves such factors as the response of vendors' maintenance services (both hardware and software).

At this point, the user is ready to step into the evaluation arena. His inputs are established:

1. A simulated job stream containing detailed processing requirements and arrival times for each of the application programs

2. Required system performance criteria in terms of throughput, response time and/or reliability

3. A set of specifications suggesting broadly what system capabilities and component sizes or types should be considered in detail

There are, today, many different processing modes—teleprocessing, remote batch, etc.—which can be used to handle a workload. Each of these will have a different price/performance index when applied to the projected workload. Unless a user is irrevocably committed to one or another of the modes, he can run some broad comparative evaluations, using SCERT, for example. He can simulate the way his projected workload would be handled by the various modes to get estimates of comparative efficiency and cost.

The systematic method is costly, but should lead to substantial savings over the system's life.

INTRODUCTION

The Postal Source Data System (PSDS) was designed to collect data at its source in selected post offices concerning (1) employee time and attendance, (2) labor-hour distribution, and (3) mail volume, and to forward this data to centralized high-speed computers for processing. The processed data was to be electronically transmitted to the originating post offices and other organizations within the management. PSDS has been described by the Post Office Department as being the largest system of its kind ever developed and an important first step in the Department's development of a Postal Management Information System.

PSDS was to be initially installed in the 75 largest post offices in the continental United States, involving about 60 percent of the total mail volume and 60 percent of the total number of post office employees, and was to be fully operational in these 75 offices by November 1968. PSDS was subsequently expanded to include an additional 35 large post offices. Although PSDS has become fully operational in some of the 35 expansion offices, it has yet to be implemented in several of the initial 75 offices. We have identified PSDS acquisition costs of about $60 million as of February 1971.

Source data entering PSDS through electronic input devices at individual post offices is transmitted over long-distance telephone lines to computers at one of five collection centers (teleconcentrator sites). The computers at these sites continuously collect data from the post offices they serve and forward the data automatically to large-scale computers at one of two automatic data processing centers (ADPCs). The ADPCs, after processing the data, transmit it to high-speed printers in the post offices to provide local postal management with print-out reports on labor-hours worked and mail volumes.

The more than 12,000 input, processing, and output devices that constitute PSDS are connected by over 115,000 miles of transmission lines leased from telephone companies. Alternate lines and dual equipment have been designed into PSDS to provide protection against possible loss of data due to equipment or transmission line failure.

INSTALLATION OF PSDS BEHIND SCHEDULE
AND COSTS ARE SPIRALING UPWARD

In February 1966 when justifying the need for funds for PSDS before the Treasury, Post Office and Executive Office Subcommittee, House Committee on Appropriations, Department officials stated that (1) the total cost of PSDS

Abridged from *Report to the Congress: Need to Evaluate and Improve Postal Source Data System Before Further Expansion: Post Office Department* (Washington, D.C.: United States General Accounting Office, 1971), 65 pp.

would be about $33 million (equipment, software, and installation, $30.2 million; first year's supplies, communication line rental, and maintenance, $2.8 million) and (2) the employee time and attendance, labor-hour distribution, and mail volume recording functions of PSDS would be fully installed in the 75 largest post offices by November 1968.

By February 1971, more than 2 years after the target date for a fully operational system in the initial 75 post offices, PSDS acquisition costs related to the initial 75 post offices had risen to at least $44.5 million (an increase of $14.3 million or 47 percent); but PSDS was not operational in several of these post offices including those in New York City and Washington.

Also by February 1971, PSDS acquisition costs—both in-house and under contracts—at 110 post offices (the initial 75 plus 35 expansion offices) totaled about $60.5 million. The target date for full installation of the three planned applications of PSDS at the last of the initial 75 largest offices and the last of the 35 expansion offices is August 1971, more than 2½ years beyond the initial target date of November 1968 for having PSDS fully operational.

We believe that the Department's decision to award contracts for the purchase and installation of equipment for PSDS in 75 post offices was premature and resulted in excessive costs. In our opinion, most of the deficiencies and spiraling costs associated with the installation of the system resulted from inadequate study and testing before nationwide installation. At the time the initial contract for the acquisition and installation of the PSDS was awarded:

1. Only limited testing had been made of a prototype source data collection system and that system was significantly different from the one contracted.

2. A study made by the Department prior to the award of the contract had not demonstrated adequately the feasibility of the proposed nationwide source data collection system.

3. Sufficiently detailed system specifications had not been prepared.

4. Site surveys to enable the Department to make realistic estimates of such items as equipment and space needs had not been made at most of the 75 post offices where the system was to be installed.

Delays and added costs resulted also from various changes in specifications and procedures for a Work Load Recording System encompassing the labor-hour distribution and mail volume system applications.

INADEQUATE FEASIBILITY STUDY

The Comptroller General and the Director of the Bureau of the Budget (now Office of Management and Budget) issued guidelines in January 1959 and March 1960, respectively, to be followed by all executive branch departments and establishments in making preacquisition (feasibility) studies of automatic data processing (ADP) systems. These guidelines, which are still in effect, describe the essential characteristics of an adequate feasibility study, including but not limited to:

1. A realistic examination of the cost of an ADP system when related to the results that can be achieved.

2. A discussion of alternative systems considered.

3. Specific recommendations directed toward both the specific problems involved in getting started and the proposed regular operation under the new system.

We believe that the June 1965 study report fell short of meeting these guidelines and of demonstrating the feasibility of the proposed source data collection system. Some of the shortcomings of the study report were:

1. The feasibility and costs of the proposed system were based on data for a significantly different system in Minneapolis and Milwaukee, a system which had neither been tested fully nor proved successful. We were informed that supporting documentation for the cost data was not available.

2. Specific problems—such as adequacy of electric power, air conditioning, space, and transmission capability of local telephone facilities—which might be involved in making the system operational, were not identified.

3. Only one data collection system was discussed and no alternative proposals were presented or considered.

SYSTEM SPECIFICATION NOT PREPARED PRIOR TO SELECTION AND PURCHASE OF PSDS EQUIPMENT

The preparation of system specifications is a necessary prerequisite in acquiring ADP equipment. Circular A-54, issued by the Bureau of the Budget in October 1961, specifically states that: *"The selection of ADP equipment will not be made until system specifications are available to serve as a basis for selection."*

Department records indicated that detailed system specifications for PSDS were not completed until 6 months after the contract for the procurement and installation of PSDS was awarded in June 1966 and that at least six major changes were made to these specifications between January and June 1967. Such changes were necessary primarily because of revised user requirements of the customer bureaus within the Department.

In our view, if sufficiently detailed system specifications for PSDS had been prepared by the Department prior to the award of the procurement contract, the Department:

1. Would have been able to make more realistic determinations of equipment requirements and the cost thereof.

2. Could have established a more realistic target date for a fully operational system at the initial 75 post offices.

3. Might have selected a different system proposed by other bidders.

In addition, if the requirements of the customer bureaus had been clearly identified before development of the initial system specifications which were later "junked," the cost of this unproductive effort might have been avoided.

SITE SURVEYS NOT MADE PRIOR TO CONTRACT AWARD

Prior to the award of the contract for the procurement of PSDS, site surveys were not made at all of the 75 initially selected post offices to determine the equipment requirements, the space needs, the necessary site modifications and improvements, and the implementation problems to be overcome. The Department sent questionnaires to the 75 offices but visited only eight offices before awarding the contract. Equipment requirements included in the procurement contract were estimated primarily on the basis of employee complements for the 75 post offices.

As late as February 1968—more than 19 months after awarding the procurement contract for PSDS—only 49 of the 75 offices had been surveyed and their actual equipment needs determined. As a result of these surveys, the original equipment quantities and the amount of the contract were increased substantially through numerous contract amendments.

The following table shows the adjustments in the quantities of equipment that have been necessary at 10 PSDS post offices and the effect the adjustments have had on the cost of PSDS. Similar equipment adjustments were made at other PSDS post offices not included in this table.

Post Office Location	Original Estimates		Deliveries to April 1, 1969		Percent of Increase in Cost
	Quantity in Units	Cost	Quantity in Units	Cost	
Albany, N. Y.	41	$ 102,500	77	$ 203,100	98.1
Birmingham, Ala.	61	148,700	94	255,200	71.7
Charlotte, N. C.	47	120,500	98	217,300	80.3
Greensboro, N. C.	39	100,600	79	180,200	79.2
Miami, Fla.	123	286,900	210	468,700	63.4
New Haven, Conn.	50	121,700	82	197,000	61.9
Rochester, N. Y.	77	193,700	133	301,500	55.5
Springfield, Mass.	53	124,100	85	208,600	68.1
Tampa, Fla.	49	127,200	86	200,000	57.0
Richmond, Va.	60	150,300	95	252,700	68.1
Total	600	$1,476,200	1,039	$2,484,300	68.3

From the award of the contract for the acquisition and installation of PSDS to December 31, 1970, 31 amendments had increased the amount of the contract from $22.7 million to $49.7 million, as shown in the table on the following page.

PREDICTED SAVINGS MAY NOT BE REALIZED

Although in 1966 the Department estimated that installing PSDS in 75 post offices would save about $36 million during the first 5 years of operation, the unanticipated high costs incurred to date indicate that savings may not be realized.

The Department's predicted cost savings were based on the assumptions that (1) estimated annual cost to operate PSDS at the 75 post offices, including amortization of equipment costs over a 5-year period, would be $14.6 million and (2) because annual employee costs of $21.8 million for the manual time and attendance and work measurement systems in operation at the 75 offices would be eliminated, the employees involved in these manual systems would be reassigned to other duties.

These assumptions, which in our view lacked validity at the time they were made because of the inadequate feasibility study, were not borne out by actual PSDS operations. Employees who were assigned to operate the manual system have not been reassigned to other duties. On the contrary, operating costs to date have far exceeded the Department's estimates, and its anticipated cost reductions have not materialized.

The Department estimated, in its 1965 feasibility study, that 740 employees would be needed to operate PSDS in the 75 largest post offices and that the annual employee costs would total $5.5 million.

Using the same basis used by the Department in its feasibility study, and recognizing the increases in employee complement and mail volume after 1965, we estimated that, as of October 1970, about 1,050 PSDS employees, at an annual cost of $10.5 million, would be needed to handle PSDS transactions at the 75 post offices. Total authorized PSDS employees, however, had reached 1,857 by October 1970, or about 800 more than our updated estimate.

We estimated also that the annual salary costs for the 1,857 authorized employees totaled $19.6 million, or $9.1 million (87 percent) more than our updated estimate of $10.5 million and $14.1 million (256 percent) more than the Department's 1965 estimate.

The Department, in its original estimate of cost savings for the system, significantly underestimated other annual operational costs for such items as supplies and services, maintenance, and amortization of equipment costs. The Department's 1965 estimate of the annual costs for these items totaled $9.1 million for the 75 post offices to be included in the system. We estimated, however, that the annual costs for these items for the 75 offices totaled at least $17 million, or $7.9 million (87 percent) more than the Department's estimate.

	Date	Description	Cost
Original Order	6-30-66	Equipment and installation	$22,699,991
Amendment Number:			
1	8-24-66	Price adjustment (decrease)	$ -80
2	11- 4-66	Equipment modifications	42,847
3	5-24-67	Additional equipment	4,589,475
7	12-28-67	do.	4,223,932
8	1- 4-68	do.	1,835,760
10	1-10-68	Equipment decrease	-104
13	6-28-68	Additional equipment	2,224,365
18	9-13-68	Equipment modifications	11,589
20	10-16-68	Additional and replacement equipment	129,000
23	1-15-69	Equipment exchange	83,000
24	1-24-69	Additional equipment	227,700
25	1-23-69	Equipment modifications	3,000
		Equipment and installation costs related directly to the initial 75 post offices	13,370,484
			$36,070,475
27	5-13-69	Additional equipment for the initial 75 post offices and 35 expansion post offices	$11,155,717
29	8-29-69	Equipment modifications	9,585
31	12- 3-70	Equipment decrease	-4,320
		Total contract equipment and installation costs	11,160,982
			$47,231,457
Costs of other contract amendments			2,502,422
		Total contract amounts as of December 31, 1970	$49,733,879

In its fiscal year 1971 budget submission to the Congress, the Department stated, as follows:

"Cost Reductions, $5,000,000:

The gross employment increase for workload is offset by a reduction of 737 positions and man-years to be achieved by improved time and attendance processing resulting from the implementation of the Postal Source Data System. This substantial reduction in the 1970 level of employment represents a savings of $5,000,000."

In view of our findings which indicate that more employees are needed to process time and attendance data under PSDS than under the former manual system, we have reservations as to whether this $5 million reduction in employee costs can be achieved under PSDS as it is presently being operated.

QUESTION

What observations do you have with regard to the Post Office Department's feasibility study of its Postal Source Data System?

PART B
SYSTEMS DESIGN

This article provides an overview of the project-management process. In particular, it emphasizes the importance of user-analyst interaction and discusses the relative role played by the two groups at each step in the process.

THE PROJECT MANAGEMENT PROCESS | 9
ARNOLD E. DITRI and DONALD R. WOOD |

What we call the Project Management Process is the specific methodology we have developed for the management of all systems applications in a company, no matter where in the company such applications may occur, or how large or small they may be. Its structured sequence of fixed phases for the accomplishment of a systems project has been polished over many years of actual experience in dozens of companies here and abroad; it is a tested and precise sequence of work steps.

No two systems projects in the same company are ever alike, just as the needs of no two users will ever be alike. For all its discipline, therefore, the Project Management Process must be flexible—adaptable to any set of circumstances. Yet despite its necessary flexibility, the Project Management Process is an established, effective modus operandi for any systems project. It works.

PLANNING VS. DOING

While essentially our methodology for project management divides the sequence structure into what we call the planning phase and the doing phase, it is worth noting that the amount of time and effort expended in planning and in doing may vary significantly from project to project. Planning deals essentially with abstracts which do not yet exist. Doing, by contrast, is the shirtsleeve work of bringing approved projects to fruition.

We use a rule of thumb to estimate the amount of detailed work the planning phase should get: it should be directly proportionate to the size of risk involved. A relatively small five or six thousand dollar systems project may get very little detailed planning, for it involves little risk. In a five or ten million dollar project,

Reprinted with permission of *Tempo*, Touche Ross & Co., September 1969, pp. 31–35. Arnold E. Ditri is Director of MS Consulting Services and Director of Computer Systems and Donald R. Wood is Partner in Charge of the MS group (Chicago office) for Touche Ross & Co., certified public accountants.

where the risk is enormous, it is possible that much of the hard detail work of preparing user specifications, normally done during the doing phase, will be included in the planning. This provides the user and management with details proportionate to the size of the risk involved.

For these reasons, the amount of work performed in each of the steps listed below may vary considerably from project to project. It is entirely possible that the second or third planning step which we describe below can be eliminated. Yet whether the risks involved are great or small, the structure—the methodology and sequence—remains the same.

Planning Step No. 1: First User/Systems Encounter. The "first encounter" between the user and a representative of the systems department may be a single meeting or several across a period of time. While the initiator might be either the systems man or the user, it must be clear in these first encounters that systems is a support function.

In this first encounter, the objective is to discuss the anticipated change—its technical feasibility, broad benefits, and approximate costs. When the discussions are over, the user and systems man may have agreed that the idea was unsound—and decide to do nothing more. Or they may have agreed that the idea has merit and the user may authorize the next step in the process.

Planning Step No. 2: Preliminary Systems Study. Now the systems representatives—with frequent ensuing dialogue with the user—make a preliminary study which, like an architect's first sketch, attempts to determine if the project selected seems really feasible, and approximately how much it would cost.

The amount of preliminary planning made by the systems people is commensurate in its detail with what they believe to be necessary to permit the user to decide whether or not to continue after this step. In essence, this study is a loose feasibility study which devotes itself to four basic factors:

1. The real need for such a project in the user's area

2. The business benefits the application would provide to the user's department

3. The timing requirements of the applications: can it be implemented in time to provide the benefits needed?

4. The risk involved versus the dollar and non-dollar benefits involved

Decision Step No. 1: User Evaluation. Upon completion of the preliminary study by the systems department, it is now imperative that the next planning step send the ball back to the user's side of the court. We call it "user evaluation" of the preliminary study. It is worth repeating that in this—and all subsequent—decision steps, the decider is always the user.

In essence, the user's appraisal of the preliminary study asks: is this a sound business venture? If I go ahead with it, is it a sound management decision for me to make for my department? Are my people ready for it? Can I afford it, both in terms of cost, and the time, including management time, which it will take to complete?

At this point in the process the user/manager has essentially three alternatives:

1. He may decide he does not like the project and stop any further work on it.

2. He may decide he already has enough information to go to management for approval to immediately start the "doing" process.

3. He may decide he still wants more detailed, more verified, more complete information.

Even if the user chooses one of the two latter alternatives, he is not yet fully committed to the project.

Planning Step No. 3: Systems Planning Study.   When a user has decided that more detailed planning is required, he and the systems representative then conduct an in-depth systems planning study of the project's feasibility. That study, when completed, might be compared to a cardboard model, made by an architect, of a building under serious consideration.

In much more detail now, it examines:

1. The technical feasibility of the project

2. The costs they will incur and the benefits they will generate

3. The number of man-months of programming and software preparation required

4. The complexity of the conversion from what exists now to what will be when the system is complete

5. The impact on the people in the user's department; the amount of training they will require to convert to the new system

6. The monthly cash flow that will result from the project

Decision Step No. 2: Management Approval.   Upon completion and submission of the systems planning study (or as noted above, perhaps before it) a point comes when the user feels he has enough detail to be able to decide to go ahead or not. Once again, the user may decide not to proceed. If he decides to go ahead, however, the project management methodology insists that at this juncture, the project must be submitted for management approval for allocation of the company's resources.

It is important to realize that management is not being asked to decide upon a highly technical proposal, couched in the jargon and expressed in the charts of the systems world. It is being asked, instead, to evaluate a business venture within the company, presented in business language, with measurable and specific business parameters of benefits and risk.

If management is required, in a given meeting, to choose between many users, certainly the return-on-investment factor indicated in each project being advocated will weigh heavily in awarding approvals. Yet a people-sensitive management may approve a project with a smaller return on investment than others, because in its judgment the people in that user's organization are far more ready for its implementation than those in another with a greater ROI.

It is impossible to overstate the significance of this fixed phase in the project management methodology. For as noted earlier, by inserting it we are including all systems technology and activity as part of the decision-making portfolio of senior management. If a project they approve requires a substantial amount of systems programming and/or new equipment costs, it is senior management now, not an unbridled systems department, which has decided to spend the money or not, in an orderly, business-oriented manner.

If management approves a user project, it will of course be the systems organization which will be responsible for the effective control of its costs. Yet, very significantly, the benefits which will be achieved will be realized by the user's organization. It will be the user who henceforth must administrate the project, just as he must for any other of his department operations. It is the user who must justify the costs of the project by producing in his organization the benefits the system promises.

THE MOVE FROM PLANNING TO DOING

What has been operative thus far in this methodology of systems management is a kind of "creeping commitment" by the user and his management. It invites increasing user involvement, increasing advocacy of the project to which he feels more and more committed. As noted above, planning, even detailed planning, takes place in a preliminary (less than final) atmosphere. Doing is the hard nitty-gritty of final irrevocable detailed decisions and actions. Doing is the hard part. One might say that when the doing begins, the project honeymoon is over.

Doing Step No. 1: User Requirements. The first significant doing step involves detailed analysis—by both systems and user personnel—of what is really involved in turning the project into reality. The systems people make final detailed analyses of systems which now exist in the user's organization. They must also specify the actual details of the new system which, when super-imposed over the old, will deliver the benefits and savings promised in the planning.

During this first doing step, the user's organization becomes increasingly involved. For their manager will have told them that once the system is installed, it is up to them—and him—to deliver the benefits. The earlier in the doing they become committed, the better.

Doing Step No. 2: Systems Specifications. When the requirements have been analyzed, it is now time for the user and his systems colleagues to make final decisions about the specific functions the system will perform. Systems specifications are prepared which spell out exactly what functions the new system will achieve for the user. In architectural terms, the systems specifications are similar to the preparation of detailed working drawings for every single function of a building under consideration, from plumbing to lighting.

The systems specifications, like such blueprints, detail exactly what the new system will contain, including such factors as:

1. Reports: content and frequency
2. Files of information required
3. User controls over the system
4. Economics, one-time and continuing costs; specific benefits
5. Outlines of new user procedures and policies
6. Machine utilization details

Essentially, the systems specifications list what processes the new system will use, and how, and when, submitted to the user in a single complete document.

Decision Step No. 3: Final Use and Approval.   If upon careful study of this more detailed document by the user and members of his organization, they become discouraged by its costs, or the insufficiency of its benefits, the user can still decide to cancel the project, and to notify management of his decision.

This is his last decision step, however. If he accepts the specifications as documented, the period of "creeping commitment" has ended. He is now committed to go forward. His decision to accept the specifications is literally a three-way contract: between the user organization, the systems organization, and top management. This moment in the methodology is not unlike approval of an architect's final blueprints, and the beginning of construction of a building with specified details and costs and functions.

The project is now firmly under way.

Doing Step No. 3: Implementation Planning.   Now both user and systems organizations must examine in careful detail how the new system will affect the present system and the user's organization. Their objective, at this phase, is to minimize the resistance and the confusion inherent in the wrenching changes which conversion to new systems almost always brings. In this phase, they plan ahead for the impact of the new system. "People considerations" are critical in implementation planning, for unless the user organization accepts the system willingly, its effectiveness will be seriously impaired.

Doing Step No. 4: Program Specifications and Programming.   The next doing step is the most detailed step in the entire project management process. It can begin either after or in parallel with the Implementation Planning work. It is the drawing of program specifications of what each computer program should accomplish for the system, and exactly how. Then the programmers sit down to begin actually writing the various programs the system will require. This step, obviously, is entirely a function of the systems organization.

Doing Step No. 5: Conversion and Training.   Even while the computer programs are still being written and debugged, the systems organization and the user organization together must begin the backbreaking task of throwing out the old and getting ready for the new. Included here is the process of converting manual information files into machine readable form—file conversion.

During this same period of time, user personnel must be trained to use the new system, according to procedures identified earlier in the implementation planning phase—in the use of new methods, new procedures, and occasionally new machines.

The user, in most cases, is responsible for training his own people—for three reasons:

1. He knows his people best.
2. Reluctance by his organization to accept the new system is highest in this training phase.
3. He must have sufficient knowledge to do this job, or he will never be able to take the next step of installing and managing the new system.

Doing Step No. 6: Systems Test.   With the programs now written and individually debugged, the files converted, the user personnel trained and psychologically adjusted to accept the new system, now comes the time to test it—to begin to make it work. Testing is one of the most critical parts of the entire Project Management Process. One of the important testing mechanisms is a process we call "fail testing." This is a technique of trying specifically to make the system fail, finding the difficult flaws—not the obvious little corrections—which will still be in the system and which must be found prior to final conversion.

The user must insist on visible proof of readiness before he considers the testing period over. Frequently, wise users prepare test data to feed through the system to convince themselves that their system is ready for conversion. But in no case will final conversion take place before systems men and user agree that it is time.

Final Doing Step: Conversion and Feedback.   When the moment of readiness arrives, it is time for final conversion from the old to the new—not unlike actual moving from old quarters into a new building.

Yet even after the system is launched, problems are bound to arise. Trouble is inherent in change. Yet if the training has been adequate, everyone who will be involved in the system should be already informed as to the kinds of problems they are likely to encounter. A formal reporting mechanism should identify for all concerned:

1. Existing problems at any point in time
2. Who is responsible for correcting them
3. What is being done to fix them

The new system, now, becomes a part of the user organization. The project management process has ended; a new system has begun, like a transplanted heart which is functioning without fail.

Yet while the new system is launched now, in a sense, it is never finished. As it operates, it evolves. It feeds back into itself improvements, and improvements upon improvements, to make it ever more efficient and dynamic and useful to the user. One might say that the end of the project is only the end of the beginning of the system.

This article elaborates on one of the steps in the project-management process: project-priority determination. It is approached first in terms of quantitative criteria and then in terms of qualitative and institutional considerations; the contents of computer-project proposals consistent with this approach are presented.

10 | COMPUTER PROJECT SELECTION IN THE BUSINESS ENTERPRISE
M. H. SCHWARTZ

With continued speeding up of both the tempo of American enterprise and the introduction of new technology, controllers and other financial managers in business and government are becoming increasingly conscious of competing investment demands. Computer projects are rapidly becoming significant competitors both with one another and with all other investment demands. For some time, it has been the rare larger-sized organization that has not generated more computer project ideas than available resources could deliver, that has not been confronted by more project demands than it could fulfill.

This problem is now filtering down to smaller organizations. Recently a bank controller told me that he could either convert his present "second generation" automated demand deposit accounting system to a lower-cost third generation system or he could automate his manual loan accounting system. He could not do both this next year. He asked my views on which to do. I advised him to do the loan accounting project for two reasons—to innovate for large new opportunities rather than improve marginally on opportunities from which the cream has already been skimmed and to focus on information potentials rather than on paper pushing.

No matter what the size of the organization, deciding what to do and what comes first is a perplexing task. In the face of increasing competitive drives and increasing competitive opportunities and threats, the financial manager must come to grips with computer project selection on a measured, analytic basis.

The effective screening, selection and evaluation of computer projects require: (1) criteria for making judgments, recommendations, and decisions about authorizing and maintaining projects, and for assigning and shifting resources and (2) a system, a method, a set of procedures. These requirements are compelling. In many ways, the requirements are identical with those associated with any major investment. Considerable thinking has been focused for years on clarifying the issues and attempting to solve the problems that have been identified. The literature on the subject, which is now quite large, emerged when business managers recognized the need for careful rationalization of decisions on plant and equipment expenditures. Improved accounting systems

---

From *Journal of Accountancy*, April 1969. Copyright 1969 by the American Institute of CPAs; used by permission. M. H. Schwartz is an assistant controller at the U.S. Atomic Energy Commission; his responsibility includes the development of an agency-wide management information system.

were of great value in improving these decisions. The literature has recently been considerably expanded in association with growth in the number and variety of competing opportunities for research and development.

We can now expect that serious attention will increasingly be given to the selection of computer projects, and we can no longer afford to plunge into the beckoning opportunity without a serious reckoning of costs and returns. We must focus on producing the most valuable output of our available human and machine resources. The role of the accountant is important, for he must shape the information that is needed for proper analysis in the selection of de novo computer projects and in the determination of which ongoing projects should be continued and which put on the shelf.

CRITERIA

Authorization for computer projects in a business enterprise should be based upon: (1) quantifiable impact on profit and loss, whether in the form of new earnings or savings, (2) qualitative factors and (3) institutional criteria. (Special cost-effectiveness analysis is required in government enterprise in lieu of P&L impacts.) "Quantifiable impact" means that we have been able to estimate, with reasonable confidence, the explicit cost/earning relationship for a project. Qualitative factors really represent implicit future dollar values—presently invisible, unspecifiable dollars that we feel reasonably confident the business will earn from improved financial analysis, improved marketing and improved operations. Qualitative factors must be analyzed not only for projects whose benefits cannot be specified in dollar terms, but also for projects measurable in dollar terms—management may frequently override dollar comparisons in favor of compelling qualitative comparisons. We should beware of monolithic dependence on the "strictly business" appeal of estimated dollar figures (whose crudeness and inadequacy are often neglected). The essence of qualitative factors is their nonquantifiable but ultimately very significant impact upon P&L in the business organization and upon the quality of performance at a given level of expenditure in the government organization.

Institutional criteria also relate, ultimately, to improved earnings and performance. These criteria are mainly concerned with keeping balance in the organization by deliberately distributing projects over the longer run in accordance with corporate objectives, corporate organization and other institutional factors.

Another factor of institutional importance is the availability of particular human resources for particular projects and the significance of projects to the human beings in the computer complex.

DOLLAR IMPACT ON P&L

Upon satisfactory completion of preliminary analysis, broad design and technical feasibility of a particular application or system, and following establishment of development plans, economic and financial feasibility may be examined. This involves a careful accounting estimation of annual and cumulated cash flows of costs and returns. Such figures bear on both the overall feasibility of particular applications and also on the priority analysis upon which choices among feasible alternatives must depend. Needless to say, the cost figures (people, equipment, etc.) should be painfully comprehensive. Too frequently many real dollar costs of implementing and running a new computer system are not adequately allowed for in systems planning. Efforts to ferret out all the potential returns are often far greater than efforts to identify and estimate all the potential costs. The potential contribution of the accountant is clearly significant.

The left-hand columns of Exhibit 1 show a possible cash-flow summary for a particular project in a way that is often presented to management. Such figures, taken at face value, may be seriously misleading, however. Is a return of $1,300,000 over five years adequate for an investment of $900,000? Is the project really worth undertaking? Is the $400,000 cash advantage fully meaningful? There are two techniques for answering these questions. One is to compute the implied rate of return on the outlay. If the rate at least equals the institution's rate of return objective, the project begins to show financial appeal. Holding other things equal, the greater the rate of return, the higher the priority of the project and the greater the resources which should be applied to it.

Rate of return calculations sometimes have tricky effects and many people, including the author, prefer to compute the "present value" of the future net earnings stream, using the institution's rate of return objective for the discount calculations. Costs for projects whose development lives exceed one year should also be discounted. The purpose of the discount is, of course, to bring consideration of the time value of money into the financial presentation. It is remarkable how neglected this imperative accounting analysis can be! The author has seen huge proposals made, even in financial organizations, that present only the unadjusted streams of earnings or savings, thus exaggerating the dimension of earnings or savings.

Exhibit 1

Cost-earnings analysis quantifiable dollar impact basis
(in thousands of dollars)

Year	Project Costs	Earnings#	Cash Flow	Cash Flow Discounted* to "Present Value"
1969	500.0	0.0	−500.0	−416.5
1970	400.0	100.0	−300.0	−208.2
1971		350.0	+350.0	+202.7
1972		400.0	+400.0	+192.8
1973		450.0	+450.0	+180.9
Five Year Total	900.0	1,300.0	$400.0	−48.3

#Net of all operating costs other than taxes
*Cash flow discounted at 20 percent return, before taxes

The right-hand column of the table shows the effect of discounting the cash flow for the illustrated project. In contrast to net earnings of $400,000 over the anticipated life of the system, discounting shows that the present value of the system is negative in sign. Compared to alternative typical uses of funds in the organization, the project will lose $48,000. On the basis of a proper accounting analysis, other things being equal, this project should not be undertaken. A more fully rounded analysis of the potentials of the project, say for the qualitative improvement of management information, may demonstrate that despite the apparent negative dollar picture, the project should be undertaken. But that is a different matter. Alternatively, more complete analysis may reveal that particularly in view of the "true" dollar implications, the project is very definitely not worthwhile. The point is that the data processing manager, the financial manager and the top manager should not be misled into selecting a project on the basis of inadequate accounting only for simple undiscounted cash flow.

ALTERNATIVE PROJECTS

So far we have dealt only with the dollar significance of a single project. Most of the time, top management must make choices from a number of alternative projects. Better decisions will be made when management is presented at planning and budget sessions with alternatives in two senses—alternative projects that would serve alternative purposes and alternative approaches to individual projects. Only then can management deal adequately with decision-making for computer activities.

When two or more possibilities are being considered, a bit more refinement of the discounted cash-flow figures is useful. A million dollar project and a half-million dollar project may show similar discounted returns, say a quarter of a million dollars. It is obvious that the half-million dollar project is preferable, other things being equal. When a large number of projects and approaches are being reviewed, the relationships are not so obvious. A relative measure of discounted returns is needed for lining up priorities. A very convenient and significant priority measure is the computed present-value dollars of net savings (or of net earnings) per present-value dollar of project costs. In strictly dollar terms, the ratio tells management what dollar output is yielded per dollar of input. Other things equal, projects should be ranked according to this measure.

A comprehensive annual budget review should also embrace ongoing projects, partly to bring new information and the lessons of experience with the projects into play and partly to determine if any existing project is of lower priority than one or more possible new projects. Should one or more ongoing projects be shelved? The ratio is highly useful in making this determination. The numerator should contain the latest revised figures of savings or earnings, discounted from the present time, and the denominator should show only remaining costs. Sometimes the financial officer must remind top management that spent costs are sunk costs—they are gone—and, while they may teach valuable lessons, they have nothing to do with determining current priorities. Thus, a project with costs behind it is worth continuing if additional costs in relation to returns are low. High past costs should not be considered as supporting a project in the effort to "make the costs good"—they are gone; nor should they work against a project whose remaining costs are now favorable in relation to payoff.

Visible, estimable dollars are not alone sufficient, however, for adequate priority determination. There are many highly desirable computer projects that management senses the need for without being able to specify explicit dollar returns. A banker, for example, may decide to put teller operations "on-line" to a computer in order to speed up window transactions, thereby reducing customer waiting time and increasing teller productivity. The costs of such a project can certainly be identified but the returns are virtually impossible either to predict in advance or to measure afterward. Compelling competitive threats or opportunities often justifiably stimulate action on qualitative grounds that importantly bear upon earnings in ways presently unspecifiable in strict quantitative terms.

The judgmental weighing of qualitative factors is the best presently available substitute for dollar measures where dollar measures cannot be made with confidence but where dollar earnings, high in relation to costs, may nevertheless be anticipated with confidence.

QUALITATIVE FACTORS

A number of qualitative factors may be revealed by study of the potential contributions of the computer to the activities and problems of a business enterprise. Increasingly, we are focusing on what can be done to strengthen management, in contrast to the focus of the past on improving paperwork processing. This article is limited to noting four broad categories of qualitative contributions of computers, the first of which is, appropriately, management information for decision-making. But before moving on to particular qualitative considerations, it should be stressed that qualitative analysis must always also present the fullest possible cost statement, because economic feasibility and economic implications are the ultimate basis for resource expenditures.

Decision-Making.   Decision-making stands upon four foundations—human attributes, skills, information and analysis. Decision-making in business occurs within many broad areas—personnel, finance, production, marketing. Improved summary statistical information and sharpened analysis will surely add to business earnings by improving decisions and hence performance. Projects that show significant promise of contributing substantially to the information flows and analytic procedures available to management should be given a high priority status. For example, an automated accounts receivable system not only provides for reduced costs of processing and speeded up billing; perhaps more importantly it can be a first step toward automating information flows that will help improve corporate cash management, that will significantly contribute to more effective use of the corporation's cash resources.

It is hard to quantify in advance the payoff of successive automation projects that increasingly enhance the financial manager's capabilities of minimizing deposit balances by the synchronization as much as possible of the streams of payables and receivables and of maximizing short-run investment earnings from freed-up cash. But a cash management information system can be a most important profit-yielding reward of computer-based financial transactions processing.

Operations.   Earnings from production and marketing are heavily dependent upon the speed, quality and accuracy of transactions data processing. Projects that show significant promise of contributing substantially to the speed, quality and accuracy of data processing should be given a high priority status. Of course, judgment must be brought to bear on the expense side—gilding the lily must be avoided. Achieving speed where speed is not profitable is a waste of resources.

Competition.   Judgments about the competition are difficult, but they are necessary in the priority setting process. Suppose a firm has to choose which of two automation opportunities to exploit this year, say systems S1 and S2; suppose further that S1 is an innovation in the industry while S2 is already in use by a major competitor; suppose the dollar cost/earnings analysis is similar for the two systems; and suppose overall budgetary considerations dictate that only one of the two be implemented this year. Management would need to analyze and judge between S1, which opens up the opportunity for leadership and an early start, and S2, which is demanded in response to a competitive threat. Even if the two systems were of greatly different dollar benefits, management would want to weigh the competitive angles in setting final priorities for it may find that it prefers the project with the lower quantifiable dollar benefit in favor of competitive intangibles.

The Firm's Image.   This is a self-explanatory qualitative factor. Nowadays all companies are eager to show leadership—in using computers as well as in other ways. This is a meritorious factor that calls for balance. No organization can be first, or even among the first, in all activities.

INSTITUTIONAL CRITERIA

Analysis of the dollar impact upon P&L and of the qualitative factors of a project deals with the more visible benefits of the project. Effective management and effective priority setting also depend upon maintaining institutional balance in the allocation of computer resources beyond the more visible benefits.

Certainly some kind of balance must be maintained among the various organizational units of a firm. Nobody, nor mathematics, can say what a "fair" share is; the solution to this problem requires great judgment and "give and take." This means, operationally, that a project of less visible benefit may occasionally be given priority over a project with presumably more visible benefit if the latter comes from an area already well endowed with projects and the former comes from an area for which little computer work has been done. The historic record is clear in too many firms: Operating potentials have starved information and analytic potentials, seemingly because the visibility of the operating payoff swamped all the rest.

There are a number of institutional criteria that make for an institutionally balanced set of projects over time. Among the criteria are:

Corporate Objectives and Corporate Plans.   Certainly no project should be undertaken that is at variance with corporate objectives or corporate plans. In a sense, overall objectives and plans are constraints. But they are more than constraints. It is the other side of the coin that is less obvious—namely, that the full spectrum of objectives and plans is often forgotten. Sometimes a costly computer project would justifiably support a fundamental business objective that bears only very generally and in no way measurably on the fortunes of the business. A commercial bank, or any business firm for that matter, may deliberately seek to develop a system in support of a community need in the interests of fulfilling an objective to participate constructively in community affairs even though the system is "unprofitable." This is a broad institutional objective. Such objectives belong among the considerations in determining project priorities.

Management Aspirations.   Management by hunch is playing a decreasing role in American business enterprise. But it is not, nor should it be, always inappropriate. The instincts of the manager are among his most valued attributes. While every effort should be made within a business enterprise to lay out the analytical basis for computer projects, if only to keep application tweakers at bay, there are occasions when an idea of a far-seeing manager should be pursued despite skimpy evidence. While this argument runs contrary to the basic theme of this article, room must be left for human beings to work out their affairs in the human context. All too often, and this is regrettable, technicians are capable of working against good ideas that come from line managers. In the same vein, top management must occasionally give in to technical drives. At least a limited number of "way-out" projects must be pursued. Overemphasis on "sure things" and on conservative criteria is likely to lead to long-run weakness. "Crazy" ideas should not be allowed to drain off resources, but ideas should be openly explored before they are classed as "crazy."

Divisions and Departments.   Some kind of balance must be maintained in project allocation among various major units of a business; there is some kind of "fair" share for each major activity. In the end, of course, division of resources must be on the basis of efficiency in their use. But how can it be ascertained that all the alternatives are being considered? One way is consciously to study potentials in relation to the structure of the organization. A bank controller might ask: Are we doing enough for loan accounting and loan management? Are we neglecting our correspondent responsibilities? What alternatives might we explore for presently unattended areas? This kind of review leads to the opening up of new potentials and to the widening of long-range systems planning.

There is no need to labor the notion of institutional criteria any further than to note that others include customers, markets, services and products, improvements vs. innovations. A final institutional criterion that merits special attention, however, has to do with the human resources that make up the electronic data processing effort.

Human Resources. Current work has to be geared to the resources available—mainly the skills and abilities of the staff. To be sure, consultant organizations are a useful extension of the existing staff, but effective use of consultants does depend in part on the ability of the user organization to negotiate with, monitor the progress of, and implement consultants' work. Consequently, some (managerial) local resources are also required for effective use of external resources. The human resources upon which computer projects depend involve:

1. Project management
    a. For internal projects
    b. For consultant projects
2. Project technical staff (could be furnished by consultant)
3. Project administrative staff
4. User area staff
5. Affected area staff

On balance, a project is best not undertaken, no matter what its seeming priority, if there is inadequate supervision and staff to prevent wholesale waste of resources. The emergence of desirable projects that the present staff cannot handle should be recognized and staff resources should be augmented or reshaped accordingly.

A CONCLUDING NOTE ON CRITERIA

The discounted cash-flow analysis, and priority analysis in general, may be extended several degrees of sophistication in the effort to portray and to cope with the uncertainty of future events: (1) ranges of costs and earnings may be specified in lieu of single figures; (2) probabilities may be assigned to the single figures or to ranges; and (3) the costs and earnings figures, along with weighted criteria, may be analyzed with the help of operations research models. Each of the three advanced methods has its advantages, notably to provide for sensitivity analysis of possible errors of estimate as well as to make clear to all parties that the estimates are in fact literally estimates and therefore subject to inevitable errors.

The notion of modeling the possible consequences and impacts of each of a set of projects and approaches is appealing, and we can look forward to improvements in project selection in the large organization along these lines. Great strides have been made in government and in a number of large corporations with the use of mathematical systems analysis for cost/benefit studies and for probing the alternative implications of possible decisions across the whole spectrum of planning and budgeting. We can expect recently developed methodologies, now actually about 10 to 15 years old, to filter down to major decisions in business generally, including decisions concerning computer systems design and implementation.

We want to fortify the judgment of top management with as sharp an analysis as possible; and management will be looking for an increasingly systematic study of alternatives and consequences. In the meantime, great improvements can be made simply by laying out the variables, their best estimated values and their likely significance to the organization.

IMPROVING PROJECT SELECTION SYSTEMS

All organizations have some kind of project selection system, whether they recognize it or not. Too many systems, however, are highly informal, non-quantitative, discontinuous, and highly personal. Many firms that study product and services development and marketing in great cost-and-earnings detail fail to give similar attention to computer project development. This we may take to be transitional, reflecting the newness of the computer in business. Sooner or later most business firms will put individual computer systems development projects through the same sort of wringer that other capital and major expenditure projects go through. In fact, a few organizations have already swung too far toward the other pole: they have selection systems that are rigorously structured to the point of inflexibility and they demand quantitative explicitness that is unreasonable.

The purely informal kind of system—which is not "systematic" and can only be called a "system" in the broadest sense of the term—is to be deplored, for its major output is frustration and misdirected efforts. The alternative extreme is much less undesirable; but when it focuses on form rather than content—a not uncommon sump for intelligence among the affairs of men—it, too, generates more frustration than enlightenment. Between the poles there is a reasonably broad band within which effective project selection is feasible.

The major ingredients of a meaningful project selection system are:

1. Selection criteria, which are the bedrock of a system

2. Project generation and formation, which stem mainly from research into potentials and problems and from planning for uses and solutions

3. Documentation, which conveys systems plans, purposes, implications, and justifications to top management

4. Organized review and analysis, which is conducted by top management against the background of explicit criteria in the contents of the annual budget cycle and long-range plans

5. Project decisions, which are made by top management

The crucial underlying element of each of the five ingredients is management involvement. Top management must lay down the criteria, must guide and support research and planning, must communicate its desires on documentation, and must become enmeshed in the review as well as in the decision-making in which priority analysis terminates. Line management must participate directly, substantively and deeply in research and planning and, of course, should contribute wherever feasible elsewhere in the range of activities that lead to priority determination. Above all, line management must share greatly in the shaping of individual computer projects: each manager is no less responsible for his information system than he is for any other aspect of his sphere of activities.

We have already reviewed selection criteria in considerable detail. Research and planning have been treated in other articles so they will not be dealt with extensively in this one.

There is one aspect of research and planning, however, that should be considered here for it is intimately tied to the project selection process. In all but the smallest organizations, the results of research and the broad planning for project proposals should be shared by some sort of users' committee drawn from line management throughout the organization. Such a committee might be named the systems planning committee or the systems steering committee. It should be chaired by either the senior data processing officer or by a superior who is either a member of top management or is especially close to top management. All proposals for computer projects should be approved by such a committee, if indeed the project proposals are not generated by this group. Final recommendations should be prepared by the committee, acting on behalf of the entire organization, for top management review and decision. The role of the committee is a vital one, for only through such a committee can an organization that has reached mature use of computers be reasonably sure that computer resources are institutionally directed in a balanced way.

This brings us to the matter of documentation of project proposals for management study and decision.

PROJECT DOCUMENTATION

For management to be adequately informed on the significance and desirability of alternative computer projects, or even of a single project if only one is proposed within a particular budget cycle, they need broad information (for each project) about (1) objectives, (2) costs and returns over the life of the application or system to be spun out of the project, (3) qualitative and institutional factors and (4) plans for development and operations. Project proposal documentation can be visualized as a four-part package, each part devoted to a major aspect of the proposal. Similar documentation should be presented for both ongoing projects and proposed projects, except that history and status information should be embedded in the documentation of ongoing projects. Finally, in addition to individual project packages, there should be the summary recommendations of the systems planning committee. While prepared last, the summary should be the initial package presented to top management.

Part I, Objectives.   The statement of project objectives is best handled in narrative form. It should specify no less than the problem and the feasibility analysis that presumably have triggered the project proposal, the various purposes to be served and the contributions of the project, the nature of the new system, the bases for financial and technical feasibility, and the place of the project in the long-range automation plans of the organization. The narrative should also point up problems that are likely to emerge, particularly the potential impacts on people, and on organizational structure. Anticipating all the problems is, of course, virtually impossible, but every reasonable effort should be made to perceive negative fall-outs both as a result of the sheer conduct of the project and as a result of implementation and operations.

Part II, Financial Overview.   Like the narrative statement on objectives, the financial overview should be presented in rather broad terms. A good overall electronic data processing framework will contain institutional standards for estimating costs and returns and presumably estimates for each project will be consistent with those standards. Proposal documentation should show annual total costs of the development project, broken down by salaries (including fringe benefits), consultant fees, machine costs, space costs, data conversion costs, training costs and all the rest. The financial plan should also present estimated financial magnitudes associated with utilizing the system to be developed.

Any proposals for replacement systems should show the annual net financial impact of the new system based upon a presented comparison of projected total costs of both the old and new systems over the anticipated life of the new system, also in terms of salaries, equipment and other major costs. Improved earnings, say from improved marketing capability, should also be specified where feasible. The mass of details that necessarily underlie summary figures should not be loaded onto management, but they should be organized and presentable in the event that the need arises for an examination of the basis for the summary estimates. The grand summary financial table for each project should be similar to Exhibit 1, shown earlier, which contains annual figures for costs, earnings or savings, raw cash flows and discounted cash flows.

It should be noted that annual cash flows are particularly important, in contrast to lump sums. The timing, as well as the magnitude, of expenditures and/or earnings may bear importantly on the selection decision. There is a danger here, however, because constant skimming of the cream in favor of short-run payoffs may leave a residue of sour milk.

Part III, Qualitative and Institutional Considerations.   Exhibit 2 shows one useful way that qualitative and institutional considerations may be brought into summary focus. For each criterion, qualitative and institutional, either "high" value or "low" value may be checked off, the choice depending of course upon subjective and intuitive measures. The purposes of the form shown in the exhibit are, specifically, to force out the analytical basis for subjective values and generally to cast qualitative and institutional considerations into as specific and analytic a framework as possible.

The form may be used in at least two ways. Projects with a large number of "high" checks are in general more valuable to the organization than projects with a small number of "high" checks. Alternatively, in the interest of bringing

Exhibit 2

Computer project proposal (Part III—Qualitative and institutional considerations)

Criteria	Value		Comments
	High	Low	
Qualitative:			
Decision making, information	___	___	___
Decision-making, analysis	___	___	___
Operations data processing, speed	___	___	___
Operations data processing, quality	___	___	___
Operations data processing, accuracy	___	___	___
Competitive factors, take lead	___	___	___
Competitive factors, catch up	___	___	___
Image of firm	___	___	___
Institutional:			
Corporate objectives	___	___	___
Corporate plans	___	___	___
Balance among firm's units	___	___	___
Customer relationships	___	___	___
Markets	___	___	___
Balance among services and products	___	___	___
Improvements to existing system	___	___	___
Innovative system	___	___	___
Human resources	___	___	___

some sort of balance into a long-range sequence of projects, certain projects may be selected because they are the only ones that give high checks to otherwise neglected particular criteria.

Many organizations that have formal procedures for selecting industrial research and development projects go so far as to assign relative weights to each criterion, compute a total weighted score for each project, and rank projects accordingly. There are certain advantages to scoring systems, but they certainly do not avoid subjective valuations—the assignment of weights and the checking of criteria are still subjective.

No doubt the handling of qualitative and institutional criteria must be shaped in accordance with the character and modes of the particular business enterprise. The choice of criteria—the table shows only one possible set—and the weighing of criteria are really evolutionary within each enterprise. The main issues are not which criteria and how to weigh them, for these issues can be worked out with experience. The central issue is criteria or not; the central issue deals with bringing as much analysis to bear as is possible in the effort to minimize ad hoc influences in the development of corporate computer and information systems.

Part IV, Plans. Three project subplans belong in presentations to top management. These are (1) the systems development plan, (2) the systems conversion plan and (3) the systems operating plan. They may be presented in broad tabular form, largely in terms of phases, stages and milestones. Overall Gantt charts or overall PERT charts are very useful supplements to tabular formats. Review of the plans helps give management insight into the whole systems development activity and provides them some firm bases for performance measurement and evaluation as well as enriching their information basis for current project selection. Plans also stimulate questions on alternative approaches, thereby contributing to the formulation of the eventual project and implementation of the new system. As in the case of the financial overview, management should not be swamped with details of the technical planning apparatus. Rather, details should be collated and held in stand-by should particular discussions call for greater detail.

Summary Documentation.   While last in preparation, first in presentation to top management should be a recommended total package. The recommendation should be structured parallel to the individual project packages so as to facilitate analysis of the parts in the context of the total. The narrative, the financial statement, the analyses of criteria and the project plans for recommended projects should be presented in aggregated form so that the entire systems effort may be appreciated as a whole both for the coming budget year and for the years ahead covered by the proposals. The recommendation should deal with ongoing projects that should be shelved and with potentially new projects that should be deferred. The individual project documents now appear as supporting evidence and justification for the recommendation.

While burdensome to prepare, the documentation is invaluable. Top management will be in a position effectively to review and to accept or modify the proposed plans and budgets either in the aggregate or in terms of particular projects. This is the final station of the project selection system—rational, measured, analytic decisions for action.

This article has been kept as practical and pragmatic as possible. It should be remembered, however, that there is a powerful theoretical foundation for solving the broad problem we have been considering. Implementation of the theoretical principle may go beyond our present accounting information-generating capabilities, but that difficulty, although perhaps presently insurmountable, should not stand in the way of conscious attention to the principle.

THE BROAD PRINCIPLE FOR RESOURCE ALLOCATION

In principle, a business should adjust expenses of each project activity—whether computer, marketing, branching, acquisitions or new products—so that estimated marginal discounted net incomes are equal throughout the firm. Budget allocations should be shifted so that a dollar spent for any project will not yield a lower net income than if it were spent any place else. This will yield the greatest net institutional income for any given total budget.

Thus, expenses for computer projects should be increased as long as the estimated marginal discounted net income from those expenses exceeds that for the rest of the firm. The principle for resource allocation among computer projects is, of course, identical: expenses for each computer project should be increased so long as the estimated marginal discounted net income from those expenses exceeds that for other computer projects and should be decreased so long as the estimated marginal discounted net income is less than that for other computer projects.

While accounting systems may not yet specify the marginal values, especially for qualitative and broad institutional improvements, the essential logic belongs in the forefront of our thinking when we attempt to determine what is the most efficient way to reach institutional profit objectives.

CASE D | LOCKHEED MISSILES AND SPACE COMPANY (A)

The external and internal requirements for more varied and detailed information cannot be generated under the conventional information systems. Each new requirement or change has to be programmed separately which is a time-consuming, laborious, expensive effort at best. As can be understood, once a system becomes operational, it essentially becomes fixed. Because of the high implementation costs, this forces you to use the mechanical program over a period of time even though it does not maintain pace with the needs from today's ever-changing reporting climate.

As an inevitable result of these deficiencies, many organizations began to develop "prop" systems to extract data from "official" reports to meet their needs. Naturally, this entailed expenditures of manpower effort and other associated costs to obtain financial and operating data for planning, reporting, and control purposes.

Equipment Aspect. Until recently, the state of the computer art was not sufficiently advanced to handle large masses of data in storage which could be updated in a timely manner and retrieved instantly on an "as needed" basis. Recent technical strides, however, have changed this situation and more sophisticated equipment with compatible program language capability is available.

Current Mechanical Program Status. Many of our programs at Lockheed Missiles and Space Company (LMSC) were generated over a ten-year period of time and in various program languages—FORTRAN, Autocode, 9 PAC, etc. Changes were difficult to make, particularly if the original person who programmed the system was no longer available to make changes or additions. Furthermore, many of the programs were inflexible for changes and, therefore, "patch type" additions to the program had to be made, which led to considerable error susceptibility.

NEED FOR A CHANGE

In view of the above, the Financial Systems and Procedures Department at LMSC conceived and designed the STARFIRE concept which will make possible the immediate accumulation of all financially oriented data, mechanically manipulate this information, and make it instantly available for retrieval to the user. This single file concept will make possible a fully integrated mechanical system which will achieve the ultimate in data processing. Its flexibility advantages will overcome the current problems associated with making changes to satisfy current as well as "unthought of" future needs.

From Michael R. Tyran, "STARFIRE—An Advanced Financial Information System," *Management Accounting*, May 1966, pp. 3–16; used by permission. Michael R. Tyran is Manager of Financial Systems and Procedures at Lockheed Missiles and Space Company.

The system, identified by its acronym—STARFIRE:

<u>S</u>YSTEM
<u>T</u>O
<u>A</u>CCUMULATE &
<u>R</u>ETRIEVE
<u>F</u>INANCIAL
<u>I</u>NFORMATION WITH
<u>R</u>ANDOM
<u>E</u>XTRACTION

organizes financial reporting so as to give us greater flexibility, report timeliness, mass storage capability, built-in controls, etc. The name is actually insignificant; it serves only as an identifier to the system.

Exhibit 1 summarizes the processing evolution which will occur from the implementation of the STARFIRE system.

Exhibit 1
Processing evolution of the STARFIRE system

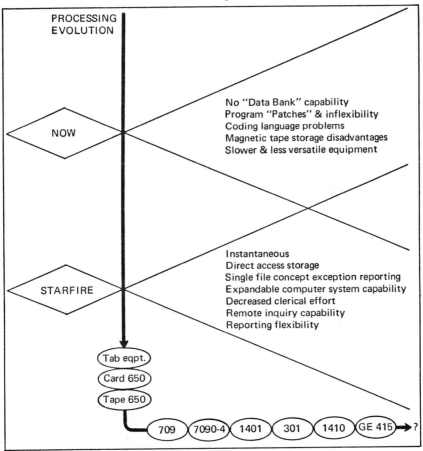

IMPLEMENTATION CONSIDERATIONS

As you can imagine, there are many activities to be considered in designing and initiating a system such as STARFIRE. The steps are outlined in Exhibit 2 and discussed below. It should be noted that the tasks are not necessarily performed in chronological order. In other words, varied tasks can be performed simultaneously by different teams.

Pre-System Design. After reviewing our data processing problems and establishing our objectives and needs, a series of meetings was held with the computer personnel to resolve programming, software and equipment requirements. The computer center management readily recognized the benefits which would accrue in their operations from the improvement and streamlining of our many current programs and systems. Decrease in computer processing time, fewer reports and reruns were the definite achievements anticipated from this system. A generalized approach to this new endeavor was formalized and presented to LMSC management for approval to proceed with a detailed system design. After management concurrence, effort commenced on this project.

Initiating Needs. Our next step was to organize a task force for this activity, composed of the systems department and programming analysts from the computation center. This made an ideal team in that all aspects of the system could be covered—from the source data flow to the preparation of the specification, programming and system implementation.

The total effort was segregated into ten functional areas of two individuals each. In other words, separate teams were assigned to the direct labor area, overhead and manpower, property, payroll, personnel, etc.

The teams familiarized themselves first with the current systems and mechanical programs involved in each area. Presentations of the program objectives and how the system would work were made to all levels of management and concerned operating organizations. Subsequent meetings were held with various data user organizations to verify their current needs and establish any new requirements. As a result of this effort, program objectives were more specifically determined.

System Design. In the review of current information available, flow charts were prepared to show the data flow, data processing and the reporting involved. Every source document was tracked from its point of origin to its resultant contribution in the reporting cycle.

Current reports, both manual and mechanical, were charted by functional areas showing report identification, recipients, issue schedules and all of the data elements contained therein. New requirements were also added to these charts so that a composite picture of all needs were reflected. This allowed us an opportunity to view the total data flow and determine duplications and irrelevancies, and streamline requirements for the overall system.

While the above effort was going on, a separate computer center team was engaged in evaluating software/hardware needs. There was close coordination among all of the personnel assigned to the STARFIRE project.

Exhibit 2

Implementation considerations

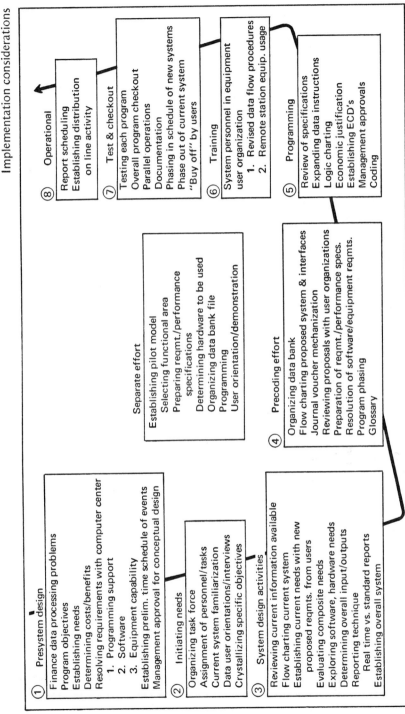

① Presystem design
Finance data processing problems
Program objectives
Establishing needs
Determining costs/benefits
Resolving requirements with computer center
  1. Programming support
  2. Software
  3. Equipment capability
Establishing prelim. time schedule of events
Management approval for conceptual design

② Initiating needs
Organizing task force
Assignment of personnel/tasks
Current system familiarization
Data user orientations/interviews
Crystallizing specific objectives

③ System design activities
Reviewing current information available
Flow charting current system
Establishing current needs with new
  proposed reqmts. from users
Evaluating composite needs
Exploring software, hardware needs
Determining overall input/outputs
Reporting technique
  Real time vs. standard reports
Establishing overall system

Separate effort
Establishing pilot model
  Selecting functional area
  Preparing reqmt./performance
    specifications
  Determining hardware to be used
  Organizing data bank file
  Programming
  User orientation/demonstration

④ Precoding effort
Organizing data bank
Flow charting proposed system & interfaces
Journal voucher mechanization
Reviewing proposals with user organizations
Preparation of reqmt./performance specs.
Resolution of software/equipment reqmts.
Program phasing
Glossary

⑤ Programming
Review of specifications
Expanding data instructions
Logic charting
Economic justification
Establishing ECD's
Management approvals
Coding

⑥ Training
System personnel in equipment
user organization
  1. Revised data flow procedures
  2. Remote station equip. usage

⑦ Test & checkout
Testing each program
Overall program checkout
Parallel operations
Documentation
Phasing in schedule of new systems
Phase out of current system
"Buy off" by users

⑧ Operational
Report scheduling
Establishing distribution
  on line activity

Precoding.   One of the main requisites of this system was to develop an overall data bank. The data banks were generated by each functional area and then consolidated. In the consolidation, there were approximately 1500 line items which were categorized by primary usage.

It should be noted further that the consolidation reflected the added feature of classifying the elements as to their involvement in the procedure of editing, auditing, sorting, updating, data collection and reporting. This bank will assist the programmer in organizing the data on disk file for the instant access and retrieval operation.

Under the STARFIRE system, it is envisioned that all journal vouchers possible will be mechanized. In some instances, it is not practical to mechanize because of the judgment factor involved in their preparation. However, even with those manually generated, the data will be inputted into the system through the input/output devices located in the area where the information originates.

One standard computer program will be prepared to handle all of the "hand-feed" type transactions. The mechanized journal vouchers, which constitute about 95% of the total, will be automatically prepared by the equipment from other information already in the computer system. The consolidated journal voucher data reflect document number, the organization preparing, processing description and ledger account detail involved. For the future, it is anticipated that journal voucher data will be outputted in the form of a listing of the debit and credit entries and the support detail will consist of mechanical reports rather than the bulky support attachments of today.

The STARFIRE system requirements generated were reviewed with the user organization. Any changes required were negotiated. The specifications reflect all the needs, if practicable and justified, of the user organizations.

The program phasing schedule indicates the programs in priority order for coding and mechanizing. This was a very necessary process in that certain programs are dependent upon others for sources and/or manipulated data.

A glossary of all terms used in this program has been compiled. It totals approximately 1,800 definitions of terms used in the STARFIRE system. This will definitely lessen the communication problems for all concerned personnel in the understanding and usage of these terms. The glossary consolidation includes an abbreviation for each term (programming and referral ease), number of characters and the definition itself.

Programming.   Some of the current programs will only require minimum adjustment to tie-in to the STARFIRE concept. In others, there will be major changes to make them compatible with the new system.

Training.   This effort is extremely important to the success of the system. In the initial implementing stage and in order to effect a successful transition, remote stations will be established only in the current information control areas such as payroll, accounts payable, property, etc. The system will be expanded to include operating organizations after they have been trained in the usage of the program and input/output devices and have established a need for a tie-in to the overall network.

Test and Checkout.   Each program will be checked out individually and then in total. Parallel operations will be a necessity before there is a "buy-off" to go productional. Phasing in of the new programs will be based on the priority of individual program data needs and their relationship to the overall system requirements. Results of the test and checkout process will govern the production schedule; however, prototype runs will be made and used as "authentic data" in the interim period.

COST CONSIDERATIONS

To undertake a system of the STARFIRE size and magnitude, a thorough investigation was required in order to establish the justification of the anticipated costs involved. The initial question posed was "will the system achieve the objectives on a paying/benefiting basis?" The answer of course is yes. In making this evaluation, our Exhibit 3 was used as a guide. The factors considered are discussed below.

Equipment.   STARFIRE could conceivably operate with the current equipment but the real-time aspect would have to be eliminated. It was determined

Exhibit 3
Cost considerations

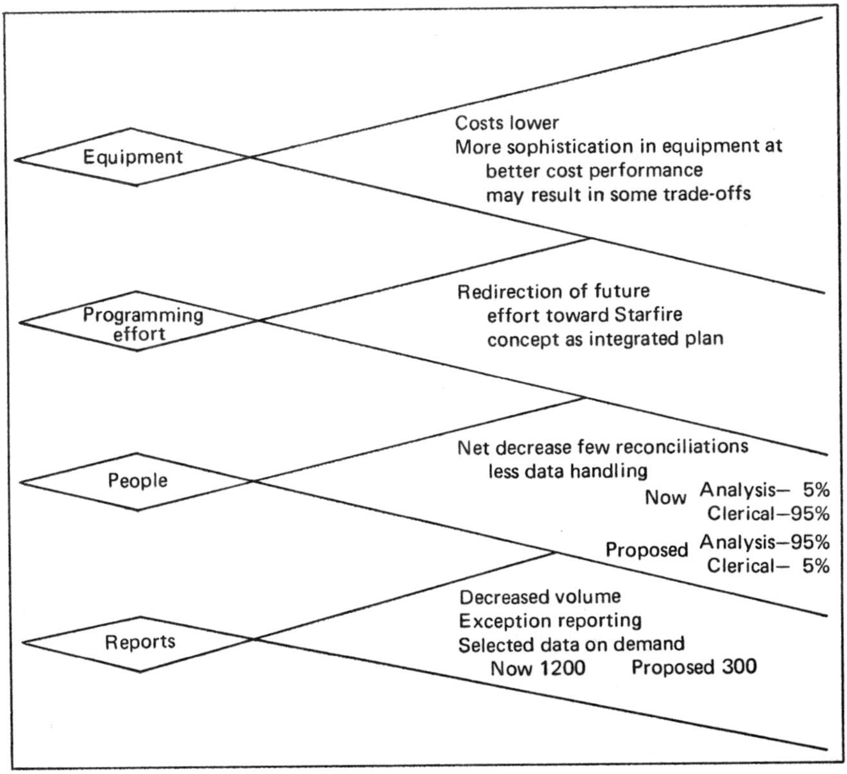

that the much faster processing of data and the improvements in the current programs would more than offset any additional requirements added to the mechanization process. Further, the reductions in current reruns and added equipment capabilities would result in dollar savings.

Programming. In essence, the initiation of STARFIRE gave us an opportunity to redirect programmer support for the development of an integrated system to meet our requirements in an organized, systematic manner. The same programming support will be used for the STARFIRE effort as on the current financial programs. Future programming will certainly decline because of program additions and improvements under the new system. Further, the language to be used is similar to English and, therefore, this minimizes programmers' effort on machine characteristics and allows greater concentration on the important system aspect of the program. Here, too, we expect programming effort savings.

People. Presently, much clerical effort is necessary. Under STARFIRE, with its mechanical implications, clerical effort will be reduced and more time will be devoted to analytical endeavors of "what does the information developed really mean."

Reports. A decreased volume is definitely anticipated because of the real-time capability and exception reporting. The concentration will be on obtaining selected data as needed which will allow for more immediate decision-making.

All of the above considerations lead us to believe that the cost savings under the new system concept will more than offset the cost of STARFIRE implementation. Further, the need for certain information to control and guide operations is immeasurable in terms of dollars. Benefits from the new program are discussed below.

BENEFITS

User Oriented. The user can now have direct access to the file on an instantaneous basis and extract data that heretofore he has been unable to obtain.

Flexibility. Changes to the system will be easier to program, more information is available and new applications can be added by increasing disk storage units and terminals. You can also custom fit the system to the job because of the capability to select the proper devices for doing the task.

Mass Storage. All data can be stored on disk for immediate access. There is unlimited storage capacity off-line, because data cells can be removed and stored. Magnetic tape, as used today, has the disadvantage of volume tape storage, dust accumulation, etc. All concerned organizations can use centralized files for data reporting and retrieval.

Decreased Clerical Effort. This results from exception and real-time reporting.

Built-in Controls. The capability to recognize program errors vs. machine malfunction and to reject data not cleared through the master audit file is built in. In addition, the input from remote stations will be displayed either on printed report or visual device for a last-minute check before it is released to the files.

Improved Operations. Data is available immediately for decision-making and the results of the decision made can be more effectively monitored and reported. More information will be available.

Revitalization of Our Reporting System. This will be achieved in order to accommodate changing management, customer, government, etc., requirements.

SUMMARY

The STARFIRE program represents a teleprocessing communication, direct access and mass storage integrated plan for financial reporting. It is an advancement in the "state of the art" of financial data processing. It is a necessary tool from both the standpoint of data needs and the introduction into the system of the new generation of equipment with its associated capabilities.

The above benefits represent only part of the story of why the trend to more sophisticated data accumulation systems, mass storage and retrieval continually advances. Competition for business is accelerating. Reduced data processing costs, more timely and meaningful information for operation effectiveness and reporting necessitate such a concept as described above—STARFIRE!

QUESTIONS

1 How do the steps discussed under "Implementation Considerations" compare with those discussed by the Systems Analysis/Design Working Party (Selection 1) and with those discussed by Messrs. Ditri and Wood (Selection 9)?

2 How do you quantify each of the various cost elements listed in the case?

3 How would you classify each of the benefits listed in the case—as tangible or intangible benefits?

VI. SYSTEMS DESIGN: INPUT/OUTPUT CONSIDERATIONS

This article discusses the manner of accumulating, summarizing, and reporting management information that is consistent with a company's organization structure. Report contents at each level of organizational hierarchy are illustrated.

11 | RESPONSIBILITY ACCOUNTING
JOHN A. HIGGINS

The subject of this article, I venture to predict, is one of which we shall hear considerably more in the next decade. The topic sounds as if it would be of primary interest to controllers and not treasurers, but that is not so. Actually, responsibility accounting is assuming greater importance with a wider range of management groups, and it is because of this that I believe it will be of interest to many persons concerned with operating problems at various administrative levels.

This modern approach to financial accounting appears to adapt itself particularly well to illustrations by use of charts, in the case of this discussion some eight being required. This new approach to accounting and reporting is the development of an accounting system designed to control expenditures by directly relating the reporting of expenditures to the individuals in the company organization who are responsible for their control. This system results in the preparation of accounting statements for all levels of management, designed primarily so that they can be effectively used by the operating people as a tool in controlling their operations and their costs. It is a system which emphasizes information that is useful to the operating management and de-emphasizes the accounting and bookkeeping aspects that clutter up so many of our accounting and financial statements today. To go one step further in the progression, no budget system is fully effective unless it is built around one basic premise or philosophy and that is that budgets and responsible individuals must be synonymous. By synonymous I mean that each responsible individual in an organization must feel that the budget is *his* budget and not something forced upon him which he might feel is unrealistic and unworkable, and unless the responsible individual does feel that it is *his* budget, he will only make a

From *Arthur Andersen Chronicle,* April 1952; copyright 1952 by Arthur Andersen & Co.; used by permission. John A. Higgins was associated with Arthur Andersen & Co., certified public accountants.

superficial attempt to live within it or use the information as a means of controlling his operations.

Now if one will accept this philosophy in his approach to budgeting, one more step must be taken to complete the picture. One must put the reporting of expenditures in phase with the budget performance responsibility, which is another way of saying that expenditures must be reported on the basis of where they were incurred and *who* had responsibility for them. Hence comes the term responsibility accounting or reporting. In effect, the system personalizes the accounting statements by saying, "Joe, this is what you originally budgeted and this is how you performed for the period with actual operations as compared against your budget." By definition it is a system of accounting which is tailored to an organization so that costs are accumulated and reported by levels of responsibility within the organization. Each supervisory area in the organization is charged *only* with the cost for which it is responsible and over which it has control.

There are three major objectives of cost accounting in manufacturing companies: (1) cost control, (2) product cost, and (3) inventory pricing. The cost systems of most companies meet the last two objectives, but for the most part fall on their faces when it comes to the objective of real cost control. Practically all of them have systems that emphasize the development of product cost rather than emphasizing the controlling of costs at the centers where the costs are incurred. Under responsibility accounting it is possible to meet all three of these objectives by first summarizing cost on the basis of "who did it" and then reshuffling the deck, so to speak, or blending the costs to arrive at product cost and cost for inventory pricing. In effect, what we are doing is putting the emphasis on the objective of cost control for the purposes of management reports but also arriving at the normal cost statements—on a greatly de-emphasized basis.

As mentioned, I have prepared a series of charts to illustrate a system of responsibility accounting and have chosen a typical manufacturing company to make my points. Our hypothetical company has been named the A.B.C. Manufacturing Company and is a multi-product metal manufacturer with annual sales of approximately $4,000,000 and some 300 employees. I have chosen the multi-product metal manufacturing plant to illustrate a general application to manufacturers using a standard cost system, although it could be applied to job costs. These general procedures, with suitable modifications, have also been applied to manufacturers using process cost accounting and also to public utilities. The theory of responsibility accounting in public utilities has been accepted rather widely throughout the utility industry. A number of commercial and manufacturing companies are presently operating under a responsibility accounting system and I believe that most of the progressive companies in the country will have adopted such a system by the end of the 50's. Inasmuch as the backbone of any responsibility accounting system is the organization chart of the company, I will first use an illustration showing an organization chart of the imaginary A.B.C. Manufacturing Company.

EXHIBIT 1

This organization chart shows a president and general manager of a single company. It could, of course, apply to a general manager of a reasonably autonomous plant or a division of a company. Three vice presidents are indicated to head up the basic divisions of a normal manufacturing business organization: production, sales, and finance. In addition to these three vice presidents, there is a chief engineer and a personnel manager reporting directly to the president and general manager. It is assumed that the vice president in charge of production has a general superintendent who is responsible for seven productive departments, each in charge of an individual foreman. Also indicated are typical service departments responsible directly to the vice president in charge of production.

EXHIBIT 2

This is the same chart blocked out to illustrate that segment of the organization around which I have built these illustrated reports. The flow of responsibility starts with the foreman in charge of the drill press department and proceeds up through the general superintendent to the vice president in charge of production and finally to the president and general manager. Obviously, I could have chosen any other segment of the organization to illustrate the build-up of responsibility for reports.

EXHIBIT 3

You will notice that on this chart I have separately set out that segment of the organization around which has been built these illustrative responsibility statements. The four levels of responsibility in the organization have been indicated and numbered. Of course, in a practical application there could be more or less than these four levels, depending on the complexity of the company organization. This chart will serve two purposes: (1) it tends to emphasize the parallel relationship of the levels of responsibility and the reports which are directed at each of the levels; and (2) it will serve as an anchor chart in this article because one will constantly refer back to this chart as each of the reports is discussed through the various levels of responsibility.

EXHIBIT 4

The first statement to be discussed is the statement prepared for the first level of supervision which in this case is the foreman in charge of the drill press department. The top section of the report consists of a listing of certain controllable expenses for which the foreman is to be held fully responsible. These costs have been previously budgeted by the foreman and now the budgeted costs are being compared with the actual costs. It will be noticed that these controllable expenses do not represent the full burden of the department.

Exhibit 1

Organization chart of A.B.C. Manufacturing Company

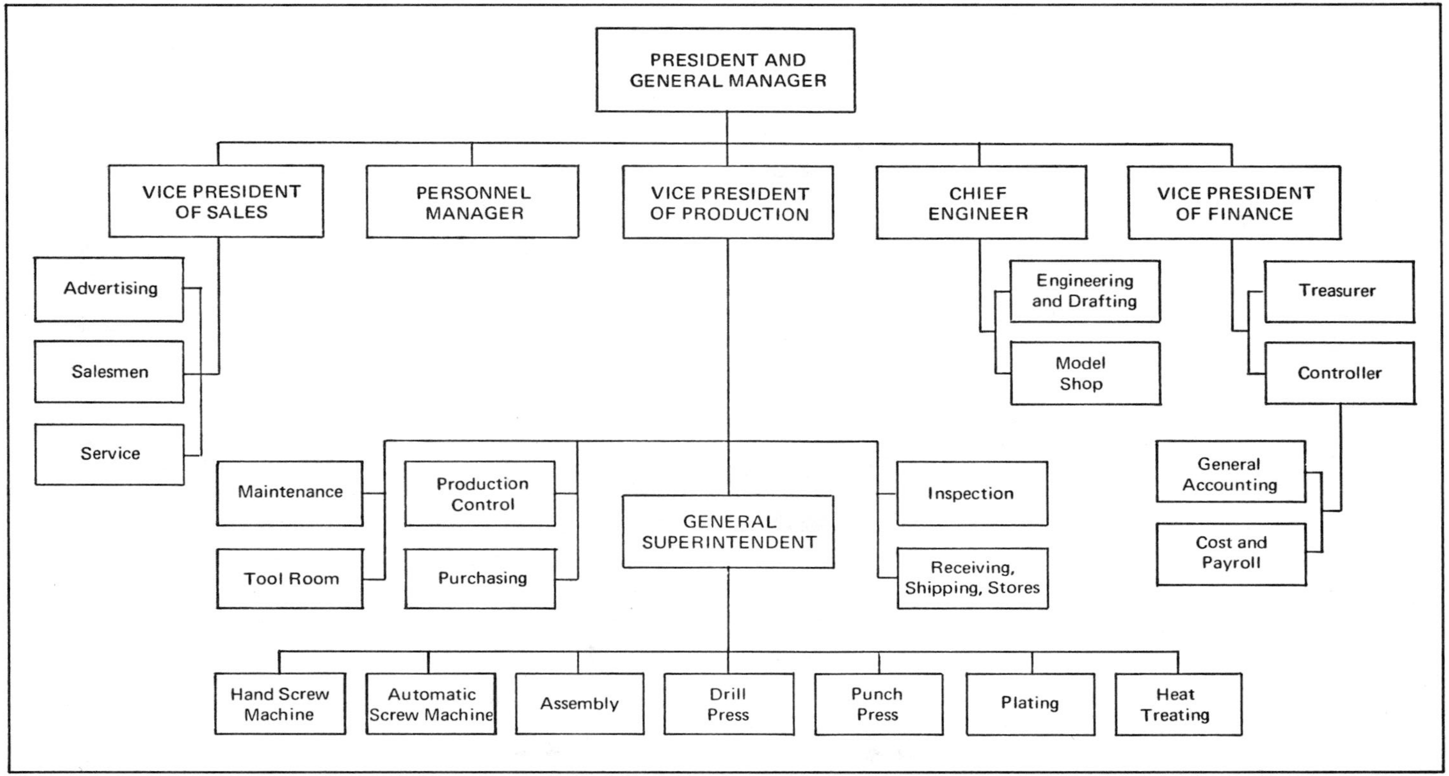

Exhibit 2

Organization chart of A.B.C. Manufacturing Company—segment used for illustrative reports

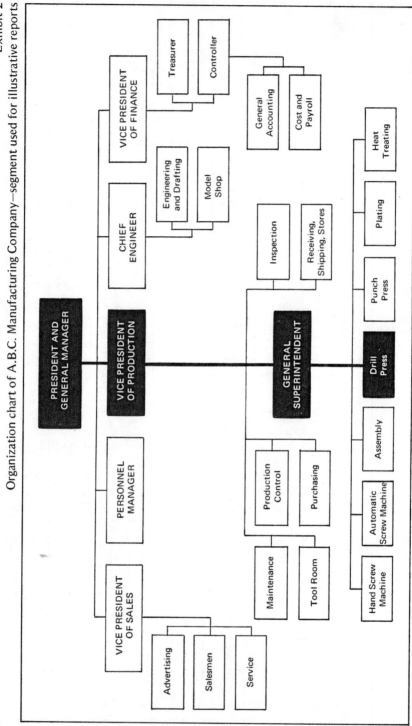

Exhibit 3

Responsibility reporting

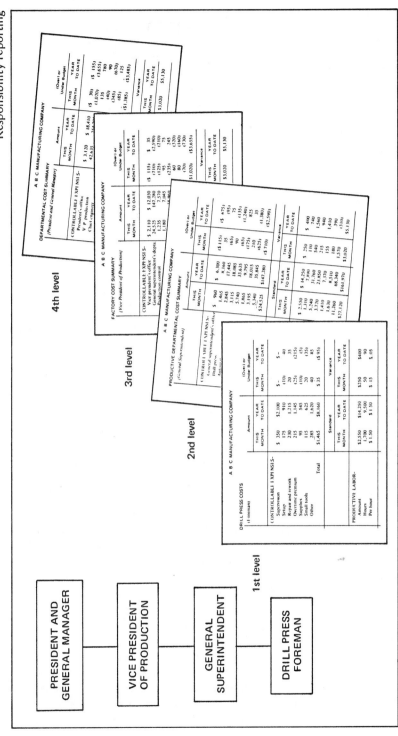

Exhibit 4
Responsibility report for the Drill Press department foreman

A. B. C. MANUFACTURING COMPANY

DRILL PRESS COSTS (Foreman)	Amount		(Over) or Under Budget	
	THIS MONTH	YEAR TO DATE	THIS MONTH	YEAR TO DATE
CONTROLLABLE EXPENSES–				
Supervision	$ 350	$2,100	$ –	$ –
Setup	175	910	(10)	40
Repair and rework	230	1,215	20	35
Overtime premium	215	1,145	(25)	(215)
Supplies	95	545	(10)	(5)
Small tools	115	625	20	(35)
Other	285	1,620	40	85
Total	$1,465	$8,160	$ 35	($ 95)

	Standard		Variance	
	THIS MONTH	YEAR TO DATE	THIS MONTH	YEAR TO DATE
PRODUCTIVE LABOR–				
Amount	$2,550	$14,250	$250	$400
Hours	1,700	9,500	50	90
Per hour	$ 1.50	$ 1.50	$ .15	$ .05

They are confined to the expenses for which the management holds the foreman completely and directly responsible. Naturally, they will vary between different organizations. Classification of these expenses is often a standard classification for all productive departments or even for all factory departments, but this is not necessary to the procedures being illustrated. This classification can be flexible so that each foreman can have reported to him his expenses in the detail and by the classification that he feels is most useful to him for controlling his own expenses. It is very important that the foreman be made to feel that he can have the breakdown of his costs made in any way that he feels will aid him in controlling and budgeting these costs. On the lower portion of this report appears the productive labor in hours and amount at standard with the variances from standard being shown. Productive labor is shown on this report because the foreman is responsible for the efficiency of the productive labor even though he is not responsible for establishing the budget of productive labor. Naturally these variances from standard can be detailed in whatever manner may be practical under the circumstances. If a job cost system were used, of course, there would be no variances and the labor reported would be actual only with perhaps a comparison to budget. It will be noticed that all through these illustrations, as I build up from the lower level to the top level of responsibility, productive labor is carried along with the controllable expenses on the theory that again each of

Exhibit 5

Responsibility report for the general superintendent of productive departments

A. B. C. MANUFACTURING COMPANY

PRODUCTIVE DEPARTMENTAL COST SUMMARY
(General Superintendent)

	THIS MONTH	YEAR TO DATE	THIS MONTH	YEAR TO DATE
	Amount		(Over) or Under Budget	
CONTROLLABLE EXPENSES–				
General superintendent's office	$ 960	$ 6,300	($ 115)	($ 675)
Drill press	1,465	8,160	35	(95)
Automatic screw machine	2,845	17,445	(65)	75
Hand screw machine	3,115	18,085	90	(135)
Punch press	5,740	33,635	(65)	(1,240)
Plating	1,865	9,795	(175)	825
Heat treating	3,195	18,015	210	35
Assembly	5,340	35,845	(625)	(1,380)
Total	$24,525	$147,280	($ 710)	($2,590)

	THIS MONTH	YEAR TO DATE	THIS MONTH	YEAR TO DATE
	Standard		Variance	
PRODUCTIVE LABOR–				
Drill press	$ 2,550	$ 14,250	$ 250	$ 400
Automatic screw machine	1,310	7,890	110	740
Hand screw machine	5,240	31,760	540	1,560
Punch press	3,720	23,850	215	940
Plating	1,410	7,370	155	1,410
Heat treating	1,630	8,510	180	390
Assembly	11,260	68,340	1,570	(310)
Total	$27,120	$161,970	$3,020	$5,130

the areas is responsible entirely for the controllable expenses but in the case of productive labor is responsible for the efficiency of that labor and, therefore, should be shown on a statement directed at each responsibility level. If one will take note of the total of the controllable costs for the drill press department, I will proceed back to our anchor chart and from there proceed to the No. 2 level of reporting.

EXHIBIT 5

Here one sees the total amount of $8,160 representing the total controllable costs for the year to date for the drill press department. Likewise it will be noted that controllable cost totals have been carried forward for the other productive departments for which the general superintendent is held responsible. Also one sees listed, under summarized controllable expenses, the cost of the general superintendent's own office, and it is also supported by a detailed statement which is not shown here. The general superintendent can have, and probably will want, statements for each of the foremen responsible to him. In the bottom section of the report, the productive labor for which the general superintendent is responsible has been summarized by areas of responsibility, the drill press department being one of those areas. Take particular note of the total amount of controllable expenses for which the general superintendent is held responsible, then proceed back to our anchor chart and from there go on to the No. 3 level of reporting.

EXHIBIT 6

This report for the vice president in charge of production has been labeled "Factory Cost Summary." Here one sees that the total amount of controllable costs of the general superintendent has been carried forward as one of the areas of responsibility for which the vice president in charge of production is to be held responsible. These other areas of responsibility, mainly service departments, which report directly to the vice president would also be supported as was the general superintendent's statement by detailed statements of the costs of the respective areas. Again one sees that the cost of the vice president's own office is set forth in total and that when it is combined with the controllable costs of all the other areas of responsibility, one arrives at the total controllable costs for which the vice president is held accountable. The productive labor has also been carried forward directly from the previous report. Again I might add that this

Exhibit 6
Responsibility report for the vice president in charge of production

A. B. C. MANUFACTURING COMPANY

FACTORY COST SUMMARY
(Vice President of Production)

CONTROLLABLE EXPENSES–	Amount THIS MONTH	Amount YEAR TO DATE	(Over) or Under Budget THIS MONTH	(Over) or Under Budget YEAR TO DATE
Vice president's office	$ 2,110	$ 12,030	($ 115)	$ 35
General superintendent's depts.	24,525	147,280	(710)	(2,590)
Production control	1,235	7,570	(125)	(210)
Purchasing	1,180	7,045	95	75
Maintenance	3,590	18,960	(235)	245
Tool room	4,120	25,175	60	(320)
Inspection	2,245	13,680	80	(160)
Receiving, shipping, stores	3,630	22,965	(70)	(730)
Total	$42,635	$254,705	($1,020)	($3,655)

	Standard THIS MONTH	Standard YEAR TO DATE	Variance THIS MONTH	Variance YEAR TO DATE
PRODUCTIVE LABOR	$27,120	$161,970	$3,020	$5,130

vice president may and probably will want to see the detailed statements supporting this summary.

EXHIBIT 7

This statement, which summarizes controllable costs by responsible departments, is the responsibility report for the top level of management, the president and general manager of the company. This statement concisely summarizes for the top executives the performance of the entire company with respect to controllable costs by comparing actual against budget by responsibility areas. If the system of responsibility reporting has been correctly tailored, these side captions will relate directly to the original organization chart. Remember that the major areas were the president and general manager, vice president in charge of production, chief engineer, personnel manager, vice president in charge of sales, and vice president of finance. Also note that productive labor has again been carried forward from the previous statement as a separate item. Now in order that one may review this build-up of controllable costs by responsibilities, it is proper to review Exhibit 8.

EXHIBIT 8

This chart sets forth the complete build-up of controllable costs from the lowest level, which was the drill press department, up to the highest or top level of

Exhibit 7

Responsibility report for the president and general manager

A. B. C. MANUFACTURING COMPANY

DEPARTMENTAL COST SUMMARY *(President and General Manager)*	Amount		(Over) or Under Budget	
	THIS MONTH	YEAR TO DATE	THIS MONTH	YEAR TO DATE
CONTROLLABLE EXPENSES–				
President's office	$ 3,120	$ 18,410	($ 30)	($ 155)
V. P. production	42,635	254,705	(1,020)	(3,655)
Chief engineer	7,520	44,830	135	780
Personnel manager	2,540	15,135	(40)	90
V. P. sales	25,860	151,380	(345)	(670)
V. P. finance	9,230	55,460	(85)	125
Total	$90,905	$539,920	($1,385)	($3,485)

	Standard		Variance	
	THIS MONTH	YEAR TO DATE	THIS MONTH	YEAR TO DATE
PRODUCTIVE LABOR	$27,120	$161,970	$3,020	$5,130

Exhibit 8
Levels of responsibility reporting

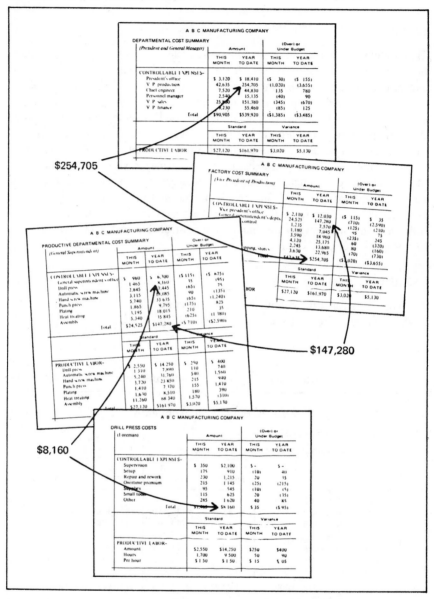

reporting. To review this build-up in detail, it will be recalled that we started with a statement prepared for the drill press department which set forth all of the controllable costs of operating the drill press department and compared these costs as originally budgeted with actual, showing the over and under budget in each case. The total controllable costs of the drill press department were then carried forward into a statement for the general superintendent. When the total cost of the drill press department was combined with the costs of the other areas for which the general superintendent has responsibility, including the costs of running his own office, one arrived at the total controllable costs for which the general superintendent was responsible. The total cost of the second level of responsibility was then carried forward in total as one of the areas of responsibility in the third level, which in this case was the vice president in charge of production. Again when this total was combined with the cost of the other areas for which the vice president was responsible, including the cost of operating his own office, one arrived at the total costs of the third level of responsibility. The total of this third level was then carried forward as one of the departments in the top level summary where all expenses of the company were summarized by departments responsible for the incurrence of the costs. The productive labor in each of these areas has been shown and carried forward from one level to the other. This build-up is not particularly complicated. It is basically simple, and one does not have to be an accountant to understand it. I should like to emphasize that what has been done here is simply to have placed reporting of costs in phase with the responsibility for the incurrence of the costs. To say it another way, cost reporting has been put in phase with budgeting.

In closing this discussion, I would like to summarize the major points. Responsibility accounting does not involve a drastic change in accounting theory or principles. It is for the most part a change in emphasis from product cost to the cost control aspects of accounting wherein the statements to management emphasize the control of costs by reporting and summarizing them on the basis of "who did it" before they are adjusted and blended for product cost purposes to obtain the conventional financial statements. To say it another way, it is a system which emphasizes the information that is useful to operating management and de-emphasizes the accounting and bookkeeping aspects that clutter up so many of our financial statements today.

After discussing the cost and benefits of having programmed checks, this selection illustrates such qualitative controls as coding checks, combination checks, matching checks, composition checks, and limit checks. These checks are presented in the context of a batch-mode, tape-oriented system.

12 | PROCESSING CONTROLS
HASKINS & SELLS

Processing controls, which are known also as programmed checks or programmed controls, are a part of the stored instructions that direct a computer's operations. To the extent that they are used, an EDP system becomes self-regulating, eliminating the need for clerical monitoring of results. This characteristic gives the computer a self-auditing capability which is superior to that of any other processing system.

THE ROLE OF PROGRAMMED CHECKING

The extent to which programmed checks are used is primarily a matter of economics: the cost of checking should be balanced against the costs of not detecting errors. This equation, although easy to state, may be difficult to apply.

The costs of checking include: (1) extra systems design and programming time, and (2) longer computer running time. Both of these are affected by the storage requirements of a checking routine. If memory space is ample, the costs may be insignificant. If it is "tight," the cost may be material because inclusion of the check may involve intricate programming and an additional computer run.

The costs of not detecting errors include: (1) manual error detection, investigation, and correction procedures; (2) various less precisely measurable factors that are peculiar to a given type of error, such as the effects upon management efficiency or customer good will. Some of these costs or possible effects are difficult or impossible to measure. Therefore, to some degree the extent to which programmed checks should be employed is a matter of judgment. In practice, the possible effects of not detecting errors sometimes are dismissed rather summarily and, as a consequence, programmed controls are minimized.

Electronic data processing requires four basic ingredients: equipment, internally stored programs, data, and human operations. Programmed checks oversee the effectiveness of each of these. Thus, the objectives of programmed checks are to monitor:

1. The accuracy of the computer,
2. The adequacy of the programs,
3. The quantity and quality of data, and
4. The correctness of human intervention.

From Haskins & Sells, *Internal Control in Electronic Accounting Systems* (New York: Haskins & Sells, 1965), pp. 73–84; used by permission.

The first objective—the monitoring of computer accuracy—varies in significance from machine to machine. The reliability of electronic equipment is extraordinarily high to begin with. This high inherent reliability is supplemented with a variety of built-in checks that automatically detect malfunctioning. Therefore, so far as computer accuracy is concerned, programmed checks for the most part merely provide comforting assurance that all is well. However, there is a recent trend among manufacturers to discontinue providing some of the built-in checks that heretofore have been considered necessary. Such a trend may increase the need to monitor computer accuracy through the use of programmed checks.

The second objective—the monitoring of program adequacy—is particularly applicable during the pre-operational stage when programs are being tested. At this stage, the checks help in the "debugging" process by proving the logic of the instruction lists. Later, when the application is operative, the checks detect deficiencies in the programs only rarely but nevertheless frequently enough to warrant their continued use. Deficiencies are frequently disclosed several months after an application is put into operation.

The third objective—the monitoring of the quantity and quality of data—is quite important from a control viewpoint. If bad input is received, bad output will result. Therefore, some check is needed at the input stage to detect loss of data and to verify the accuracy and consistency of various fields of information. The customary practice is to make a series of checks as the records are read in for processing. Some of the checks are quantitative in nature, while others are qualitative. The quantitative checks serve a double purpose. They determine whether or not the number of detail records received agrees with the control count established outside the data processing activity (if such a control was established) and they establish counts for use in controlling subsequent data processing operations. When agreement is not reached, a message is usually written out indicating the type of proof attempted, the specific control figures, and the differences. The qualitative checks test the validity, appropriateness, and accuracy of data. Records that fail to pass a qualitative test usually are rejected from further processing and printed on an error listing.

The fourth objective—monitoring the correctness of human intervention—is likewise an important element of control. Inadvertent mistakes made at the console often can be detected through use of programmed checks. Deliberate manipulation can also be detected in some instances, although more positive detection is obtained through use of console typewriters that provide an automatic record of intervention.

Programmed checking also promotes operating efficiencies in the machine room. Costly reruns can be avoided. Adherence to established schedules is facilitated by internal screening of data and self-checking of results. These benefits of the program checks warrant their use even when they may not be essential from an internal control viewpoint. For example, the accounting department may set up rigid controls over data sent in for processing and over the results that are received back. In such a situation, the data processing center should incorporate corresponding balancing steps into its programs.

QUALITATIVE CONTROLS

Qualitative controls relate to the data content of the individual records. They test the consistency of record arrangement ("record format"), the presence or absence of specified items of data, the accuracy of data that can be proved arithmetically, and the reasonableness of certain kinds of data. When the tests relate to incoming data, they are often referred to as input editing checks. When they relate to the manipulation of data or the generation of output records, they are referred to as processing checks.

Input Editing.   Input data are normally "edited" rather completely within the computer before they are passed along for main-line processing. Most of the screening merely tests the compatibility of the data—that is, its suitability and acceptability in terms of the program—although some of the tests do check the reasonableness or apparent validity of specific segments of information. In this latter sense, editing checks test the quality of data. However, machines do not have the capability to detect a fictitious entry that meets the programmed editing tests. They can detect only the items that cannot meet the requirements of a set of predetermined rules.

Editing checks vary widely because they relate to the requirements of specific applications and the character of the individual input records. They do not test the accuracy of the machine since their function relates solely to the incoming data.

Some of the commonly used checks are:

1. Coding checks
2. Combination checks
3. Check digits
4. Matching checks
5. Composition checks

Terminology for these checks has not been standardized in the industry.

Coding checks reject data codes that do not conform with established coding lists. For example, suppose normally there should be only three types of entries in a given procedure—A, B, and C. If a given entry is neither A nor B, a positive test establishes whether it is C. In Exhibit 1, a check is made to see whether the

Exhibit 1
Coding check

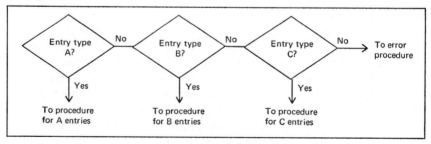

entry is C. If it is not, an error exists that otherwise would not have been detected. However, the procedure cannot detect an improperly coded entry if it is coded A, B, or C.

Combination checks are an extension of coding checks. Under program control, a computer can recognize valid relationships between two fields of coded information and reject impossible combinations. To illustrate, assume the following assignment of territories to salesmen:

Salesman	Territory
Jones	Illinois and Iowa
Smith	Illinois
Brown	Iowa and Missouri

If the coded representation of these combinations is stored internally, a computer can detect improper relationships, such as an entry that purports to credit Jones with a Missouri sale. It should be noted, too, that this look-up ability can be utilized to eliminate initial coding (and keypunching) in many situations. For instance, assume the following arrangement:

Salesman	Territory
Jones	Illinois
Jones	Indiana
Smith	Iowa
Brown	Missouri

Here the territories are exclusive, although one salesman, Jones, can sell in two states. If the input entry is coded for territory, the computer can supply the saleman's code (and name, if desired), making it unnecessary to code this information in the input operations.

A variation of this method of editing is sometimes used to verify the coding of account numbers. Where the chart of accounts is relatively complex, requiring long account numbers, the entire chart may be stored in the computer's memory. This provides a table of acceptable numbers against which the incoming record may be checked.

When an extra digit has been assigned to coded numbers as a *check digit,* a computer can perform the arithmetic needed to establish the probable correctness of the number. This would eliminate the need for the special device that otherwise is required to be attached to the card punch machine. Under this method, however, the errors would not be detected until a later stage in the processing cycle.

Matching checks detect improperly coded transaction numbers in file maintenance programs that are processed sequentially. The basic logic of the operation is shown in Exhibit 2. If both the transaction and master file records

Exhibit 2
Matching check

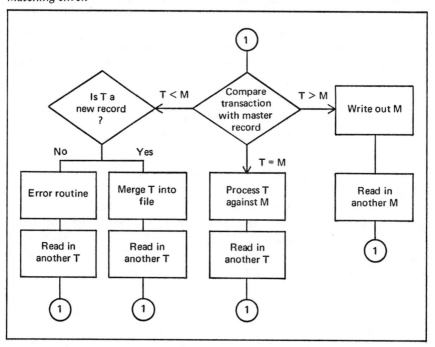

are intended to be in ascending numerical order, a determination that the transaction number is less than the master number, followed by a determination that the transaction is not a new record for the file, is an indication of some type of error. Investigation will disclose that the transaction number is out of sequence, that a master record for the transaction should have been added to the file previously, or that the transaction number is incorrect.

Composition checks test the appropriateness of data in a variety of ways. Data fields may be tested for blanks to determine whether any significant information is missing from the input records. Numeric fields may be tested to locate extraneous alphabetic characters. Amount fields within a record may be crossfooted where it is possible to prove the accuracy of the individual fields. In general, the character of the job and the skill of the programmer will determine the number, nature, and effectiveness of the composition checks that are employed.

Internal Operations Checks.   After records have been screened and allowed to proceed into the main processing steps, certain controls can be programmed to assure correctness in manipulating the data. Such checks are used sparingly, because the reliability of the hardware is sufficient assurance of processing accuracy in most situations.

Posting checks are a case in point. As their name implies, these checks are provided to avoid mispostings, which in electronic data processing may have serious consequences. For example, in random-access files the storage address of a record often is calculated by the computer from an actual number, such as a part number or a customer's account number. There are several arithmetical methods of doing this, but none of them guarantees generation of separate or unique addresses for every number. The methods recognize the probability that duplicate addresses will be computed on occasion. Therefore, a check must be made after an address has been calculated to determine whether or not the record at that location is the one that is really wanted. This is done simply by storing the actual number in the file record and comparing it with the incoming data.

The same principle often is applied in sequential processing. When there is a possibility that the input identification number may be incorrect—as there is when the number is manually coded without a check digit—the advantages of the technique should be considered. A comparison may be made of any field of information that is common to the file and the data to be processed. For example, in an accounts receivable application that employs a master file of open items, the input and file records would first be matched on customer number. It may then be appropriate to compare invoice number and invoice date in addition to invoice amount before changing the master file.

It is now generally considered unnecessary to check the arithmetical operation of a computer. However, arithmetical proofs are often programmed as a means of checking the reasonableness or completeness of overall processing. The most common checks are the limit check, the crossfooting check, and the sign check.

Limit checks test the reasonableness of data by comparing them with established tolerances. The tests may be applied to input records as they are read. They may also be applied to output results as they are written or used to update a master file. For example, in a public utility billing application the reasonableness of metered consumption (input) can be tested by calculating "high-low" limits for each account, based on historical usage, seasonal variations, and other factors. Similarly, payroll computations can be compared with predetermined maximums, invoice extensions exceeding a prescribed amount can be flagged for attention, and issues from a storeroom in unusually large quantities can be marked for special consideration. In theory, limit tests can be applied to nearly every business factor involving time, money, or other quantitative units. In practice, they are applied selectively.

Crossfooting checks prove the arithmetical accuracy of individual records and/or a group of records. Just as a clerk checks a schedule by crossfooting columnar totals, a computer can crossfoot individual records, such as gross pay to net pay, accumulate the respective amounts, and crossfoot the final totals. The technique is a simple way of establishing overall completeness and accuracy. It is especially effective at the conclusion of lengthy jobs, since these may be subject to interruption for mechanical or scheduling reasons and thus may be vulnerable to restart errors.

Sign checks, as their name implies, test the algebraic sign of a field of information. For example, the machines can detect a negative balance in inventory, an excess of payroll deduction over gross pay, or a change in an account balance from debit to credit. The checks frequently are used to indicate a failure to receive data. This could be the case, for example, when issues from stock are deducted before the receipt of goods is processed.

Real-time computers present a special control problem. When many point-of-origin devices are connected to a central computer, some definite measures should be provided to prevent insertion of erroneous data, incorrect modification of master files, or the reading out of unauthorized information. The design of the devices usually restricts usage to some specified function, and for nonaccounting applications these built-in controls are adequate. But when on-line stations become prevalent as channels of accounting information, additional control techniques must be developed. Programmed checks may prove to be one of the more effective methods of controlling the use of the on-line devices.

The general and detailed steps involved in the development of the STARFIRE system are discussed in the following presentation.

THE OVERALL CONCEPT

Exhibit 1 depicts the overall system. As can be seen, remote stations located in various concerned organizational units such as payroll, cost accounting, budget and forecast, etc., make daily input to the files from their locations. This information is entered through card media, magnetic tape and input/output devices.

Authorized input and output organizational units are established. Only those thus designated have the means to enter data in certain files and retrieve that information to which they are authorized. This eliminates the problems of security (need to know, entitled to, responsible for, etc.) concerned with data development and usage.

Exhibit 1
Data flow under STARFIRE

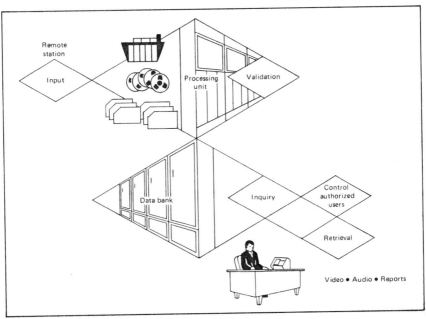

From Michael R. Tyran, "STARFIRE—An Advanced Financial Information System," *Management Accounting*, May 1966, pp. 3–16; used by permission. Background information and the implementation and cost considerations were discussed in Case D.

The transactions are validated against the master audit file which checks for data completeness, proper charge numbers, valid organizations, employee numbers, etc. Incorrect data are rejected and an error message is sent back automatically to the inputting units. The correct data enter the various data banks where program routines update, add or delete information in the files.

Each day the processing unit forwards to each of the submitting organizational units a listing of the transactions made that day. These listings then serve as checklists for their verification and future reference.

The information is obtained through devices such as video display, input/output keyboard print, audio (in the future) and routine reports. The reporting can be either on a real time basis (instantaneous) and/or batch processing. The main consideration in this whole system is that it be user oriented—give the responsible organizations the capability for immediate access and retrieval of routine or unique information that they need to perform their function effectively.

THE CURRENT SYSTEM VS. STARFIRE

Under our present system, we input various data as shown in Exhibit 2. This is done through transmittals to keypunch from the concerned areas.

The information is processed and the resultant report data is outputted, "massaged" and in many instances re-inputted to obtain the final result.

Exhibit 2
Current data process vs. STARFIRE

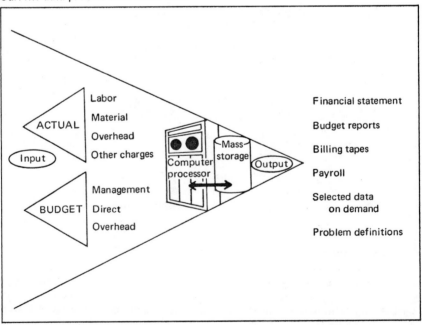

This is necessary because we have no mass storage capability for complete processing of the data to its ultimate end from the initial source document. Under STARFIRE, this capability is available and will give two additional features that we do not possess today—capability to "call out" of the files only that specific information we need and exception reporting. By exception reporting, it is meant that there will be programmed parameters in the system which will automatically report deviations from the norm. For example, if the actual direct labor hours against a contract exceed the budgeted allotment by a certain percent, then this information will be automatically reported to the concerned organizational unit for investigation and subsequent action.

Data Flow.   In Exhibit 3, you will note that, under our current system, time card information is processed weekly and reports are generated. The problem is that the result is only achieved through continual resubmission of data in order to obtain the next hierarchy or summary level of reporting. Weekly summaries are received and resubmitted for monthly totals. Monthly totals are used to prepare journal vouchers which data is then submitted to generate financial statements. Under STARFIRE, the time card data will be accumulated daily, stored and manipulated to achieve financial statement output on a one day, month end processing cycle.

Exhibit 3
Data accumulation and report generation

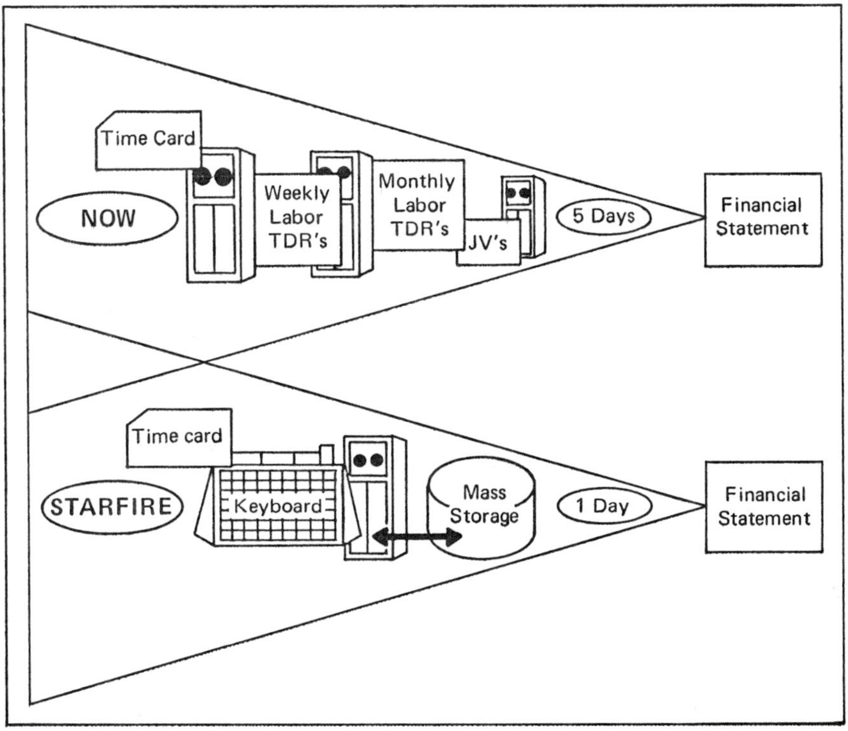

Data Retrieval.   Exhibit 4 shows one of the techniques to be employed in extracting data from the files on a video display device. It works like this—if you were an authorized user of certain data, had a problem in the detail of your financial statement and wanted to analyze the situation, you would insert your data authorizing badge into a device which would then display the Master Index Chart of data to which you were entitled for access. With a "light ray" pencil device you would select in Step A of Exhibit 4 "Financial Statement," then the "year to date" time period in Step B and "Actual vs. Management Budget" in Step C.

Your next display would be a listing of all your financial schedules. Since you predetermined that your problem was in the profit-and-loss area, you would select that schedule in Step D.

Now you have in Step E a profit-and-loss schedule, year-to-date period and a comparison with the management budget. Your review of this information indicates your unexplained and largest variance to be in your cost reimbursement contracts. In Step F, therefore, you select "Cost Reimbursement Contract" for more detail which would be a listing of CRC contracts with their associated variances from budget. A review of this listing would reveal that Contract AF21 is the problem area and so your next step is to obtain all of the cost detail on this contract. This is not really an involved process and having done it a few times, you could go from the beginning inquiry to the desired end in seconds. The same procedure as above holds true for obtaining personnel, organization and operating data.

Exhibit 4
An example of a STARFIRE technique

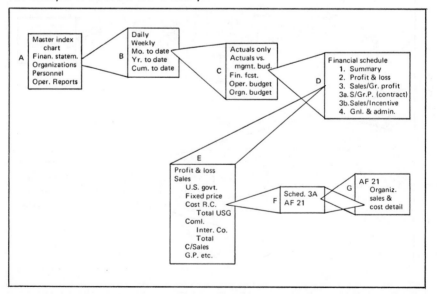

DATA BANK CONCEPT

The STARFIRE concept as applied to the overall financial recording and reporting system is new in that it represents an integrated program for achieving real time, direct input access as well as instantaneous retrieval. A generalized process flow is reflected in Exhibit 5 (page 169).

STARFIRE SYSTEM OPERATION

As described above and shown in Exhibit 5, responsible control agencies or stations are accountable for the input of all data into the system, its manipulation, validity, monitoring and distribution control of the output. The flow of the data, as shown, is through remote station located input/output devices. Input will be on a daily basis (as is possible) with file updating occurring on off shift hours. Listing of all transactions will be outputted to the concerned organizations daily. Program routines will manipulate the data into the various usage files so that "update" can be accomplished in a number of areas simultaneously.

As you will note in Exhibit 6 (pages 170 and 171), the detailed elements of the source documents (Reproduction Department) are shown along with the files and reports with which they are associated. For example, certain reproduction request data is entered in Journal Voucher 291 (Reclassification of Reproduction and Photographic Charges), sub-ledgers (Cost Reimbursement Contracts, Work in Process, Expense, Billing), cumulative cost file and various batch reports. No real time reporting is required in the reproduction area. A single transaction can, as stated above, "trigger" the appropriate entries in all of the affected files.

Detailed element files are maintained and updated daily (direct labor, material, etc.). The data banks are also updated to reflect certain summary information which will be used to prepare financial statements, operating reports, budgets, customer billings, etc. The complete process from source document to the final reports will be mechanical under STARFIRE and the data bank concept.

PILOT MODEL

In order to determine what the problems might be from the standpoint of a STARFIRE system implementation, a pilot model operation was conceived and placed into operation. An input/output device was obtained and located in the financial systems' area. It was tied in to a remote computer file in order to simulate a typical STARFIRE process of accumulating and retrieving information on a real time basis as well as batch processing. A series of charts was prepared for demonstration purposes which showed the data transmission parameters, a general system flowchart of the operation and the format for inquiries as well as what the response messages would look like. Exhibit 7 (page 172) shows one of the charts used in this demonstration.

This pilot model was prepared to reflect all conditions that might occur in a "live" situation. Detailed specifications were prepared and programmed. Many problems were encountered before successful "runs" were made. This model will assist us immeasurably in implementing the overall program. All concerned user organizations have been oriented to the equipment usage and also given an opportunity to observe first-hand the operation of the STARFIRE concept.

QUESTIONS

1 What processing controls are used to check input data in this case?

2 How does the STARFIRE technique shown in Exhibit 4 compare with the reporting technique discussed in the Higgins article (Selection 11)?

Exhibit 5
STARFIRE data bank concept

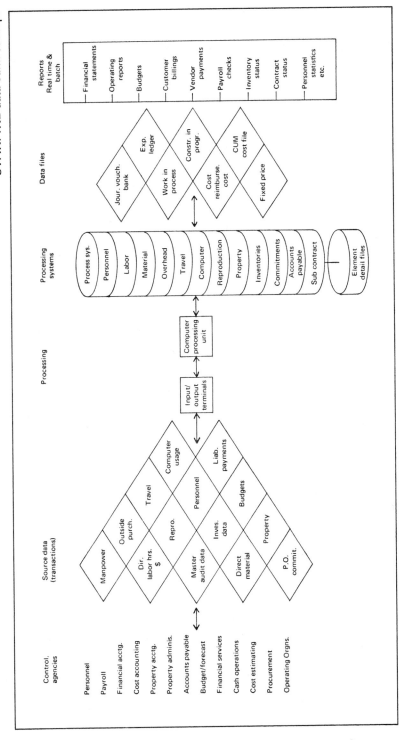

Exhibit 6

Data element source to output relationship chart for Reproduction Department

Source Document/ Process/etc.	TC	Data Element In (X)	Data Element Out (O)	JV 291	CRC	WIP	EXP	Billing Date	Cum. Costs	Real Time	A	B	C	D	E	F	G	H	I
Reproduction request		Plant (Facility)	Converted repro. charge no.	O					X		X	X					X	X	O
Engineering job		Requesting orgn.	Major class	O					X			X		X	X		X	X	O
Release ticket		Request date	Project	O								X		X	X		X	X	O
Blueprint request		Major class	Work order	O		O	X		X		X		X			X	X	X	
		Minor class	Work authority						X		X		X				X	X	
		Project	Minor class (B)		O	O		O	X			O	O	O			X	O	
		Work order	Reproduction amount, week			O	X	O	X			O	O				X		
		Work authority	Reproduction amount, month	O		O	X		X			X		O			X		O
		Segment/task	Responsible project orgn.		O	O			X				O				X		
		Source document number	Responsible work order orgn.		O	O			X			X					X		
		Units (quantity) reproduced	Journal voucher number	O	O												X		
		Reproduction cost code	General ledger account no.	O	O	O			X					O			X		
		Vendor cost	Subsidary account no.	X				X			X	X			X		X	X	
		Indirect analysis code	Orgn. O. H. pool identifier														X		
			Group code						O				O	O		O	X		
			Labor (reproduction) amount						O		O		O				X		
			Analysis/element code								O						X		
			Dir. repro. amt., last 12 months						O			O	O	O			X		
			Reproduction amt., year to date						O				O				X		
			Repro. amt., contract to date						O				O			O	X		
			Indiv. (repro.) amts. by O. H. pool (3 months)						O					O			X	O	
			Suspense code					X									X		
Reproduction cost code/ rate transmittal		Cost code, total rate (price)	Reproduction amount, week	O	O	O	O		O		O	O	O	O	O	O	X	O	O
		Cost code, labor rate (price)	Reproduction amount, month						O		O	O	O	O	X		X	X	
		Reproduction type	Labor (reproduction) amount		O				X								X	X	
		Reproduction cost code	Dir. repro. amt., last 12 months						X										
			Reproduction amt., year to date						O		O	O	O				X		
			Repro. amt., contract to date			O	O	O	O		O	O	O			O	X	O	O
			Indir. (repro.) amts. by O. H. pool (3 months)	O	O				O		O	O	O	O				O	O
			Suspense code						O										

File	Data element									
Reproduction budget Transmittal	Major class		x		o o o o x x x x	o x x	o o x x	x	o o x x x x x x x x		x x x x
	Minor class		x		x x x	x x	x x x				x
	Project										
	Work order										
	Work authority										
	Segment/task										
	Requesting organization				x x x	x	x x x x	x	x		
	Responsible project orgn.										
	Responsible work order orgn.				x x x	x x x x	x x x x x	x			
	Budget amount, month										
	Scheduled completion date										
	Estimated completion date										
	Year to date budget amount										
	Contract to date budget amount										
	Schedule status (indicator)										
	Variance project to date										
Labor distribution system	12 month direct labor hours				o	o	o		x o o		x x
	Major class								x x		
	Project										
	Repro. rate per direct labor hour										
	Dir. repro. amt., past 12 months										
Master audit file	Converted repro. charge no.		x					x	x x x x x x x x x x x x		x
	Major class		x x								
	Project										
	Work order				x x	x					
	Work authority										
	Responsible project orgn.		x			x	x		x		x
	Responsible work order orgn.										
	Gen. ledger account number										
	Orgn. O. H. pool identifier										
	Subsidary account number			x							
	Division										

Note: Although Journal Vouchers and Ledgers indicate a monthly update above, it is anticipated these will be updated more frequently than this, possibly daily.

Exhibit 7

Input transactions to update system records

	INPUT FORMAT	RESPONSE MESSAGES
ORIGINAL IDENTIFIER ENTRY	Note: Character input in all fields is mandatory; i.e., date 1/9/65 is "keyed in" as 01/09/65, etc.	Acceptable—Document No. assigned Non-acceptable—Error message
ACTIVITY INFORMATION ADDED TO THE ABOVE IDENTIFIER RECORD	Note: Any number of cost code/units combinations up to a max. of 5 can be transmitted. Units need not be right-justified by operator, i.e., 10 units are "keyed in" as 10, etc.	Acceptable—Notified complete Non-acceptable—Error message
COST CODE RATE CHANGE	Note: Character input in all fields is mandatory, i.e., if desired rate is $1.50, must be transmitted as 01500; cost code 6 is transmitted 06; etc.	Cost code in file—Advised of new rate, etc. Cost code not in file—Advised
BUDGET INPUT (OR ADJUSTMENT) AT WORK AUTHORITY/ORGANIZATION LEVEL	Note: Character input in all fields is mandatory; i.e., budget amount of $10.00 is "keyed in" as 00001000, etc.	Acceptable—Advised of new budget amount Non-acceptable—Error message
BUDGET INPUT (OR ADJUSTMENT) AT DETAIL RECORD LEVEL	Note: Character input in all fields is mandatory, i.e., budget amt. of $15.00 is "keyed in" as 00001500, etc.	Acceptable—Advised of new budget Non-acceptable—Error message

This article emphasizes the importance of good program design in systems building. Modularity and generality in program structure are discussed, and the relationship between main modules and subroutines is illustrated.

EFFECTIVE PROGRAM DESIGN | 13
DAVID W. PACKER |

This discussion of computer program design promotes the idea that the success and ultimately the cost of any computer program is critically related to its design; that is, that the design is, by far, the most critical aspect of program development. The EDP community often talks of design and the concepts of modularity, generality, flexibility, and maintainability; yet many programs are not well designed, and others are not designed at all, but simply written. It is my belief that the design of a program is much different from its coding, and is a creative task involving many—if not all—of the same elements as systems design.

GOOD PROGRAM DESIGN RESULTS IN GOOD SYSTEMS DESIGN

A further extension of this view is that one who learns to design programs well gains valuable training in systems designing as well. The only basic difference between the program and the system is that the program is a smaller unit, and consequently there is less risk from bad design of it. A system is nothing more or less than a set of programs with logical and physical inter-connections, in much the same way as a program is a set of routines with the same sort of connections. I believe that program design is, over the long run, a most essential ingredient of an effective systems job, for well-designed programs are fairly insensitive to the inadequacies of the particular coding techniques used and tend to make the system flexible and easy to modify.

The lip-service paid to program design manifests itself in a number of misconceptions about what constitutes good design. This, coupled with the fact that the computer can do "anything" (i.e., that even the most poorly designed program can be made to work), detracts from the importance of program design

From *Computers and Automation*, July 1970, pp. 37–41. Copyright 1970 by Berkeley Enterprises, Inc.; used by permission. David W. Packer is Manager of Information Systems and Data Processing at Digital Equipment Corporation.

today. Why should programs be designed well—or maybe more practically, why should programs be designed at all and not just coded?

I think it is clear to anybody who has worked with large numbers of programs that have existed for a long time that well-designed programs are easier to write, to document, to review, to control, to understand, to debug, to test, and to maintain.

Today, many programmers are being thrust into their jobs with only a brief indoctrination into programming techniques (a course that more often than not has nothing or little to do with design), with a manual that answers only the technical questions of the specific language being used. Very little education or emphasis has been or is being given to effective design of computer programs. Thus, the development of programmers' creative skills (which in turn would provide a solid base for future systems work) is being minimized.

Another important consideration is that EDP installations are operating at an unnecessarily high cost level, and they are often unresponsive to users' needs because of the time required to change, revise, and write new programs. The EDP business today is characterized by a tremendous shortage of programming and technical talent so it is highly desirable to educate the available talent in an organized way and to develop at the earliest time the creative and technical requisites for high productivity, fast response, and advancement in the organization for people currently in programming jobs.

It is my intention in this article to discuss program design, to show concrete examples of what constitutes good—and poor—design, and to show how fundamental the design process is to the whole programming job, and in effect to the whole systems job. My comments derive from COBOL-oriented business-data-processing operations; but I do not believe they are restricted to COBOL users nor to business applications programmers. The following sections focus on concepts of modularity and program structure. From these elements, I will seek to outline the straightforward approach to program design that results.

MODULARITY

The concept of modularity is at the heart of effective program design. It is also the concept most often not carried through to a meaningful end, although the programmer thinks that it is.

A rather theoretical definition of a program module is that it is a set of instructions that perform a clear-cut function that can be described largely independent of other program steps. Essentially, a module is a set of instructions that is meaningful within itself.

The degree of modularity that a program achieves relates to how close it comes to consisting of a number of independent modules, each with a meaningful function and with no interactions with other modules. In other words, the output of one module is in no way dependent upon what is happening or has happened in other modules. It depends only on the input to the module and the function of that module. As a result of logical independence, any program error can be traced to a malfunction of a single module, and by correcting the module the program malfunction will be completely corrected.

USING SUBROUTINES

Modularity implies the use of common routines (or subroutines). However, heavy use of subroutines by itself does not mean that one has a modular program. To be truly modular, two key points are required:

1. Each module of the program has a small number of interactions with other modules.

2. Each module has clearly defined functions, which are related specifically to the logical function of the program.

For example, consider a program that is updating a master file with transactions from three transaction files. When the program was first laid out, it looked very complex, because the updating functions were different for each transaction type and because the process of reading the transaction files to determine which transaction type should be updated next was inherently complicated.

The program was redesigned with the following key modules:

1. A section that processed the transaction files to find the next transaction to be processed and delivered it to a common working storage location.

2. A section that received each transaction and updated the master file accordingly.

Now each module could be written independently—when working on the transaction matching one did not need to think at all about the updating functions; when working on the updating, problems of matching multiple transaction inputs could be completely forgotten—the problem was simply to post one transaction at a time. Thus overall complexity was considerably reduced.

Maintenance was also easier. If, for example, a new transaction file was added, it was clear where to make changes and what changes to make. The chance of "subtle" problems emerging was reduced; we knew that a new type of transaction would appear as input to the update, and it was clear how to accommodate it. For the update module itself was modular; i.e., it contained a set of simple sections that provided for the processing differences between transaction types.

A good test of modularity is independence among modules. The test involves the following questions:

1. Can each module be reviewed and specified in detail without regard to other modules?

2. Can each module be coded by a different person (this is not desirable but may be necessary) based on a simple set of specifications and with very little (ideally, no) communication required between the programmers?

PROGRAM STRUCTURE

Conceptually, a well designed program consists of two types of routines. They are:

1. "Mainstream" or control modules.

2. Subroutines, each a module with a function that is only a part of what the entire program does.

MAINSTREAMS

The "mainstream" modules direct the program's operation. They are the basic control sections, calling various subroutines to do detailed jobs. By reading the mainstream code, one can get an overview of the entire logical function of the program.

For example, consider a typical sequential update. Below is the COBOL Mainstream section. The update is sequentially matching a transaction file to a master file, updating the master when a match occurs (by adding to totals in the master), and rejecting transactions (printing an error message) when a transaction has no matching master. The matching is done on fields within the records called TRANS-KEY and MAST-KEY.

```
MAINSTREAM SECTION.
COMPARE-TRANS-TO-MAST.
     IF TRANS-KEY EQUALS MAST-KEY GO TO UP-DATE.
     IF TRANS-KEY GREATER THAN MAST-KEY PERFORM WRITE-NEW-MASTER THRU WNM-EXIT
     PERFORM READ-OLD-MASTER THRU ROM-EXIT
     GO TO COMPARE-TRANS-TO-MAST.
TRANS-LESS-THAN-MAST.
     PERFORM ERRONEOUS-TRANS THRU ET-EXIT.
READ-TRANS.
     PERFORM READ-NEXT-TRANS THRU RNT-EXIT.
     GO TO COMPARE-TRANS-TO-MASTER.
UPDATE.
     IF TRANS-KEY EQUALS HI-VALUE GO TO ENDING.
     PERFORM ADD-TO-MASTER THRU ATM-EXIT.
     GO TO READ-TRANS.
```

As exemplified above, the mainstream section consists mainly of decision logic (IF's, GO TO's) and calls of subroutines (PERFORM's). This section, surprisingly enough, is often quite short; yet it provides a clear description of the entire logical function of the program.

SUBROUTINES

Each subroutine is a program module with a smaller function than the entire program. Each is essentially a small program, and will itself consist of a mainstream and may use other, lower level subroutines.

Referring to the example, note that every routine that is PERFORMed is a closed subroutine. For example, the ERRONEOUS TRANSACTION routine is a program whose input is a transaction in an input area and whose output is, in this case, an error printout. The routine might look like this:

```
ERRONEOUS-TRANS.
      MOVES SPACES TO PRINT-LINE.
      MOVE "NO MASTER FOR THIS TRANSACTION" TO PRINT-LINE.
      PERFORM WRITE-PRINT-LINE.
      PERFORM MOVE-TRANS-TO-PRINT-LINE.
      PERFORM WRITE-PRINT-LINE.
ERRONEOUS-TRANSACTION-EXIT.   EXIT.
```

The statements above are the "mainstream" of the subroutine. It, in turn, calls other simple routines for output and for formatting. But its operational functions are clear from the mainstream section alone.

Subroutines can be overused—often to the point where documentation and clarity degrade. This happens when key logical functions appear in a subroutine rather than in the mainstream, where they logically belong, or when subroutines are written for tasks that are short enough to be included in the mainstream.

For example, in the update program, if certain transactions are being selected or deleted from the input file, this logic (or at minimum a PERFORM of the logic) belongs in the mainstream, not in the READ-NEXT-TRANS subroutine, because it is an important function of the program.

Thus, it is critical that the designer not be carried away by subroutine usage. A common misconception is that any use of subroutines is good because it means modularity. A program that overuses subroutines—reducing mainstreams to meaningless levels—is as bad as an undesigned program where everything is included in a long, complex mainstream section.

Subroutines are a tool to break a program into a set of meaningful building blocks with a minimum of interactions among them. Like a program itself, each should do a job that is related to the logical breakdown of tasks of the entire programming system.

Conceptually, both mainstream and subroutine modules are a set of "building block" programs that can be written, tested, and maintained by themselves— they are highly independent.

OVERALL PROGRAM STRUCTURE

The block diagram shown in Exhibit 1 is a convenient way to represent the hierarchical structure of a program. Each box indicates a program module. Along the top are mainstream modules, which are always in control of the program's operations. Note that there may be several mainstreams; typically there is an initial section (initialization, setup, etc.), followed by the main processing section or sections (if the program is doing a series of sequential jobs), and an ending section (wrap up, final totals, closes of files, etc.).

At the next level are what I call first level routines, the major subroutines referred to in the mainstream. Since these are in fact programs, they may use

Exhibit 1
Typical program structure

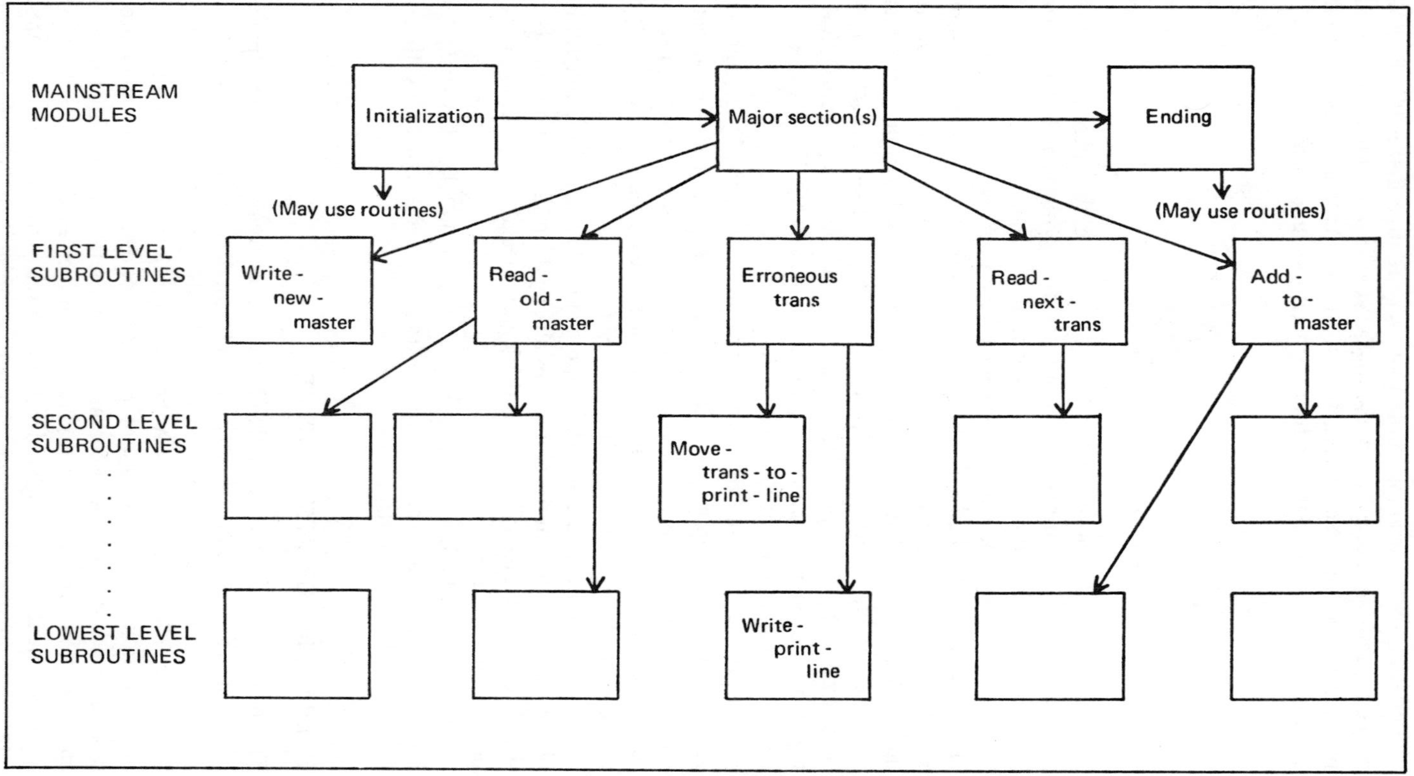
MAINSTREAM MODULES
FIRST LEVEL SUBROUTINES
SECOND LEVEL SUBROUTINES
LOWEST LEVEL SUBROUTINES
Initialization
Major section(s)
Ending
(May use routines)
(May use routines)
Write - new - master
Read - old - master
Erroneous trans
Read - next - trans
Add - to - master
Move - trans - to - print - line
Write - print - line

more detailed routines, creating a structure several levels deep. As one goes deeper into the structure, one normally finds that routines have functions of increasingly limited scope. For example, at the lowest level are subroutines that do such things as write print lines, read tape, read disk files, etc.

The block diagram representation of a program is a useful tool for teaching and for stimulating good design concepts. It shows every module of the program and will quickly bring to light fallacious design concepts (for example, an undesigned program will show up as one monstrous block), excessive use of subroutines, etc.

DESIGN CONSIDERATIONS—AN EXAMPLE

Here, let me discuss a representative example of program design consideration. It is typical of a wide variety of rather general design questions that come up in a broad range of programs.

The design consideration is how to handle the several possible outcomes of a modular subroutine. For example, the mainstream may say, "PERFORM READ-CUSTOMER-RECORD." Then the question is how can we account for the possibility that the customer record will not be found by the subroutine that is "performed"?

There are two approaches: First, to have the subroutine handle the error condition; i.e., go to an error routine that returns to the mainstream section. Second, to have an indicator set at the end of the subroutine that will tell the mainstream logic whether the record has or has not been found. If the error indicator is set or "on," then the mainstream logic can handle the error condition. I believe that the indicator is usually the better method, because it puts back into the mainstream logic for a condition that is in fact a part of the broad function of the program—what to do when an error is found. Thus the mainstream may read:

```
PERFORM FIND-CUSTOMER-RECORD
    IF ERROR INDICATOR IS ON, PERFORM CANT-FIND-CUSTOMER.
```

"CANT-FIND-CUSTOMER" is another program module that would print the program messages and take appropriate action. Thus again the reader of the program knows, from the mainstream alone, that errors can occur and how they are handled.

In most programs, there are many such design considerations. The good programmer will find the opportunity for creativity, innovation, and personal satisfaction if he recognizes such opportunities and exploits them.

GENERALITY AND FLEXIBILITY

An important design consideration that does not relate directly to program structure is that of generality. Essentially, this means setting up a program to do a general task, rather than a series of highly specific jobs. Generality buys flexibility, for it creates programs that are adaptive, without modification, to the normally changing business environment.

Almost every program of any substance contains opportunities for generality. For example:

Don't include today's specific numbers in programs (like stockrooms, parts, orders). They may (and usually will) change. Include them as parameters, or data, that serve as inputs to the program and can be changed at run time.

Make dates printed by programs in the format "N week period ending MM-DD-YY" so that the same program can be used for weekly, monthly, quarterly, or yearly reports as a function of the input data. Allow for full dates (decades do change, about once every 10 years).

Format reports in a way that allows expansion. Normally a vertical arrangement is best; printing summary items across the page limits expandability and means program changes whenever an item is added or changed.

Don't cut corners based on current requirements. Always design for the general case. For example, if there is a four-digit account number, where the first two digits are constants (today), don't set up records and programs to use only two digits ("But, the other two don't matter!"—today). Use the whole number. Avoid the crises of "But, that means revising 30 programs!" by designing it for the general spaces—you will need them sometime. Don't lump items together unnecessarily ("They say they only need the total, so why keep an extra field in the master file?"). The keynote is:

Think ahead

Understand why

Design systems that live in the world of change

Avoid future crises

Of course, there are tradeoffs. A highly generalized system is expensive to build and operate. In many cases, however, a general approach is as easy to implement as a specific one. It just requires more thought in the design stage. Sometimes (often) it's even easier, because the extra thought results in generality that avoids programming specifically all the oddities of the way things work now.

THE DESIGN PROCESS

How does one really set to work to design a program? I think the answer to this question is relatively simple, and it takes the form of evaluating various alternatives to good program design. The first step normally is to start drawing flowcharts. These should not be detailed flowcharts; and in fact, even in the case of relatively complex programs, it should not take more than ten to twenty blocks to show what is really being done. In other words, the flowchart blocks should all fit on a single piece of 8½" x 11" paper, if the designer is thinking broadly about the function of the program and is really starting at the highest level before becoming enmeshed in detailed design of individual portions of the program.

The basic approach here is to think in terms of alternatives and to draw flow diagrams at a general enough level so that it is possible to re-think and re-draw until one finds a design that is satisfactory. The process one goes through here is like many other creative processes. One starts with some assumption of how the total program should be structured and starts to diagram it. In the process, one will often see difficulties and objections with that particular method. From these objections one will get ideas for another way that will make the logic look simpler and more easily implemented.

Because of this process, it is important to start at a fairly general level. By "general" I do not mean vague. It is important to be precise but not to worry about too many of the details. If one starts drawing a detailed flowchart, one thing that often happens is that the effort to revise it evokes a normal emotional bias against really examining alternatives.

The flow diagram at this stage will normally be a detailed diagram of the key mainstream section, showing all of its decision logic and showing all first level subroutine modules, each with a brief description.

Many programmers do not begin design at this level, an indication of a nonmodular approach to the problem. Instead, the tendency is to just start drawing a detailed flowchart, solving each problem as it occurs. This is analogous to building a house without a plan—one brick at a time. The result in either case is likely to be the creation of a monster.

If we are to have well designed programs, the concept of design as a discipline must be accepted, taught, and developed. The concept of design is essentially unrelated to the material in the programming manuals; the information there provides only the raw materials that design converts to reality.

This article looks at some of the problems facing a prospective buyer of proprietary software. Considerations relating to make-or-buy alternatives and guidelines for evaluating software packages are discussed.

14 | HOW TO BUY PROPRIETARY SOFTWARE
LARRY A. WELKE

This article will look at some of the problems and pitfalls facing the prospective user of proprietary software and give some guidelines for the intending purchaser. Perhaps the most obvious place to begin is with the simple decision to make or to buy a software package.

THE MAKE-OR-BUY DECISION

There are two major considerations in the make-or-buy decision—cost and competitive advantage. If your in-house team can design software that will give you a distinct advantage over your competitors then it is obviously better to generate your own software. If this is not the case, then relative costs should be compared. This is not as easy as it may sound since a true evaluation should include not only direct costs but also overhead costs associated with your in-house activities. Indirect costs may be hard to evaluate. There will inevitably be some intangible factors such as the effects of tying up your software development group on a project that could be purchased. The purchase would free the group for other work. However, your programming group may have to modify your own systems to mesh with the purchased program.

However, if you can satisfactorily estimate your own costs, you should also keep in mind the following points:

1. Your in-house effort may never reach fruition whereas a package that exists can be tested almost immediately.

2. In-house developed programs often lack documentation but a packaged program will have documentation that can be checked before buying.

3. A project begun in your own shop may go well over the budgeted costs but proprietary software is usually offered at a set price.

4. A purchased program may cause you to incur costs for data or system conversion, although these can be covered by your purchase contract.

THE THREE-PHASE METHOD

Assuming you have concluded that buying software will ease your systems headaches, there are three areas that you will need to consider, namely your own

Reprinted from *Computer Decisions*, February 1971, pp. 14–16. © 1971 Hayden Publishing Co.; used by permission. Larry A. Welke is President of International Computer Programs, Inc.

characteristics, the vendor's characteristics and, of course, the package's characteristics.

Start by analyzing yourself. Determine what your needs are in terms of the end-user department, in the light of your present and intended equipment configuration and the capabilities of your staff.

Make sure that you consider the real end-user. If the package is a payroll program then the real end-user is the payroll or accounting department. If the package is a utility program then the real end-user is the data processing group. If you don't know the needs of the end-user, then you cannot satisfy the want. Similarly there is no point in buying a program that can only be used for six months because of changes in your equipment configuration.

The capability of your staff should be considered particularly with respect to maintaining the package. If it is written in a language that is not used in your computer center, then you will have difficulty in having your staff perform any maintenance. It is also important to ensure that the systems and programming staff understand why software is being purchased. Some analysts and programmers will feel that buying casts a slur on their ability. There have been several examples of good programs that became inoperable because someone didn't want them to work.

The next stage is to consider the vendors. First you have to find who supplies the kind of package you need. There are several organizations that publish surveys of this field. Trade journals publish new software developments as they become available. Consultants and software-brokers can also be helpful.

When you know the vendors then make sure that they display technical competence and financial reliability, and have installed at least one of the packages that you are interested in. Most software companies are quite small so you should be able to deal with the principals and be able to meet the program's principal developer. If the developer has 'just left' the company then be really careful!

Financial reliability is a very important question. If the company has been in business for some time you might be able to get a rating from Dun and Bradstreet. If not, then check out their latest financial report and see if you can estimate that they will be in business for at least the period of the program's warranty.

The vendor should be able to point to at least two or three places where his product is performing satisfactorily. You might also ask for the names of two establishments where the program has been sold but is not being used—just to keep your vendor honest.

Next you should check out the packages that you think will meet your requirements. Here, there are some questions to be answered:

1. Where did the program come from? Be sure that the seller has the right to sell the program, particularly if you feel that the development was done by another company.

2. Who will maintain it and for how long? Most warranties will be for one year. Longer program maintenance will be a subject for negotiation.

3. Is the program operable? If possible, have a demonstration on your own system with your own data. If not, try benchmarks (i.e. test runs) but make them exhaustive.

4. Will the package run on your equipment and under your operating system? If not, will the vendor modify the program?

5. Who is using this package? Someone has to be first. It had better not be you if this is your first purchase of proprietary software.

6. Are there restrictions on the use of the program? Can one of your subsidiary companies copy the package? Can it be used in a multiple computer installation?

7. What is the price structure? Is installation, documentation, training, etc. covered by the price?

You may not be able to get all these questions answered fully. However, the package that comes nearest to answering them all is likely to be the one that will have the staying power for your use.

When you've been convinced that you should buy a particular package then ask to have a contract drawn up. This contract should include the terms of the installation, the maintenance and educational support to be provided by the vendor as well as the more obvious items like price and delivery and penalties for late delivery or inadequate performance. If you require the vendor to make modifications, have them specified in the contract. You will have to agree to clauses restricting copying and multiple usage.

There are seven points to successful software buying:

1. Determine what is available. Don't start and end with saying there is only one package available on the market. Find out how many. If there is only one, question hard; you probably will find there are more than one. It is going to be rare when you find only one package to cover a particular problem area.

2. Inform your staff of what you are doing and get their support. Let them know that you are evaluating a package to solve this particular problem and let them know the advantages of so doing. Let them know the role that they will be playing on it. Some excellent packages have gone down the tubes because the staff, in one way or another, fought them until they didn't work.

3. Be methodical in your approach. Be absolutely methodical and don't vary from it. Admittedly, it may take all the romance out of buying the package—and that's the way it should be.

4. Let the seller know exactly what you are doing. It is to your advantage to let him know exactly how you are measuring him and his package.

5. Know and get everything possible in writing. Make it a matter of record. All too often, serious problems develop because someone didn't bother writing it down.

6. Document what you are doing throughout your evaluation process so that you can make an intelligent report of your activity and your conclusions to your management, to your accountant and to your attorney. Before you finally sign off on a piece of paper that you are going to buy something, all three of these should know what you have done and how you have arrived at your conclusions. Some people who buy software claim their attorney or accountant doesn't understand software. Well, your management doesn't understand any more than the accountant and the attorney, yet you have to convince them. The onus is upon you to prepare information in such a manner that those people can understand what you are about to do.

7. Finally, throughout this entire procedure, do everything possible to minimize the cost of evaluating the proposed package. There have been cases where the package cost $4,000 and the evaluation to get it cost $16,000. Some people will just go on and on and on, evaluating forever, because it's a lot of fun.

The experiences of software purchases are increasingly positive. Both the seller and the buyer are becoming sophisticated in their respective roles. And all of this is good because purchasable software can go a long way to easing some of the problems of the computer user.

CASE F | TITLE INSURANCE AND TRUST CO.

This case looks at the general procedure of making cost and payback analysis of a computer project. The case is a personal trust accounting system for a trust department servicing over 4,000 accounts. This trust accounting system was to perform the following activities:

1. Accounting for all assets held in trust including securities, real property, businesses, and other assets

2. Posting pending and final securities transactions to appropriate accounts and distributing dividends

3. Pricing securities each month and preparing statements for clients

4. Preparing client tax returns

5. Recording trust officer time charged by account

6. Analyzing and reporting account performance

7. Preparing client billing

8. Controlling disbursements to trust beneficiaries

Accounts range in size from $50,000 to $1,500,000 and the total assets controlled are close to two billion dollars. Before the new system, the trust accounting was handled by a unit record installation with files containing over 500,000 cards. An investigation indicated that development costs in banks which had programmed their own systems had run from $500,000 to $1,000,000 and more. It was therefore reasonable to assume that development of this system would involve a similar expenditure.

Because of the scope, complexity, and potential cost of the new system, a detailed preliminary study was undertaken to select the alternative courses of action and determine their costs. This study occupied over one man-year of systems analyst time as well as the time of personnel in the user department. The company performs this type of cost, benefit and payback analysis for all proposed projects costing over $25,000.

CHECKING THE ALTERNATIVES

After identifying the problem, several alternative solutions were examined. Initially these alternative solutions ranged from "blue-sky" approaches to minor

---

Reprinted from Louis Fried, "How to Analyze Computer Project Costs," *Computer Decisions*, August 1971, pp. 22–26. © 1971 Hayden Publishing Co.; used by permission. Louis Fried is Manager of the Information Services Division of Title Insurance and Trust Co.

changes in the existing routines. Each alternative solution was first analyzed in a cursory fashion to identify and eliminate those which were obviously unattractive or not feasible.

After a rough design of the alternative solutions, each design was analyzed to determine its impact on personnel, available resources, computer time, organization performance, and established organization goals. Tentative operating costs were established and compared to the actual costs of the present operating methods (which represented one possible alternative). No decision, or a decision not to change, is actually the selection of the present method as an alternative.

One element of the operating cost of alternatives must be the amortization of the implementation and conversion costs of the new system over the anticipated life of the system. Implementation and conversion plans had to be developed for each of these alternatives that passed an initial test of feasibility on the basis of operating cost and the impact on the organization.

The operating costs for the computer portion of the system were estimated in a variety of ways. For software packages, present users were consulted and computer times were projected for our transaction volume on the basis of their experience. For functions not performed by the packages, we estimated the transaction volume and the consequent input-output time necessary on the computer for the number of programs involved. The computer times developed were priced at our internal billing rate for the computer.

With the aid of line management, we determined the number of clerical staff required. Clerical costs were based on actual salaries paid at the present time.

Cost estimates were also prepared for all the recognized elements, such as systems analysis and file conversion, involved in implementing the system and converting to it. In this process some alternative solutions were eliminated for some of the following reasons:

1. The technical capability for the proposed solution did not exist or was extremely new and untried.

2. The environment of the organization was not suitable to the proposed solution or it required more resources than the company was willing to commit.

3. The time required to implement the system eliminated some more complex or time-consuming alternatives.

4. Some alternatives were politically or psychologically unpalatable.

These activities resulted in a list of requirements or specifications characteristic of the proposed solutions available. The specifications were rated as to degree of importance and priority for installation. This accomplished, implementation methods for alternatives were considered.

The two most common alternatives are to design and program the system in-house or to obtain a packaged system—the classic "make or buy" decision.

During the past three years the growth of the commercial software package market has been such that any firm seeking a solution to a common problem can frequently find that solution in a packaged form. In fact, the firm may have the choice of several alternative packages from which to select a "best fit" to its existing organization. There are many factors, including reduced cost and shorter implementation time, that encourage the purchase of package. On the other hand, the unique needs of the organization might tend to encourage the development of a new system in-house.

After technically feasible make or buy alternatives had been identified, it was then necessary to compare them to each other. This involved field work in which the analyst and members of line management visited companies that had installed their own systems and companies that had installed packages that were under consideration. This developed into an extremely valuable phase of the investigation since it provided actual case histories on which to base our estimated costs of design and implementation for each of the alternatives. After applying what was learned in the field studies to our own situation, it was then necessary to compare the estimated costs of each alternative to each other in such a manner as to permit the organization's management to make an intelligent, informed business decision. This required examining the comparative impact of the alternatives on company resources, profit, cash-flow, and benefits attained. It also required the presentation of these considerations to management in a concise, understandable manner. For this application it was decided to buy a software package. All the estimates, to be given later, are for the "buy" case. The use of a software package turned out to be considerably less expensive than similar in-house designs.

This presentation described the basic concepts of the existing system and its major problems. It outlined the concepts of the proposed alternatives, its major objectives, and the primary benefits to be derived from its approval. A comparison of the operating cost of the present system to the estimated operating cost of the proposed alternative was illustrated and the cost of implementation and conversion for the alternative was clearly indicated. The effect of the present system and the proposed alternative on the cash flow of the company was described. A payback analysis for the alternative was presented. The impact of the alternative on company practices was clearly set forth. Finally, the carefully considered recommendations of the group making the presentation were delineated. These recommendations identified the alternative selected as being the most desirable and described the specific steps that should be taken to implement the recommendation.

EVALUATING THE BENEFITS

The benefits of any proposed alternative can be either tangible or intangible. The tangible benefits can be calculated and put in tabular form (Exhibit 1). Only one set of charts is shown for each alternative. It may be necessary to present several

Exhibit 1
Comparison of costs: present system and proposed system

Year	Present System	Alternative System		
		Total Cost	Saving (loss)	Saving (loss)
1	$1,125,942	$1,290,526	$(164,584)	$(164,584)
2	$1,238,536	$ 945,796	$ 292,740	$ 128,156

cases to management but, in this case, only the present system and its most desirable alternative were presented. The Implementation Cost worksheet (Exhibit 2) was prepared for the analysis of all elements of implementation cost for each alternative. System implementation costs were divided into major task groups which included:

1. System design and programming if the alternative was to make the system

2. System modifications if the alternative was to buy the system (in this case it was decided that purchasing a software package was most economical)

3. Preparation for conversion which included review and clean-up of the present file whether manual or automated

4. Preparation and publication of clerical and operating procedures

5. Conversion of manual files to machine readable form or conversion and reformatting of existing computerized files

6. Training of the personnel who would utilize the system

7. Pilot operation of a small segment of the data in the new system and/or parallel operation of the new system with the old

8. Miscellaneous project tasks

9. Capital expenditures for equipment or packaged software

A sub-total was taken at the end of those items which are usually charged to expense in the year in which they occur. The final total included capital expenditures which were to be amortized over five years.

Personnel costs such as those associated with system analysis, programming, user personnel, and project management were based on actual salaries paid plus overhead. Keypunch and computer costs were based on established internal billing rates. Since it was decided to buy a software package, there are no entries in the Implementation Cost worksheet for system programming. Programming to adapt to the package is included under "System modifications."

Once all costs had been accumulated it was necessary to indicate their occurrence over time by the use of a PERT chart or Gantt chart. A development schedule was prepared for the proposed system and as the costs for each task were analyzed they were estimated on an optimistic, most likely, and pessimistic

Exhibit 2
Implementation cost worksheet

Project Tasks	Cost Elements									
	Systems Analysis	Programming	Key-punch	Computer	Forms & Supplies	Out-side Contract Services	User Adminis-tration	User Person-nel	Project Manage-ment	Total
Systems design and programming										
System modifications	$13,500	$16,000		$ 5,200			80			$ 34,780
Preparation for conversion			$ 1,600	1,250		$8,200		$11,860		22,910
Clerical and operating procedures	9,750	750			$1,000			840		12,340
File conversion	2,675	2,050	9,660	16,075			200	3,350		34,010
Training	1,875						240	1,560		3,675
Pilot and parallel operation			900	5,250			540	1,400		8,190
Other project tasks									$14,800	14,800
Sub-total	$27,800	$18,800	$12,160	$27,775	$1,000	$8,200	1160	$19,010	$14,800	$130,705
Capital expenditures		38,000								38,000
Final total	$27,800	$56,800	$12,160	$27,775	$1,000	$8,200	1160	$19,010	$14,800	$168,705

basis. While the Implementation Cost worksheet shows the optimistic total cost only, separate worksheets were developed for the most likely and pessimistic estimates as well as for the out-of-pocket costs. The different levels of estimated costs could also have been approximated by the application of contingency factors to the various cost elements in the initial worksheet.

The various levels of costs were not consolidated into an average for presentation to management. Instead they were presented in a manner that clearly showed management the extent of the risk involved in the proposed project. The anticipated variance from the most likely estimates was from 13 percent under to 15 percent over.

A second worksheet was used to analyze annual operating costs (Exhibit 3). This sheet was prepared for the anticipated life of the system or for five years of operations, whichever is shorter. The example illustrates five years' costs only. The elements of the annual cost of operation are:

1. Computer costs, generally based on time against an hourly rate or representing the total cost of equipment dedicated to the application

2. Supplies including cards, magnetic tape, forms, and similar computer or general office items

3. Operating personnel, generally user organization members and administrative management

4. Maintenance cost of the system including systems and programming personnel, computer time for test and assembly of programs, and other expenses

5. Overhead including floor space, electricity, telephone service, and labor related costs

6. Amortization of system implementation cost including capital expenditures

A subtotal was taken at the end of those elements which represented cash costs (or costs that affect the profit and loss statement) with a final total that included the "non-cash" costs of implementation that have been charged to expense when they occurred.

Only employee count and dollar amount were shown for the present system. These two measures were also used for the proposed alternative, but within the alternative, an optimistic, most likely, and pessimistic figure was shown. The alternative costs varied from the most likely figure by 8.2 percent under to 8.8 percent over.

These annual worksheets were consolidated into a five year operating cost chart for presentation to management. The annual costs reflected the impact of increased levels of business expected in future years. The totals indicate that a savings in operating cost of 30 percent of the cost of the present system is most likely (Exhibit 4).

Exhibit 3
Operating cost worksheet

Elements of Annual Cost	Present System		Alternative System					
			Optimistic		Most Likely		Pessimistic	
	Employees	Amount	Employees	Amount	Employees	Amount	Employees	Amount
Data processing	14.5	$ 254,600	2.5	$ 30,000	3	$ 36,000	4	$ 48,000
Supplies & forms		13,300		10,700		11,900		12,800
Operating personnel	94	583,425	76	482,175	85	527,550	90	561,825
Overhead		252,817		208,942		228,602		243,457
Maintenance cost;								
Personnel	0.2	4,800	0.3	7,200	0.3	7,200	0.3	7,200
Computer time		17,000		10,000		11,700		12,300
Other								
Amortization of special equipment or software				7,600		7,600		7,600
Sub-total	108.7	$1,125,942	78.8	$756,617	88.3	$830,552	94.3	$893,682
Amortization of implementation cost				26,638		23,034		35,229
Final total	108.7	$1,125,942	78.8	$783,255	88.3	$853,586	94.3	$928,911

Exhibit 4
Operating cost summary

| | Present System | | Alternative System | | | | | |
| | | | Optimistic | | Most Likely | | Pessimistic | |
Year	Employees	Amount	Employees	Amount	Employees	Amount	Employees	Amount
1	108.7	$1,125,942	78.8	$ 783,255	88.3	$ 853,586	94.3	$ 928,911
2	119.5	1,238,536	81.9	822,418	91.8	904,801	99.9	1,003,224
3	131.4	1,362,389	85.2	863,539	95.5	959,089	105.9	1,083,482
4	144.5	1,498,628	88.6	906,715	99.3	1,016,635	112.3	1,170,160
5	158.9	1,648,491	92.2	1,045,336	103.3	1,077,633	119.1	1,263,773
Total	158.9	$6,873,986	92.2	$4,421,263	103.3	$4,811,744	119.1	$5,449,550

Capital Expenditure $38,000

CASH FLOW AND PAYBACK ANALYSIS

The cash-flow analysis shows the present system and the proposed alternative for a five year period. The projected operating costs of the present system are brought forward from the worksheet previously prepared. For the proposed alternative the implementation costs are also brought forward from the worksheet. Operating costs included the cost of operating the present system until it would be replaced by the proposed alternative system (1.25 years in this example) and the operating cost of that system brought forward from the worksheet. Earnings directly attributable to this system resulted from the anticipated sale of new services and were entered as negative figures (enclosed in parentheses) with the total being a net amount. This chart used the "most likely" figures from previous charts, but it could have been repeated for each of the three levels of cost estimated. On this basis a cumulative savings of $1,895,901 was projected for the five-year period (Exhibit 5).

Exhibit 5
Cash flow analysis

Year	Present System	Alternative System			Total
		Implementation	Operation	Earnings	
1	$1,125,942	$164,584	$1,125,942	—	$1,290,526
2	1,128,536	30,120	921,676	$ (6,000)	945,796
3	1,362,389	—	891,998	(28,000)	863,998
4	1,498,628	—	945,517	(33,000)	912,517
5	1,648,491	—	1,002,248	(37,000)	965,248
Total	$6,873,986	$194,704	$4,887,381	$(104,000)	$4,978,085

The final exercise was a payback analysis. Only two years need to be considered to arrive at a positive figure in the cumulative savings column (actually, one year and one month). The costs of the present system were brought forward from the annual totals for the alternative in the cash-flow analysis. The savings (loss) column was computed for each year by subtracting the total cost of the proposed alternative from the cost of the present system. The payback period was determined by the point at which the cumulative savings (loss) column becomes a positive figure (Exhibits 1 and 6).

There are several areas of intangible benefits that should be presented to management decision makers. While these were not used in our example, they could also include the following. The morale of the user organization staff may improve (with resultant increased output) as a result of the attention paid to employees in the area during design and implementation of a new system. As the famous Western Electric (Hawthorne) studies indicated, increased output frequency results from increased management attention without regard to actual improved working conditions.

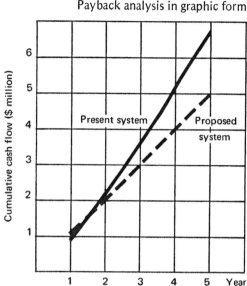

Exhibit 6
Payback analysis in graphic form

Improved statistical information may add to business earnings by improving decisions and performance. The ability to control operations such as production is heavily dependent upon the speed and accuracy of processing data. A cybernetic feedback loop can only be effective if the required data arrives in time to properly control the process being measured. The implementation of computer oriented systems may serve to improve the firm's image or by analysis of sales and market research data to more properly direct the thrust of the company's marketing efforts.

Although the foregoing items are classified as intangible benefits, it is not unreasonable to ask user management to place a dollar value on some of these benefits. These dollar values can be estimated on the basis of such things as improved operational capability, decreased product rejection rate, increased marketing potential, and similar items. Estimates of dollar value so created can be presented to management by inclusion in the earnings column of a cash-flow chart and in a payback analysis chart. Such charts should be clearly labeled to indicate that they included the estimates of value placed on intangible benefits.

QUESTIONS

1 How are the figures established for each cost element shown in Exhibit 2?

2 How does the make-or-buy decision-making process in this case compare with that discussed in the Welke article (Selection 14)?

3 What is the purpose of presenting optimistic, most likely, and pessimistic cost figures?

4 How does the payback approach compare with the discounted-cash-flow approach?

PART C

SYSTEM IMPLEMENTATION AND SYSTEMS MANAGEMENT

VIII. SYSTEM IMPLEMENTATION AND POST-IMPLEMENTATION REVIEW

This selection presents a sociologist's view of the factors influencing people's attitudes toward technical change. Four variables affecting the success of EDP implementation are identified: degree of stability, user perception, strategy for change, and role perception of the systems analyst.

IMPLEMENTING EDP SYSTEMS—A SOCIOLOGICAL PERSPECTIVE | 15
ENID MUMFORD

Systems analysts and sociologists have an important common interest—they are both concerned with the problems of implementing technical change. But the two specialisms have different approaches and objectives in relation to technical change: the systems analyst is primarily concerned with designing and introducing new methods of work which will help a company better to achieve its business objectives; the sociologist is interested in the consequences of these new methods for the work groups associated with them and in ensuring that systems are designed and implemented in such a way that the human individuals who form part of the system are not degraded or made to suffer undue stress and anxiety. The sociologist maintains that companies will more easily achieve their business objectives if attention is paid to the human element and change is introduced in such a way that it does not cause resistance to develop in groups on the receiving end. Resistance to change is also of the utmost importance to the systems analyst as his carefully designed and rational systems will come to naught if people refuse to operate them. If the argument of the sociologist is correct, and experience of computer introduction to date seems to support it, then systems analysts and sociologists need to get together to discuss their common interests, analyze the factors in work situations leading to resistance to change and to decide on the best methods for meeting this problem.

Set out below are the ideas of one sociologist on the factors influencing people's attitudes to technical change. The author would be delighted to hear the views of systems analysts on whether her arguments have any validity from their point of view and also on how they cope with the difficulties she identifies. In order to clarify the argument a number of diagrams are used. (It must be pointed out here that sociologists do not draw diagrams in quite the same way as do systems analysts. In the diagrams that follow, arrows signify relationships between variables and are not intended to indicate inputs and outputs.)

From *The Computer Bulletin* (U.K.), January 1969, pp. 10–13; used by permission. Enid Mumford is a lecturer in Industrial Sociology at the Manchester Business School.

Studies of computer introduction in a number of firms suggest that the four variables shown in Exhibit 1 have a major influence on the attitudes of employees to technical change. These are:

1. The degree of stability in the user system. By this is meant the extent to which the organization of a user department meets the personal needs and aspirations of the staff employed in it.

2. User perceptions of change. How the staff of a user department believe that the new computer system is going to effect themselves and their interests. These perceptions will not necessarily bear any relation to the realities of what is going to happen.

3. Strategy for change. The levers used by the computer innovating group to change the user department from a manual to an EDP system. This change will involve altering employee attitudes and behavior as well as departmental technology.

4. Role perception of the computer innovating group. How the systems analysts responsible for introducing the new technology perceive their role and how these perceptions affect their attitudes to user personnel and the strategies they adopt to get the change implemented.

The last three of these variables can be manipulated, that is they can be altered to meet the requirements of different situations. But in order to be able to manipulate these variables successfully, systems analysts must be aware of the pre-change attitudes which exist in the user department so that implementation strategies can be designed which fit in with user group needs. If this is not done then inevitably there will be considerable resistance to change.

Exhibit 2 provides a more detailed model of what is meant when we talk of the 'stability' of the user department. In order to design strategies for change which are likely to be successful it is desirable for systems analysts to make a

Exhibit 1
Key variables for study of implementation of technical change

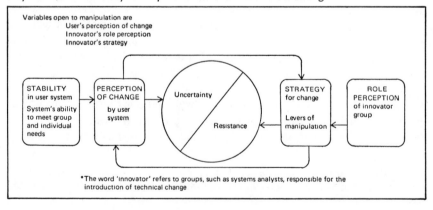

preliminary assessment of this stability factor. It can be explained as follows. At work we all try to meet a large number of personal needs; the nature of these needs depends on many factors related to our upbringing, education, responsibilities and personality; thus the needs of routine clerks are likely to be different in many respects, although not all, from the needs of, for example, highly qualified scientists. We all require money and security, but those of us who are married and have to support young families will have a high need for these two things—hence the triangle in the diagram marked 'external demands.' But we look to work to provide us with many things besides the money and security necessary to care for our families and some of these other 'wants' are listed in the triangle 'internal needs.' We want adequate rewards for the level of work we are called upon to do; we want status—and some of us in addition want power and responsibility; we want interesting work and we want pleasant social relationships within the work situation. But the extent to which we, as individuals, require all or some of these will depend on the kinds of people we are.

The degree to which our needs within work are met affects our attitudes to our work and leads to the formation of what sociologists call 'group norms.' These are attitudes and ways of behaving of which the work group we belong to approves and to which it expects its members to conform. For example, in many shop floor situations, being too friendly with the boss is seen as a betrayal of group interests and is not permitted by the group norms. Anyone who breaks this code can expect some unpleasant retribution from the rest of the group. Similarly a very strong norm in most groups is that the identity of the group shall be preserved at all costs. This fact presents particular problems to systems analysts because invariably the reorganization associated with EDP breaks up the

Exhibit 2
Pre-change model
Variable = Degree of stability in system

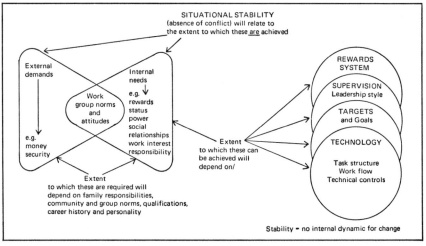

existing user department group structure and requires the formation of entirely new work groups.

If the needs of groups at work are being met by the departments in which they work then we can say that the situation is 'stable.' People will get satisfaction from work and there should be little conflict: managers will talk about having a department in which morale is high. However, employee needs can only be met providing that the work situation is designed to permit this, and whether the work situation does permit this will depend on a number of factors related to the structure and organization of the department. These factors are set out on the right hand of Exhibit 2. All departments will have some kind of technology although this can range from a very simple manual system to a highly complex type of automation. The nature of the technology will influence the way work is carried out, the kinds of controls that are used to see that it is carried out and the social structure of the groups in which it is carried out. If the nature of the technology leads to dull and routine jobs, while the needs of the labor force are for interesting and varied jobs then, inevitably, there will be conflict and people will take some kind of action to try to change an unpleasant situation: this action may take the form of labor disputes, absenteeism or quitting the company. Technology is probably the most constraining factor on the way work is organized and the amount of satisfaction it can offer to the employees involved in it, but there are others. Three factors also affecting the satisfaction of employee needs are shown in the other circles. These are the nature of department targets and goals, the leadership style of the department's supervisors and the reward system, that is the methods which are used to reimburse employees financially for the effort they are making to meet the department's targets. If targets are tight and difficult to meet then supervision may introduce tight controls and these may thwart employee needs for status and responsibility. Again, if a work group wishes to be consulted on work affairs but has an authoritarian and undemocratic supervisor, then needs will not be met and there is likely to be conflict and low morale. Similarly, certain reward systems, in particular incentive schemes based on piece work, may produce high production but do this at the expense of work interest and social relationships.

Systems analysts reading this article are now probably asking what all this has to do with them and with the introduction of EDP. The sociologist would reply that a knowledge of the factors influencing people's attitudes to their work, and an ability to analyze particular departments in these terms when implementing EDP systems can make all the difference between success and failure. For example, if the pre-change situation in a user department is 'stable,' that is people like their work and it is meeting the majority of their needs, then there is no internal dynamic for change. People will want the comfortable and satisfying methods of work to continue and a systems analyst entering this kind of situation can reckon on a great deal of non-enthusiasm for what he is trying to achieve. His problem is then to change apathy and disinterest towards change into positive feelings of enthusiasm. If, in contrast, the user department situation is unstable before the change, that is employees have a number of strong grievances related to unfulfilled needs, then this knowledge is vitally important to the systems analyst. His proposed new system will be seen in one of two ways. Either it will be interpreted as a possible way of righting some wrongs, because it can change the organization of work in a way which will better meet people's needs, or it will be seen as making an already bad situation worse. The challenge for the systems analyst is to make it the first rather than the second and this involves (a) knowing that the problem exists, (b) designing the EDP system so that the needs of the user department can in fact be met, and (c) devising implementation strategies which will not only tell the user department employees how they will gain from the new EDP system but also identify them with the changes which are about to take place. This is not easy to do; and systems analysts may argue that it is not worth doing as most people will eventually adjust to anything. However, accountants might support sociologists in suggesting that an approach which increases job satisfaction and hence decreases industrial unrest, absenteeism and labor turnover, and which at the same time increases people's toleration of technical change, can make substantial differences to a firm's profit and loss account.

For the moment we will abandon our consideration of 'unstable' situations, which are clearly very complex to handle, and return to a consideration of the problems of introducing EDP systems into 'stable' situations; that is, situations where employees are reasonably happy and satisfied with the status quo and do not have any particular enthusiasm for change.

Exhibit 3 shows that a major problem for the systems analyst is now the degree of uncertainty which the suggestion of change induces into the user department situation.

Exhibit 3
Pre-change model
Variable = Degree of uncertainty introduced into system
Uncertainty is a product of perception

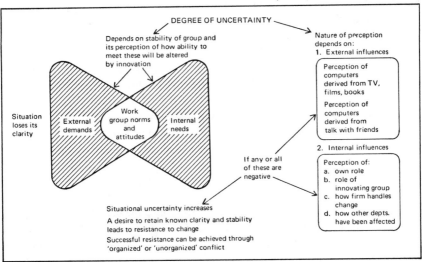

When presented with the prospect of change the first question people always ask is 'How is this new arrangement going to affect me?' The nature of their answer to this question depends on a number of factors which have a powerful influence on attitudes. Some of these factors are to be found in the community outside the firm and some in the firm itself. Clearly the systems analyst hopes that the answer to the question will be 'for the better' but whether this is what happens will depend on many things. Few people are without any views on computers; most of us have a number of strong impressions of what computers are and do which we have derived from popular communication media such as films, TV and books. Many of these impressions are frightening or threatening and the author of this article now has a collection of anti-computer cartoons derived from *Punch*, the *New Yorker*, etc., which she can use to illustrate this point. The film *2001* at present travelling the cinema circuits must bring home to many people the fact that computers are projected as becoming both all-powerful and psychotic, a not very reassuring prospect. The systems analyst must therefore be aware that in giving people information about computers he is starting from a negative and not a neutral position and that he will have to overcome preconceptions of a frightening kind.

Within the firm there are many factors which will influence the attitudes of staff to the idea of a new computer system. First of all there is the nature of their own role. If they are engaged in routine work which has always been completed in more or less the same way, then they will not be used to change and they will not want change. If, in contrast, change and variety is an integral part of their existing work and they have a responsibility for developing and improving their jobs then they can be encouraged to see the computer as a mechanism for helping them to do this more rapidly and effectively.

Secondly, there is the manner in which the role of the innovating group is perceived by the firm's employees. If systems analysts are seen as cold, calculating men who will introduce change at any price, then their overtures are likely to be resisted. Similarly, if they have the reputation of good hearted bunglers then the same resistance will be evoked. Thus the kind of image projected by the innovating group is of the utmost importance. The third factor is the history and reputation of the firm in the handling of change. If it has a reputation for always taking careful account of employee needs then staff will expect that it will do the same over the introduction of the new computer system. If, in contrast, it has a reputation for ruthlessness then uncertainty over the consequences of the new EDP system will be very high and there will be a great deal of anxiety. If the firm has already computerized other areas of the business then the experience of these departments will be known and discussed at great length. Because of the number and complexity of these variables affecting attitudes, sociologists would suggest that realistic strategies for implementation can only be designed if there is a sound knowledge of the amount of uncertainty that has been introduced into the user department by the suggestion of an EDP technology. In addition the reasons for this uncertainty must be ascertained. This approach presents the systems analysts with yet another analytical task in the human relations area.

The third major variable affecting the attitudes of the user department to the proposed change is shown in Exhibit 4 and is what can be called the 'role perception' of the innovating group. This covers not only how systems analysts see their own role but also the point referred to above—how their role is seen by the members of the user department. Exhibit 4 sets out the possible variations in this innovator-user relationship. The role behavior of the innovator group will always be modified by constraints exercised by the company in which they are working; for example, although they may see their function as maximizing computer usage in the company, top management policy may prevent them from introducing any new system which will cause redundancy. Similarly, user department staff will not worry about losing their jobs if they know that their firm will not take any steps likely to cause labor displacement.

At present, by virtue of their training and the demands of the firms in which they work, most systems analysts see themselves in what can be called a 'technical-rational' role; that is, they see their primary responsibility as designing efficient and streamlined systems and they do not concern themselves too much with the effects of these systems on the personal needs of staff in user departments. This approach may continue for some years yet, but it seems unlikely that it will be acceptable on a long-term basis. Society is becoming increasingly concerned about the 'good life' and is unwilling to accept innovation which increases profits for the few while decreasing satisfaction for the many. (Already the employment implications of mergers are causing concern at government level.) Also, innovation which does not take account of human needs is likely to meet with increasing resistance and whilst it is true that this

Exhibit 4
Change period model
Variable = Role perception

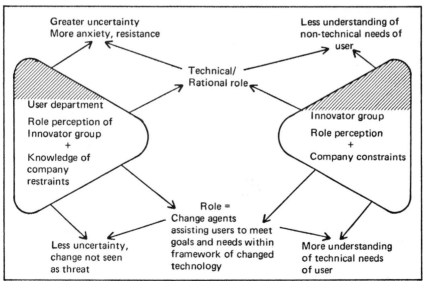

resistance has not shown up so far in relation to EDP, this is because largely female clerks have been on the receiving end of new computer systems. This is a group with little power influence or job investment. But more powerful groups will be affected in the future and their ability to frustrate change of which they do not approve will be high. EDP change in the future will therefore become much more complex to handle and will require the use of skills which have not been needed to date.

It seems likely that the systems analyst of the future will see himself very much more as a 'change agent' than he does at present; that is, he will set out to move people from one kind of stable situation to another equally stable and satisfying. In order to do this he will need to have a wider perception of his role and responsibilities and a much greater understanding of the non-technical needs of employees who are on the receiving end of technical change. He will design systems not only to meet the technical needs of the firm but also simultaneously to meet the human needs. This will not be easy but it can be done and modern society is likely to demand that it is done.

Exhibits 5 and 6 show two change situations, in one of which there is a high level of conflict and in the other of which there is a low level of conflict. The conflict here is between EDP innovators and EDP users for we are assuming that the pre-change situation is stable and that change is not desired. The high

Exhibit 5
Change strategy model
Variable = Levers of manipulation

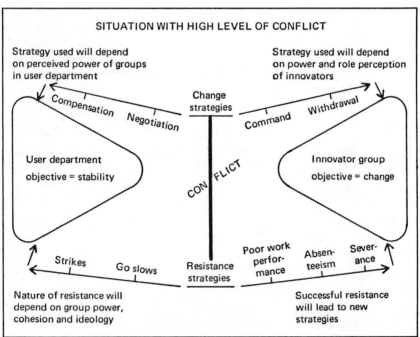

conflict situation is one that the author has observed in many firms introducing computerized systems of work where there has been little understanding of the human relations variables operating in the change situation.

In the kind of situation set out in Exhibit 5 the change process frequently becomes a straight power battle. The systems analysts design their system without any meaningful consultation with the user department and then decide on their change strategies in the light of the user department's ability to resist. In turn the user department decides on its own resistance strategies in terms of the realities of the power situation. If the user department is seen by the innovating group as weak and unlikely to exert much influence on higher management then, once persuasion has failed, it is likely to adopt an authoritarian approach and insist that the new system goes in. The weak user department will retaliate by activities including non-cooperation, poor work performance, and absenteeism or by individuals leaving the company for other more congenial jobs. If, on the other hand, the user department is recognized as having the capacity to put up considerable resistance to unwanted change and to influence top management attitudes through its ability to hold up production by means of strikes or go slows, then the innovator group will adopt different strategies. These may include compensation—associating the new EDP system with something the employees want, for example, a pay increase. It will certainly involve negotiation

Exhibit 6
Change strategy model
Variable = Levers of manipulation

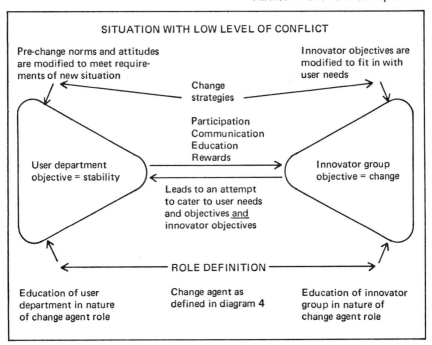

between the two parties and, if the user department is still powerful and resistant, it may involve the withdrawal of the innovating group and the abandonment of the proposed EDP system. Whatever happens, transactions concerning the change are likely to be prolonged and difficult and this kind of situation is costly and undesirable. Sometimes it cannot be avoided but often it can by the use of sound analytical and strategic techniques. Power battles are likely to become an increasing feature of EDP change as computers move away from the office into other parts of the firm.

Ideally, however, the innovating group will start from a low conflict situation or will be able to transform a high conflict situation into a low conflict one. At all costs the reverse of this last point must be avoided. The strategies associated with keeping conflict at a low level are set out in Exhibit 6. The EDP system designed by the systems team will be a result of joint discussion and participation by the user department and so will embody tasks, procedures and controls which still meet the personal and group needs of the staff of the user department. If necessary the systems analysts will abandon some of their technical objectives in order to achieve this reconciliation of EDP with user needs, and they will do this willingly because of their definition of their role as that of change agents. Their strategies for change will depend heavily on self and user education, and in positive communication and involvement. By using this kind of approach they will be able to modify some of the pre-change attitudes of the user department so that uncertainty is reduced and users are convinced that the new system will meet their needs equally as well as the old. Change will thus be introduced in an atmosphere of knowledge and approval. Uncertainty and resistance will be reduced and the user department will believe that gains not losses are a product of EDP change.

These then are the views of a sociologist on the factors influencing people's reaction to change; factors which the author believes need to be taken into account when designing and implementing EDP systems. These views may not be correct or they may not be acceptable to systems analysts, but they perhaps warrant some discussion. If systems analysts think that there is some validity in an analytical approach to the introduction of technical change then a whole new set of problems arises. These include consideration of how systems analysts should be trained and whether it is they or some other group in the firm who must accept responsibility for the human relations aspects of change. What do you think?

This article directs attention to the importance of reliability in computer operations. New control concepts are introduced, internal and external security measures are mentioned, and internal auditing techniques are presented.

PLUGGING THE LEAKS IN COMPUTER SECURITY | 16

JOSEPH J. WASSERMAN

Many companies are working to develop new business applications for electronic data processing (EDP). All too often this effort is not accompanied by a proportional effort to develop computer control systems which will protect the company's assets from misuse or error. Yet the importance of effective computer control is increasing, for a number of reasons:

1. The growing size and complexity of EDP systems, which make errors more costly and more difficult to detect.

2. The sophistication of third-generation hardware, where original documents may exist only in the form of magnetic records within the computer, placed there directly from remote terminals. (This development presents many new problems, such as security of data, and it increases the number of sources where incorrect inputs can be generated.)

3. The growing reliance of management on information generated by computer systems, not only for financial data but also in such areas as marketing, production, engineering, and forecasting.

4. A continuing shortage of skilled computer personnel, which leads to rapid turnover and the hiring of marginal workers.

When management does think of computer control systems, it tends to focus mainly on fraud, and there have been some widely publicized cases of this. But the real problem for most companies is not fraud but ordinary human error, which can cost a company millions of dollars without criminal intent on anyone's part. Computer security thus involves a review of every possible source of control breakdown—a highly demanding, but not impossible job.

NEW CONTROL CONCEPTS

One factor that has made the job more difficult is lack of awareness by many executives of new control concepts required for computer systems. EDP systems are so new that few top executives have had much first-hand experience with them. While computer manufacturers do attempt to give executives an

From *Harvard Business Review*, September–October 1969, pp. 119–129; used by permission. ©1969 by the President and Fellows of Harvard College; all rights reserved. Joseph J. Wasserman is President of Computer Audit Systems, Inc.

understanding of computer capabilities, the introduction is often quite general, and the need for controls is not sufficiently emphasized.

Because of this basic misunderstanding about EDP systems, many companies have eliminated traditional controls for checking human calculations—"the computer doesn't make mistakes." But computers are programmed and operated by humans, who still do make mistakes. Therefore, traditional control techniques still can be important and should be evaluated in terms of their usefulness to EDP systems. In addition, new control concepts must be devised to use the powerful capabilities of the computer. Although top management has the primary task of formulating a basic control policy, all employees connected with an EDP system have a responsibility to ensure that data processing is adequately controlled.

One slowly developing trend that fosters this approach is the strategic placement of a qualified top-level executive whose primary responsibility is to direct the corporate computer efforts. With this technical know-how available on the executive level, the company has taken a positive step toward establishing an up-to-date control philosophy. The company can then establish meaningful procedures to protect computer programs and data against error, malice, fraud, disaster, or system breakdowns.

In this article, we will analyze these potential problem areas and show how a combination of good judgment and machine capabilities can control them. Exhibit 1 summarizes the problems and the primary elements in an adequate control system.

Getting Off to a Good Start

Testing is vital to the success of a system and, therefore, is worth careful scrutiny. In particular, the last test phase, where all elements of a new installation are tested as a unit, indicates whether the system is reliable. Here the best method is to run the new and old systems in parallel, comparing results where possible. For example:

Parallel testing was successfully applied to a telephone company operation involving rating and billing of toll messages. When the new system was considered ready for use, the design staff extracted 300,000 toll messages that were prepared for processing by the old system. The 300,000 messages were adjusted so they could be entered as inputs to the new system.

The results of processing these messages through both systems were compared by the computer to determine whether the new system was capable of rating, filing, and billing the toll messages correctly. Any toll messages that created exceptions not encountered in the old system were traced by the systems design staff to discover the cause of discrepancy, and corrective action was taken before the new system was introduced.

If a parallel test is not feasible, the operation of the new system may be checked

Exhibit 1
Steps toward a secure computer system

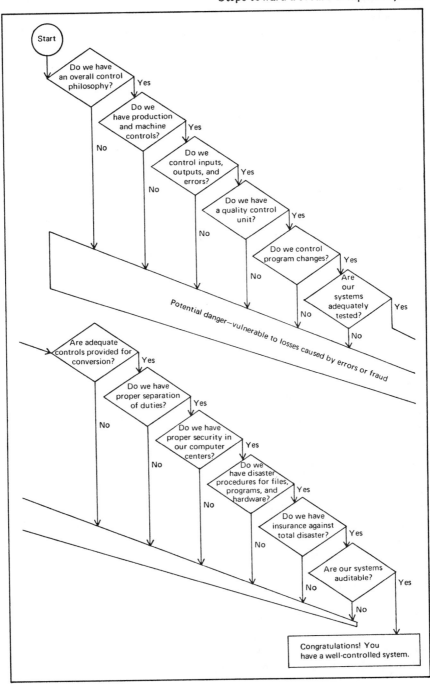

by a test deck consisting of fictitious transactions especially designed to test the system's logic. The test deck should be as complete as possible, since minor oversights can cause major losses. In one instance, an organization that pays benefits to large numbers of people neglected to include a test case to ensure that a check on the termination data for benefits was part of the computer program. As a result, many millions of dollars were paid out to persons whose benefit periods had expired.

Canvassing of Data

Finally, during the changeover to the new system, a careful check should be made to ensure that all data are converted as required. This may sound elementary, but it is very important. For instance, one major corporation, when making a changeover, failed to convert all the data from its old system; and this failure cost the company nearly $3 million.

The controls also should ensure that data are converted only once, or a company may find itself duplicating asset records or billing its customers several times for the same item.

A final check should be made to ensure that the data going into the new system have been verified and are as complete and error-free as is economically feasible. Control totals of items such as dollars and units based on the old system should be checked as the records are converted. One way of doing this is to write, prior to conversion, computer programs that will edit individual records for missing data and invalid codes; this step amounts to "scrubbing" (i.e., cleaning) the data in the old system. For example, prior to converting to a new payroll system, the employee records from the old system should be checked to ensure that significant data, such as tax codes and social security numbers, are present and valid. The problems of converting to a new system are great enough without adding the burden of erroneous data.

QUALITY CONTROL

As part of a plan for monitoring an EDP system, a quality control unit should be established to sample the accuracy of data both before and after computer processing (see Exhibit 2). Such quality control units were common in the precomputer era, when it was possible to follow the flow of data by checking documents as they were processed manually. The era of large-volume computer input and output makes quality control even more important.

The degree of training needed for the quality control unit depends on the sophistication of the system. The unit's major function is to spot data that are obviously unrealistic. For example, if the number of errors is increasing, the quality of incoming data should be scrutinized more carefully at its source to determine the cause(s) of error. This type of control and analysis will detect minor problems before they become major and will indicate where the system needs to be reinforced through additional training or improved controls.

Exhibit 2
Relationships among control groups

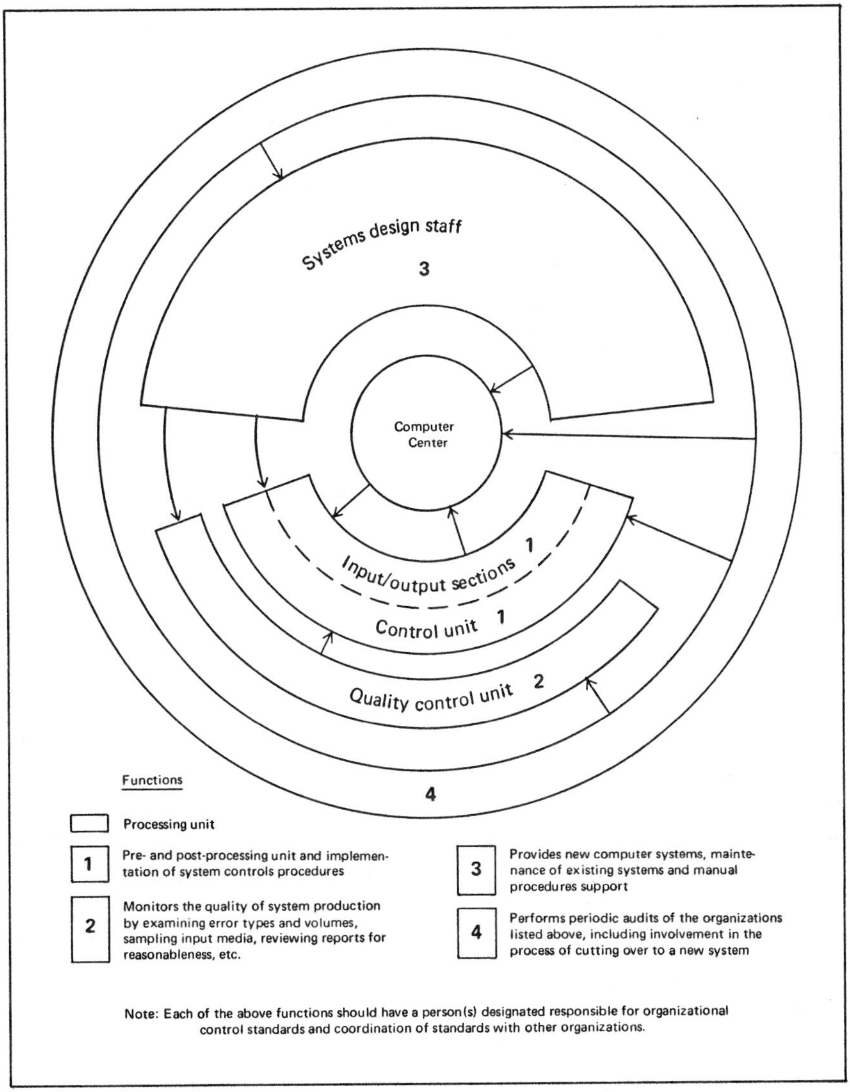

Systems design staff

3

Computer
Center

Input/output sections   1

Control unit   1

Quality control unit   2

Functions

4

☐ Processing unit

| 1 | Pre- and post-processing unit and implementation of system controls procedures |
| 2 | Monitors the quality of system production by examining error types and volumes, sampling input media, reviewing reports for reasonableness, etc. |

| 3 | Provides new computer systems, maintenance of existing systems and manual procedures support |
| 4 | Performs periodic audits of the organizations listed above, including involvement in the process of cutting over to a new system |

Note: Each of the above functions should have a person(s) designated responsible for organizational
control standards and coordination of standards with other organizations.

Input, Output and Errors

As part of the control unit, an input section (see Exhibit 2) should maintain
positive controls over all transactions it receives and, wherever possible, should
identify them by type, source, and date. Once such controls are established, they
should be part of an interlocking system of control totals which serve to assure
that data accounted for as input are not subsequently lost or distorted.

As for controlling the accuracy of a system's output, care must be taken to ensure that machine controls cannot be overridden because of human error. To illustrate:

Although it possessed an apparently foolproof system, one company came close to a disastrous loss of records stored on a master computer tape because of an operator's mistake. The tape was updated daily by adding the latest day's results to the master file. A computer operator once mistakenly used the previous day's master tape, which was kept as a backup. The computer program recognized that the wrong tape had been mounted and printed out a message saying so, but the operator ignored the message and pushed the restart button. The fact that one day's results were missing from the master file was not discovered until 20 days later, and reconstructing the master file was extremely costly.

When the serious consequences of such an error were recognized, the internal auditors requested the systems design staff to change the program so that the master file could be processed only if the proper tape were mounted.

Output controls over receipt and distribution of data will ensure reasonableness, timeliness, and completeness of computerized results. Output data should be balanced against machine-generated control totals when practical.

While some errors in an EDP system are inevitable, the manner in which they are corrected and reentered may determine the success or failure of the system. Even when the fact that errors are being made is noted, system designers often neglect manual and machine methods of correcting the mistakes. A good control system should provide a built-in method of error analysis, including information on the type, quantity, value, and age of errors, so that the source can be determined and corrective action taken.

In the case of systems that process large volumes of data and, as a consequence, are subject to a significant number of mistakes, management should consider maintaining a master file of detected errors that provides a positive control of errors, records, their magnitude, quantity, source, and age. Statistics from this file will provide management with a computerized indication of error trends, which can then be countered by appropriate controls.

Other Checks and Safeguards

There should be written instructions for all machine operations. These instructions should be kept complete, current, and understandable; and computer room managers should ensure that their operations personnel are following the procedures outlined. The best control system is no better than the performance of the people who run the computer operation, so records of the performance of both men and machines should be kept. Supervisors should also periodically review operator interventions, machine halts, and other occurrences indicating unusual conditions. Records of machine performance, preventive maintenance periods, and schedules of operation should, of course, be kept current. All this falls in the category of what are often called "production and machine controls."

The EDP library deserves more attention than it usually gets. Many companies fail to realize the size of their investment in programs and data files for an EDP system. The loss of a production or program tape can be very costly, so careful controls should be established to ensure that tapes are removed from the library only when needed, that only authorized personnel have access to the library, that all tapes are clearly labeled, and that records of tape use are kept.

Library controls should also include maintenance of backup tapes (usually referred to as "grandfather," "father," and "son," depending on how far back they go). Such backup data can restore current data files in case the latest tapes are damaged or destroyed.

The problem of maintaining backup files is more complicated for the newer random-access computer systems, in which outdated information is erased as new data are processed. However, magnetic tape can duplicate the various files contained on storage devices (such as disks, drums, and data cells) so that the system can be restored to its most current status in case of hardware or program failure.

Program Changes

In view of the possibility of major losses resulting from minor program changes, management should limit the number of people who are authorized to change operating programs or internally stored program data. The slightest change can have extraordinary effects. For instance:

At Cape Kennedy a space launching failed recently because, during a program change, a computer symbol equivalent to a comma was inadvertently omitted from the program. The omission sent the rocket so far off course that it had to be destroyed.

In company operations, the possibility of fraud through unauthorized program changes is obvious. To illustrate:

In one bank, a programmer altered a savings account program to transfer the "round off" fractions of cents in the interest calculation to an account he maintained under a fictitious name; he was able to withdraw large sums of money before his scheme was detected.

Yet as far as internal security is concerned, losses from fraud are dwarfed by losses from honest mistakes resulting from unauthorized program changes. The likelihood of loss from mistakes can be substantially reduced if programs are changed only by those persons having the proper authority.

An adequate security system should make clear the type of information to be made available to each employee. Classified information, such as data relating to customer credit, shareholders, payroll, marketing, and manufacturing processes, must be categorized by appropriate security levels.

Today, setting up a security program is complicated by the growing use of remote terminals. It is not uncommon for a company to have its computer in one center, data transmission points in several different cities or states, and assembly of final reports in still another location. When employees hundreds of miles away are in direct contact with the computer files, there must be controls to ensure that the files are not changed from remote locations without authorization, and that classified or sensitive data are available only to authorized personnel in those locations. For instance:

1. The number of remote terminals through which computer files can be changed should be limited.

2. Identification codes for each terminal and authorization codes should be used for the limited number of employees who are authorized to operate remote equipment. The computer should be programmed to check the validity of the codes before it accepts or gives information. Since personnel turnover is high, identification codes should be changed frequently.

3. The adequacy of controls themselves should be checked. One way is to have supervisors try to gain access to a remote terminal without authorization. If they can use the terminal without being challenged, so can others.

EXTERNAL SECURITY

While fraud tends to be overpublicized as a problem of internal security, just the opposite seems to be the case in matters of security against outsiders. Yet knowledge about computer systems is widespread enough that numerous persons outside the company may use a system's weaknesses for their own profit. A striking illustration of how this calls for controls occurred when banks introduced computerized accounting systems:

In these systems each customer had his account number preprinted in magnetic ink on his deposit slips and checks. A supply of the preprinted deposit slips was sent to all bank customers, and blank deposit slips were made available at the bank. Several cases of fraud came to light in which customers defrauded the bank by interspersing their magnetically coded deposit slips with the bank deposit slips provided at the bank. An unsuspecting customer using the defrauder's deposit slip would have his deposit credited to the defrauder's account, because the computer would apply the deposit to the account number that was magnetically inscribed on the deposit slip. After calling the bank to find out the balance in his account, the defrauder would withdraw his supposed funds. Many thousands of dollars were stolen until a system of controls was developed.

This simple but ingenious fraud is typical of the new challenges to security systems that EDP advances create. Even the concentration of vital records, programs, and equipment in a single location—an obvious security problem produced by having a centralized EDP operation—often goes unnoticed by management.

Guarding the System

There is every reason to keep unauthorized personnel and visitors out of the computer room. Yet many companies view their computer installations as showplaces, welcoming visitors with relatively little supervision and failing to provide even minimum security precautions. These companies apparently have not considered the possible losses from damaged files or lost programs and the consequences of having equipment out of service.

Protection from Disaster

The EDP system control plans should include protection against disruptions ranging up to major disasters.

One of the most obvious protective measures—and hence one that is often overlooked—is simple observance of fire prevention rules. There should be well-established and frequently practiced procedures for protecting files, programs, and hardware against fire hazards. As far as is possible, duplicates of all vital files, programs, and related documentation should be maintained in another location. Provision should be made for emergency use of backup equipment and even temporary manual processing of critical data.

Most companies are aware of the risks inherent in fire, flood, or natural disaster, but other potential hazards may not be so obvious. To illustrate:

Lack of a complete set of backup files caused a serious problem for one company. An employee, who was cleaning the interior of a magnetic drum cabinet, attached his magnetic flashlight to the frame of the unit. The magnet destroyed a portion of the data on the drum, a portion which the company did not ordinarily duplicate. The company lost six days of computer time reconstructing the lost data. In addition to the need for backup files and programs, this situation points out the need for proper training of personnel who maintain computer equipment.

Equipment or program failure is a continual problem. With high-speed EDP systems, the possibility of losing, duplicating, or misprocessing transactions because of these failures is great. "Recovery/restart" is the term applied to the programs and procedures used by a computer system to isolate and correct failures and to continue processing after a failure has occurred. These procedures may range from a simple rerun of the job being processed to a very elaborate and complex system involving programs designed specifically for this function.

Adequate Insurance

Increasing investments in program development, computer hardware (if owned), and stored data make it important for management to evaluate a company's insurance coverage. Is there enough insurance to avert substantial financial loss in the event of an EDP system disaster from causes such as fire, natural disaster, and vandalism? Recent unrest on college campuses has accounted for three serious situations involving computer centers:

1. In Montreal, Canada, at Sir George Williams University, students set fire to the computer center, causing an estimated $1 million damage to computer equipment.

2. At Brandeis and Northwestern Universities, militant students occupied the computer centers. In both of the latter situations the students held the computer as a hostage, so to speak, and were not destructive.

A number of insurance companies offer EDP policies. In calculating the amount of coverage needed, the insurance and data processing managers should determine the cost of reconstructing files (both revenue producing and administrative data) in case they are destroyed, and of carrying on normal business while this is done. The added cost of using backup equipment should also be taken into account.

CONTROL OF / BY PEOPLE

In data processing, one employee can perform functions that were previously assigned to several business units. Unless there are proper controls, such as those mentioned, knowledgeable but unscrupulous employees can manipulate programs for their own benefit, and incompetent employees can cause lasting damage by making errors. If duties are properly separated, the possibility of such damage is minimized, since each employee will have only a limited role in the entire system's operation.

However, management has tended to overlook separation of duties because of the rapid growth in computer use and the general shortage of personnel. Separation of duties may also be overlooked when a reduction in EDP staff or a combining of functions is carried out as a means of cost saving with the new system. These factors often make management dependent on a handful of experienced EDP people who "grew up with the system" and have a monopoly on operating know-how. This increases the vulnerability of records and makes it difficult to assess individual performance and pinpoint weak spots in the EDP system.

Only one person or operating group should be responsible for an operation at any one time. Ideally, this means drawing lines between the employees who authorize a transaction and produce the input, those who process the data, and those who use the output for reports or for other management purposes. The same controls should cover scheduling, manual and machine operations, maintenance of programs, and related functions. For example, programmers should not have access to the entire library of programs, if only to guard against the possibility of malicious damage.

An equally important control measure is rotation of employees within the EDP group. This has a twofold value:

1. It prevents an employee or group of employees from so dominating one area of operations that losses from fraud or error are not detected.

2. The high rate of turnover among computer personnel makes it prudent to avoid relying on any individual. Every employee should be replaceable by someone with a working knowledge of the position.

New Role for Auditors

The advent of computers caught the audit world unprepared. Most executives still envisioned the auditor doing the traditional finance-oriented audit; a few managements had their auditors take a look at the new computer world, but the auditors lacked the knowledge and know-how they needed to master it. Thus there was a scarcity of auditors grounded in computer system principles and equipped to effectively deal with computerized operations.

In the Bell System, an executive decision was made in 1959 to utilize the internal auditing staff as an important new influence in the development of future computer-control systems. Bell realized that computer processing imposed new control requirements, new areas of audit interest, and the elimination of some traditional audit concerns. In order to establish an effective EDP audit function, management selected a staff of EDP auditors who had a good grasp of auditing principles and sufficient aptitude for and knowledge of the EDP field, and it gave them the following objectives:

1. Develop new computerized audit techniques and have them built into the system wherever possible.

2. Develop control requirements and techniques and emphasize to the systems design staff the need for an adequate control system.

3. Evaluate the effectiveness of the control system while it is still in the design process.

4. Evaluate all other areas, such as system testing and conversion, where controls are essential.

In general, the EDP auditor was not to assume responsibility for the development of a control system but was to evaluate the procedures and facilities being designed. This was an important point, for management saw that if the auditor did design control systems, he would lose his objectivity and, in effect, end up auditing himself. Similarly, he was not to be responsible for enforcing control procedures, but only for evaluating the effectiveness of these controls. The EDP auditor thus became a "devil's advocate" on behalf of top management.

The new approach to EDP auditing was called "preconversion auditing." It provided management with an independent control appraisal of future computer systems.

In an approach like the preconversion audit, management is called on to mediate between the systems design and auditing viewpoints. If there is a difference of opinion on a control question, it is up to management to listen to both points of view and make a decision by weighing the cost of controls against the degree of risk involved.

Making the System Auditable

It is the auditor's responsibility to ensure that computer systems are auditable when they become operational. He should be continually on the alert for possible effects that the proposed new system will have on internal controls, and should develop audit requirements accordingly. It has become increasingly difficult to audit using conventional techniques, because hard-copy printouts are being substantially curtailed and very often source documents are not in a readily usable sequence. More often than not, information required by the auditor is no longer readily available without additional costly computer runs, and computer time is becoming more and more difficult to obtain. For these reasons, it is essential for him to make his audit requirements known to the systems people at the earliest possible time.

It seems clear that the EDP auditor should attempt to make optimum use of computer technology as an audit tool. He should attempt to have audit techniques and routines built into the computer system, where it is feasible and economical to do so. In this manner much of the auditing work can be performed as a by-product of the regular operation at little or no extra cost.

The Mini-Company Test

As indicated earlier, the test deck is one useful method of checking a new computer system. The method is popular among auditors. A refined and more sophisticated method is what I call the "mini-company" test. A mini-company can be defined as a means of passing fictitious test transactions through a computer system simultaneously with live data, without adversely affecting the live files or outputs. In other words, it is a small subsystem of the regular system. A separate set of outputs, including statistics and reports, are produced for the mini-company. This not only ensures that the test material does not interfere with any outputs concerning the real company, but also enables the auditor to check that statistics and reports are being prepared correctly (see Exhibit 3).

Let us see how the mini-company concept might be applied to a hypothetical payroll system:

Suppose the computerized payroll system of the hypothetical company has a master tape file that contains a record for each employee in the company. Each pay period, a payroll computation program is run which has as its input the current master file and transactions consisting of employee time allocation

Exhibit 3
Testing the main system with a mini-company

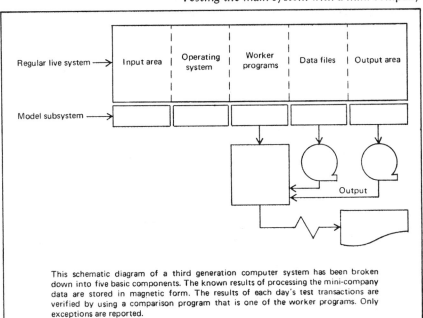

| Regular live system ⟶ | Input area | Operating system | Worker programs | Data files | Output area |

Model subsystem ⟶

Output

This schematic diagram of a third generation computer system has been broken down into five basic components. The known results of processing the mini-company data are stored in magnetic form. The results of each day's test transactions are verified by using a comparison program that is one of the worker programs. Only exceptions are reported.

(hours worked, absence, vacation days, and so forth) during the pay period. The program produces three output tape files: (a) an updated master file, (b) a payroll register and check file, and (c) a reports file.

To define the mini-company, a fictitious Department 9999 is established. It of course consists of fictitious employees. Records must be established for the employees on the live master file. Once the master records are established fictitious transactions will be prepared to be applied to these records. The fictitious master records and associated transactions constitute the mini-company base and must be designed to test as much of the payroll system's program logic as possible. Mini-company transactions are entered into the payroll computation and run right along with live transactions.

The mini-company data are separated from the live data in a subsequent computer run. Then the live data or "output files," as they are called, are processed in the normal manner, with checks printed and scheduled reports made. Similarly the mini-company data are processed to produce a payroll register, checks, and reports. The results produced by computer processing of the mini-company's input are compared with results previously calculated outside the computer to determine if any irregularities in controls or processing have occurred.

This concept is particularly advantageous because it permits continuous testing of the system on a live basis. Auditors will utilize the mini-company for periodic system reviews, and a quality control group can use the continuous-testing capabilities to great advantage in meeting its daily responsibilities for monitoring the quality of system production.

Other Auditing Techniques

In addition to the mini-company, other special audit programs can be developed. Briefly, here are some special programs which can be used by the auditor on either an off-line or on-line basis:

Comparison—matches two duplicate files contained on magnetic tape, cards, or disks; determines if they are identical; and identifies any unmatched records. (This type of program has been used in the Bell System to verify rating tables for toll messages. In one instance tape files containing tables of approximately 35,000 rating points were compared in approximately ten minutes using second-generation computer hardware. The advantages of the comparison program are its ability to perform 100% verification and identify for the auditor any exceptions for more detailed review.)

Sampling—samples records in a file on a random basis.

Extraction—extracts specific records from the file.

Compilation—checks mathematical computations made by the computer, such as adding or subtracting related fields of data or multiplying a data field by a constant. (This type of program is particularly useful in verifying the proper application of formulas in computer runs. For example, if employee group insurance deductions are developed in a payroll system by multiplying annual salary by a fixed rate, the compilation program can make these calculations independent of the regular programs. The comparison program just outlined can then be used to determine if the results of the compilation program and the regular payroll runs are in agreement.)

Systems that are auditable also should meet the requirements of public accountants and various government agencies. For example:

Certified public accountants need the ability to audit computerized records of assets, liabilities, expenses, and income for yearly financial statements.

Internal Revenue Service auditors want to check on how transactions are handled, whether expenses are correct, and whether all income is stated properly.

Department of Defense contract auditors want to check that expenses are properly allocated to government contracts.

CONCLUSION

The establishment of a well-controlled and auditable computer system no longer should be the impossible dream of the executive. Management might picture a computer control system as a control maze (see Exhibit 4). Each control function should complement another function, so that a breakdown in one area is corrected by controls in another area. Most losses through error or fraud can be prevented by such interlocking controls.

No one group should bear complete responsibility for protecting the computer system. The need for controls should be instilled in the entire organization, starting with top management and extending to all personnel.

Exhibit 4
The control maze

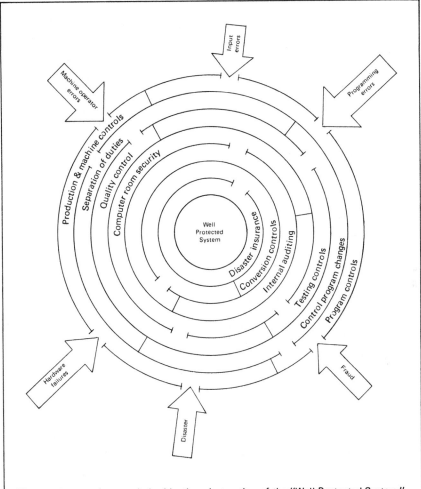

The attack arrows have as their objectives destruction of the "Well-Protected System." If the system is properly controlled, each of the factors represented by an arrow will be interrupted and negated by applicable control elements as it attempts to penetrate the control maze.

INTRODUCTION

Pinchin Johnson and Associates Ltd. is a leading paint manufacturer in Britain, supplying paint to industry and for domestic use. The Company has a number of sales divisions each specializing in sales to particular industries. Six years ago the Company had a total of ten sales divisions. Each sales division was largely autonomous, operated under a separate name, had its own forms and stationery, employed its own representatives and had its own order, invoice and sales ledger departments. A number of warehouses served each region of the country.

At this time there were nine factories, each tending to specialize in the formulation and manufacture of paints, varnishes, and lacquers for individual industries such as motor vehicles, ships, aircraft and domestic appliances. However, specialization was not complete, and, in practice, selling divisions found it necessary to place orders on every factory from time to time, and factories to place orders on each other. The problems involved in controlling production were many and difficult of solution by a set of formal rules.

In 1961, the management recognized that with the development of second-generation computers there was increasing scope for introducing computer processing to the Company to take over existing procedures and to provide more sophisticated management control information. Pinchin Johnson is a large member firm of the Courtaulds group of companies; thus it was possible to call upon the assistance of the Group Management Services department in carrying out a computer feasibility study. Because of the complexities of production control it was agreed that the area of investigation should comprise the data processing requirements of the sales divisions and of the accounting administration at Head Office.

THE FEASIBILITY INVESTIGATION

Initially, a systems analyst from Management Services (the writer) was asked to undertake a short feasibility survey to determine the specific functions within which more detailed investigations should be concentrated and the approximate savings in personnel which might result from the adoption of computer processing techniques.

Procedures were examined in outline at several sales divisions and discussions were held with a number of executives in the sales divisions and the accounting administration. Procedures varied slightly from division to division, but those set out in (a) to (c) below are typical of those in relation to home trade orders.

From Norman Smith, "Systems Analysis Problems Encountered During a Large Computer Application," *The Computer Journal* (U.K.), February 1966, pp. 230–237; used by permission. At the time this article was written, Norman Smith was with Courtaulds Ltd., of which Pinchin Johnson and Associates is a member firm.

(a) *Preparation of Works Orders*

Customers' orders were received in the order department by letter, printed order form or notes of telephone conversations. Since they usually contained insufficient detail for factory purposes, they were vetted by order clerks who inserted customer codes, product codes and descriptive detail about customers' special requirements from each customer's file. The customers' orders were then sent to the order typists.

Order typists prepared factory order masters from the vetted customers' orders, and from these masters, sets of production order copies were duplicated. The number of copies varied for different factories and types of product, but one copy was always sent to the costs department at Head Office, where ad hoc analyses were carried out as required.

The production copies of the factory orders were sent to the designated factories, and one copy of each order was filed in the order department. The order masters were sent to the invoice departments.

(N.B. In the above procedure the point at which credit control took place varied widely from division to division. However, each existing customer had a credit limit against which new orders were checked, and normal procedures were followed for establishing the credit status of new customers.)

(b) *Preparation of Invoices*

When dispatches were made against orders, dispatch note copies of the factory orders were returned to the sales division. A further editing process now took place. Goods were supplied at the price ruling at the date of dispatch. Therefore, it was necessary to check that the prices stated on the orders were still the current prices. Also, sometimes the exact products ordered could not be supplied because of changes in technical specifications of products, and equivalents were substituted. After this editing had been carried out, the dispatch notes were passed to the invoice department.

Within the invoice department, comptometer operators extended each item on the dispatch notes and entered the extensions and total values. Then they sent the dispatch notes with the corresponding order masters back to the order typists, who typed the amounts onto the masters, marked order items not dispatched "to follow," and ran off invoice copies which they returned with the other masters back to the invoice department.

The invoice department checked the typing and distributed the invoice copies.

(c) *Posting the Sales Ledger*

The sales ledger invoice copies were used as the posting media to each division's sales ledger.

Mechanized book-keeping was in operation in most divisions, with the ledger card as a copy of a "flimsy" statement. Statements were sent out monthly. Remittances were reconciled with the ledger but because of the volume of transactions and the fact that a single remittance might be made to cover receipts from several sales divisions, reconciliation was difficult and represented a continual problem for the Company.

(d) *Preparation of Sales Statistics*

The sales statistics invoice copies were sent to the sales statistics department at Head Office. The work of this Department was centered around a Powers-Samas 65 column punched-card installation, which included an electronic multiplying punch.

A card was punched and verified for every invoice item and the statistical analyses set out in Exhibit 1 were prepared at each month end, showing quantity sold, sales value and cost value for every line printed.

The overall totals on each analysis were built up to show the cumulative position for the current quarter and for the year to date.

A staff of about a dozen operators under a supervisor carried out this work, hampered to some extent because none of the invoice formats in use was laid out in such a way as to maximize punching speeds.

(e) *Warehouse Orders*

Procedures in respect of orders supplied from the Company's warehouses from finished stock were considerably simpler than the above but in every case invoice copies were sent to the division's sales ledger department and to the sales statistics department.

(f) *Export Orders*

For export orders much more complicated documentation was required. In view of this and the low volume of orders involved it was decided to exclude the procedures of the Export Division from further investigation.

FEASIBILITY ANALYSIS

Over eighty personnel were engaged in the preparation of orders, invoices, the sales ledger and sales statistics.

Investigation was carried no further at the feasibility stage. Effort was now directed towards determining the form which a computer application might

Exhibit 1
Sales statistics tabulations

Analysis No.	Major Sort	Intermediate Sort	Minor Sorts
I	Sales Area	Representative	—
II	Factory of Origin	Product Code	—
III	Representative	Product Code	—
IV	Customer's Account No.	Sales Area	Trade Group
V	Trade Group	Sales Area	—

take. It was obvious that the earlier the stage at which a computer could be utilized the greater would be the advantages. The first suggestion was therefore that basic data about each order should be coded and punched into cards so that the computer could produce the factory order set. The principal objection to this was that the production function regarded a daily computer run to produce factory documentation as essential whereas the economics of computer operation indicated that weekly processing was desirable. The additional set-up costs involved in daily runs were sufficient to outweigh the advantages of using a computer to produce factory orders.

The next possibility was to prepare order masters on typewriters producing punched paper tape as a by-product. These tapes could be matched with similar tapes produced at the dispatch stage, and the combined information used by a computer to produce invoices. The snags hinged round the fact that in order to identify the item dispatched much of the information to be punched into the order tape would have to be repeated, and thus the advantage of punching this information at the order stage would be lost.

In view of this, it was decided that the starting point for the application would be the stage at which under the existing procedures dispatch notes edited by the sales divisions were passed to invoice departments. This had the advantages of simplicity. It would not be necessary to instruct staff in many locations in a completely new system. The documentation might change, but the procedures prior to invoicing would be much the same.

The scheme envisaged at the end of the feasibility study was as follows. At the Company's sales statistics department at Head Office, all the 65 column card punches, verifiers, the sorter, the tabulator and the electronic multiplying punch would be replaced by 80 column card punches and verifiers. Dispatch notes would be sent to the installation daily from all the Company's dispatch points. A card would be punched for each item dispatched, and also for each credit allowed on returns, for amendments to master files and for ledger postings. Weekly, these cards would be sent to a computer service bureau. The computer would assemble and print invoices, post invoice totals to a sales ledger posting file and each invoice item to a sales statistics file. There would be a weekly ledger posting run, and statements would be printed monthly. Sales would be analyzed in different degrees of depth at weekly, monthly and quarterly intervals. It was envisaged that the existing punch and verifier operators could cope with the volume of input providing that document layouts were improved. The gross savings in staff were estimated at 42, and it was anticipated that the computer could provide far more management control information than would be available from a manual system.

THE DECISION ON FEASIBILITY

The feasibility study described above was carried out in December 1961 and January 1962. The conclusions reached were discussed at length with the Company's management, who considered that more detailed investigations were justified by the potential clerical savings, irrespective of the possible value of more sophisticated control data. The management did not ignore the value of such data, but obviously management are more easily persuaded of the benefits of computer applications that yield high clerical savings which can be measured in monetary terms, than when the benefits take the form of intangibles the value of which is a matter of judgment, even when the latter may be of greater importance in the long run.

THE SYSTEMS SURVEY

It was now necessary to proceed to systems analysis which would culminate in the preparation of a detailed computer systems specification.

Pinchin Johnson wished to play an active part in designing the system. They did not want to be put in the position of having to accept or reject a system designed by outsiders. Therefore, they took a decision to appoint one of their senior accounting executives to act as Company "watch-dog" over the application. This decision probably contributed more to the success of subsequent work than any other single factor. The executive concerned was Chief Accountant of a division of the Company and Cost Controller for the Group. It was agreed that investigation would be undertaken by Management Services who now attached a second systems analyst to the project. It was also agreed that contacts within the Company would be arranged initially by the accounting executive appointed to look after the application. He would make decisions on points of principle and detail as they arose in the course of the investigation, either on his own initiative, or after consulting his colleagues. This simplified the task of investigation considerably. One of the major problems in designing new systems is usually to reconcile the incompatible requirements of a number of executives. In this case, in effect the Company resolved these difficulties internally. Individual executives might frequently present the systems analysts with divergent requirements, but if these could not quickly be resolved, there was a senior executive charged with the responsibility of reaching agreement among his colleagues. Thus the main task of the systems analysts was to design a system capable of meeting the Company's requirements. As a result, investigation proceeded faster than would normally have been expected. Procedures were examined in detail in four typical sales divisions, and discussions were held with executives throughout the Company on their requirements as regards computer output. By the end of April 1962, it was possible to prepare a systems specification which the top management could use as a basis for making a final decision on whether to proceed. The main features of the system proposed are outlined in the following sections.

(a) *Preparation of Works Orders*

It had been agreed that the application should start at the stage where dispatches were invoiced. This would involve punching details of each dispatch as shown on the dispatch note. However, the latter was a copy of the works order master. Thus, it was necessary to design a new works order set which could be used throughout the Company's divisions, and which was laid out to maximize punching speeds for data recorded on the dispatch note copy. A suitable revised order master and works order set was designed and agreed by the Company. Because of the simplification achieved an incidental benefit was that the costs of works paperwork was reduced. To facilitate computer processing the Company agreed to introduce a new product code, and to revise its customer coding method. These codes were to appear on the works order master and hence on the dispatch note which would then contain all the variable data needed by a computer to produce an invoice.

(b) *Preparation of Invoices—Punching*

As stated previously, the intention was that dispatch notes and credit notes should be sent in daily batches from each factory and warehouse to the Company's Head Office where details would be punched at the re-equipped punched-card installation. Since this department would no longer produce sales statistics its title would be changed (it is referred to hereafter as the punched card department).

Bearing in mind the volumes of data to be processed it was thought that efficient operation of the system would depend on early detection of invalid data. Hence, each batch would be pre-listed on sales volume, product price rate, and three other quantity fields by a comptometer operator at the dispatch point. Product and customer codes would have check digits attached. On receipt by the punched-card installation each batch would be briefly examined for obvious errors, and details of the batch would be entered on a control book. Then cards would be punched and verified for each item dispatched. (Exhibit 2 illustrates the amount of detail which could be required.)

Finally, the cards for each batch of dispatch notes would be passed through a non-printing tabulator, to show the accumulated totals for the punched card fields corresponding to the dispatch note prelisted batch totals. During the weekly input run the computer would again accumulate these fields to ensure that no cards were lost prior to the run. Similar controls were designed for other forms of input.

(c) *Preparation of Invoices—Processing*

As a preliminary, the two master files would be updated. Then dispatch (and credit) cards would be read by the computer, edited, and written to magnetic tape. Editing would include verifying check digits on product and customer codes, and calculating totals for control fields on the cards. These totals would be printed for comparison by the operator with the list of batch totals submitted by the punched card department. The latter check would ensure that all cards were input and that none were omitted or read twice.

Next, the input magnetic tape of valid card images would be sorted to product code order and passed against a product master file (see Exhibit 3). The

Exhibit 2
Summary of dispatch/credit card layout

Field Description	Columns	No. of Columns
Batch number	1–2	2
Card class	3	1
Entry type	4	1
Debit or credit	5	1
Factory order number	6–12	7
Date of dispatch/receipt	13–16	4
Dispatch point code	17–18	2
Account number	19–24	6
Delivery address code	25–26	2
*Extra invoice set signal	27	1
*Discount code rate	28–29	2
*Representative number	30–32	3
*End use code	33–34	2
Product code	35–43	9
Number of packages	44–46	3
Package size	47–51	5
Quantity	52–55	4
*Number of returnable drums	56–57	2
*Charge per returnable drum	58–61	4
Method of extension required	62	1
Product price rate	63–67	5
*Sterling field	68–74	7
*Carriage charge	75–78	4
Blank columns	79–80	2

Fields marked with an asterisk (*) were optional to be punched if required.

data stored in this file against the matched product codes would be incorporated in the input records.

Thereafter, these input records would be sorted to customer code order and passed against the customer master file (see Exhibit 4). Here relevant information would be incorporated in the record and invoices assembled.

Items would be extended in accordance with one of four methods, charges would be made for containers where appropriate, and invoices would be totalled, trade discounts being calculated (if applicable) from a look-up table. The Company had agreed to the use of a common stationery for all sales divisions. Two print image tapes would be created and from these invoices could be printed two-up.

Two points are worth noting about the above brief summary of the invoicing routine.

Firstly, at the start of the investigation, it was widely supposed that invoice

Exhibit 3

Data stored in product master file

1. Product code (including product group code).
2. Product description.
3. Product standard cost.
4. Unit of measure code (indicating whether product sold in gallons, pounds, yards, etc.).

Exhibit 4

Data stored in customer master file

1. Customer's account number.
2. Name and invoice address.
3. Name and statement address (if different from above).
4. Delivery address codes and delivery names and addresses (up to 100).
5. First two letters of customer's surname (for sorting statistical analyses).
6. Representative number. ⎤   But these could be over-
                         ⎬   ridden by data punched into
7. End use code.   ⎦   the Dispatch Card.
8. Settlement terms.
9. Computer credit limit.
10. A signal to identify accounts selected for regular statistical output.
11. A signal to identify accounts for which an extra invoice set is required.

extension was a matter of multiplying quantity times price. This did not prove to be the case. Sales were made in a number of units of measure, of which the most common were liquid (gallons and pints) and weights (lbs. and oz.). The unit of sale varied (e.g. per package, per pint) and a variety of provisions had to be made for special products and special circumstances. Invoicing is often not as easy an application as it looks at first glance.

Secondly, it took more time to reach agreement that invoice stationery should be standardized throughout the Company than it did to reach a similar decision on works order documentation. This is not surprising. The effects on the customer of changes in stationery have to be carefully considered by those responsible for sales. It was in dealing with this sort of difficulty that the advantage of having a senior executive of the Company specifically responsible for the application was very marked. It is much easier for a Company executive to assess the merits of the arguments advanced and to argue out a decision with his colleagues than it is for any outsider.

(d) *The Sales Ledger*

At the end of the invoicing routines the computer would post invoice (and credit note) totals to a ledger posting file. Thus most of the data required to post the sales ledger was already on magnetic tape at this stage. However, details of cash postings and journal vouchers would still have to be sent to the punched card department for punching. Controls followed a similar pattern to those for dispatch notes.

It was also planned to incorporate a reconciliation scheme into the system. This would be essential if the computer records of sales ledger transactions were not to expand continuously, resulting in ever increasing processing times. The intention was to give sales ledger clerks the facility to specify either (1) that all items should be reconciled up to a given date, or (2) that stated items were to be reconciled.

Internal reconciliation of the ledger by the computer was considered but for various reasons was rejected as unworkable for the Company, though it was recognized that this was the ideal solution to the problem of reconciliation.

There was to be a weekly ledger posting run during which all transactions were to be posted to the appropriate ledger accounts, and reconciliations made as specified. All customers were to be assigned computer credit limits (lower than the real credit limits) and it was planned that each week the computer would print a list of customers whose computer credit limits had been exceeded. This would call the attention of sales ledger staff to these customers before their real credit limits were exceeded, and it would thus facilitate credit control.

At the end of each month, statements would be printed two-up, with separate statements for "goods" and "container" accounts. A copy of each statement would form the sales ledger. In addition to statements the computer would also print a list of all items outstanding on each account. That is, it would print a breakdown of opening balances. It was thought that this would assist reconciliation of the ledger considerably, since it would render unnecessary any reference to previous months' transactions in the ledger.

(e) *Preparation of Sales Statistics*

The range of sales statistical tabulations which could be produced by the 65 column punched-card installation was limited because of the time required to sort and tabulate. With a computer those times could be shortened considerably and thus it was possible to provide far more information. Statistics produced by the punched-card installation were also limited in regard to calculation because of the restricted facilities available. Moreover, output had to be in customer account number, product number, or other code order. It was not possible to print descriptive information. When it was made clear to executives that they could specify virtually any form of analysis of sales, an almost insatiable demand for more and better statistics was revealed. The senior accounting executive of the Company watching over the application had to resolve the conflicting requirements, and the systems analysts were forced to stress continuously the difficulties which executives would face in absorbing all the information requested. Finally, the Company decided that nine statistical analyses of sales were necessary.

In these analyses, selling margins replaced cost values. The 65 column equipment had been restricted to calculating the latter, but the only purpose was to permit subsequent calculation of margins. It was also possible to show the year-to-date cumulative build up for every line printed. This was a considerable step forward as compared to the statistics produced by the punched-card installation. Two completely new analyses related to sales by package size. It was thought that these would assist both the sales divisions and factories in future planning.

The Company was insistent that in analyses in which customers' names were output, the names should be in alphabetic order. (This was a considerable advance over the punched-card tabulations in which customers were printed in account number order.) It was argued that a completely alphabetic sort by the computer would be impractical, and a compromise was reached. All customer output would be presorted on two letters to be designated by the Company (usually the first two letters of the surname). Within this, the order would be account number.

Another new facility offered was that of selecting important customers for regular statistical output. A moveable signal identified these customers. The intention was that sales in respect of other customers would be grouped. The significance of this facility was that it would reduce the total volume of statistics to be presented to executives for their appraisal.

CONSIDERATION OF THE PROPOSALS

Top management considered the report in which these proposals were made, and accepted them. A major factor in this decision was undoubtedly that the proposals embodied the requirements specified by the Company's own executives, agreed by them in advance. It was not a report setting out what an outside body thought the Company's requirements should be. The benefits both in clerical savings and in the provision of better control information were also accepted by the Company's executives. The scheme had the tremendous initial advantage of being "their" scheme.

PROGRAMMING

Group Management Services was asked to assist in implementing the scheme. Two computer service bureaus were asked to quote for the work and the quotation of the Honeywell London Service Bureau was accepted. It was agreed that their H800 computer should be used and that programs should be written in FACT language by the Service Bureau programming staff. FACT was a relatively new language in this country at that time and it was believed that only by making use of Honeywell's own knowledge could the writing of the programs in a reasonable time be guaranteed. During program writing Company staff asked for many minor additions to computer processing requirements. In the writer's experience this is a cross which has to be borne by computer staff. As executives continue to think about their requirements, and their knowledge of the capabilities of computers grows, so they request changes which test the ingenuity and patience of the systems analysts and programmers. When many such changes are made the whole application is put in danger if the overall consequences are not carefully thought out and minuted by the systems analysts to all concerned. A successful application has to be controlled very closely by the systems analysts responsible for design and implementation. Slapdash methods are likely to result in an application which never gets beyond the parallel running stage.

Programming for the application was completed within seven months by a team of Honeywell programmers. Concurrent with programming the Company was making preparations for the change-over. The information about products and customers to be stored in the computer's master files was transcribed onto standard input forms. Punched-card service bureaus were employed in converting this information to punched cards. All the documentation was prepared and staff instructed in the revised procedures. Arrangements were made for a parallel run in respect of invoicing and sales ledger with one of the Company's sales divisions. If this was successful, the relevant work of this division would be taken over by the computer in the following month. Thereafter, at least one division would transfer its invoicing and sales ledger to the computer each month until the take-over was completed.

PARALLEL RUNNING

The parallel run began exactly one year after the start of the feasibility study. Daily, the selected sales division sent a batch of invoices to the punched-card installation. In addition to the normal controls, these invoices were pre-listed on total value. After each weekly run, the computer-produced invoices were compared with those produced by the sales division and reconciled on total value. The principle was that the total value of the sales division's invoice should be equal to the total value of the computer-produced invoices plus the value of the dispatches rejected by the computer because of failure to meet editing conditions. Several residual errors in the invoicing programs were detected as a result of this exercise. At the end of the month a similar exercise was carried out to reconcile the sales division ledger with the computer statements. Now the vital decision was taken to "drop off" the manual system in respect of this selected sales division. From this point on each month new divisions transferred their work to the computer. Within six months the scheme was completely operational.

BENEFITS ACHIEVED

The Company's sales ledger was centralized in its Head Office, with a considerable savings in personnel overall. Invoicing had ceased to exist as divisions transferred this function to the computer. It had not proved necessary to expand the punched-card installation staff. All the forecast savings in staff had not been made at this stage because of the enormous volume of work involved in the changeover. However, once the new system was working efficiently it was possible to concentrate on achieving savings. In practice there was no redundancy, the problem being solved by staff transfers and natural wastage.

SYSTEMS RE-STUDY

After a few months, when it was established that the computer system would operate smoothly, plans were made to transfer the work to a Honeywell 400 computer newly installed by the parent Company, Courtaulds Ltd., to replace their NCR 405 computer. The opportunity was taken to restudy the system in the light of experience. The principal improvements decided upon were as follows.

(a) *Controls*

There was a need to improve controls. Those upon input were satisfactory except that if the single totals printed out by the computer as the sums of the controlled fields on the punched cards did not agree with the prelisted totals it was difficult to pinpoint errors. Therefore, it was decided that the computer should accumulate and print individual batch totals. Output controls had originally been negligible. Experience proved this to be a hazard. Therefore it was decided that the computer should repeat the accumulation of quantities in controlled fields and print out the totals at the end of each pass and also at the stage of creating print image tapes.

(b) *Account Numbering*

Some customers had accounts with several sales divisions. Under the system operating prior to the use of a computer these customers had received separate statements for each sales division. This procedure had been incorporated into the original computer system. As the change-over was to be gradual no other procedure could be followed. However, once the sales ledger was centralized, there was a clear need for these customers to receive one statement in respect of all their dealings with the Company. Therefore, it was agreed that the computer master customer file should be split into two files, a master invoice file and a master ledger file (see Exhibits 5 and 6).

As part of the invoicing run, during the pass against the customer file, the appropriate ledger account number would be incorporated in each input record. On the subsequent ledger posting run, invoices would be posted to this ledger account number. This new facility would make it possible not only to dispatch to a large number of delivery points, and to invoice any number of branch offices, but also to post these invoices to any other selected ledger accounts.

Exhibit 5
Data stored in master invoice file

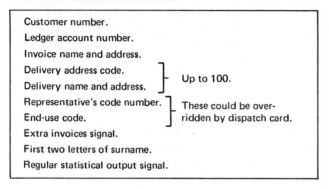

Customer number.
Ledger account number.
Invoice name and address.
Delivery address code.
Delivery name and address.   } Up to 100.
Representative's code number.] These could be over-
End-use code.   ] ridden by dispatch card.
Extra invoices signal.
First two letters of surname.
Regular statistical output signal.

Exhibit 6
Data stored in master ledger file

Ledger account number.
Statement name and address.
Credit limit.
Settlement terms.
First two letters of surname.
All unreconciled ledger postings.

(c) *Reconciliation*

As stated previously, the original concept had been that the computer would store all ledger postings until they were reconciled, and that a cash receipt would reconcile either all items prior to a certain date or selected items. In practice this system imposed too heavy a burden on the sales ledger clerks. In the revised system it was proposed that a cash receipt would pay:

1. the balance as at a certain date; or
2. the balance as at a certain date, plus indicated items; or
3. the balance as at a certain date, less indicated items; or
4. selected items, listed individually; or
5. all items except those listed individually.

(d) *Invoice and Statement Layout*

Because the H400 computer printer printed across 120 print positions as compared to the 160 provided by the Honeywell Service Bureau H800 computer, two-up printing of invoices and statements ceased to be feasible. Therefore, these documents were redesigned to minimize the additional printing time which would result. The H800 invoices had, on average, 12 lines and were printed two-up. However, since the parallel invoices very often did not contain an equal number of product items in practice two invoices required about 15 printer lines. The redesigned H400 invoice had, on average, 10 lines, so two invoices required 20 printer lines. The above ignores the time required to skip over unprinted portions of the invoices, therefore it understates the comparative advantage of two-up printing, though only slightly.

(e) *Sales Statistics*

Finally, the sales statistical output was revised. Experience of using a computer had demonstrated not only the range of statistics which could be obtained, but also the volume of paper which a high speed printer could generate. Attempts were made to reduce the frequency of the larger returns and to improve the effectiveness of the returns generally. In particular, quantities dispatched, which might be expressed in a variety of units of measure, were converted to a standard unit of measure by the computer during the statistical runs.

Some difficulty had been experienced by the Company in deciding which were the first two letters of each customer's surname. In practice, the decision was usually taken by junior clerks and this could result in statistics appearing in tabulations at the most improbable points in the alphabet. For instance, British Railways, Southern Region, might be allocated "SO" or "SR" rather than "BR," while Western Region, BR, might be allocated the correct letters. A. B. Metals might be allocated "AB" and XY Metals might be allocated "ME." The Company decided to continue with this method of sequencing output, because it avoids the necessity to cross-reference account number to Company name, but the expedient has definite drawbacks.

RE-PROGRAMMING

Programming did not now become the responsibility of the Group Management Services systems analysts associated with the project, although operation and programming of the computer was a function of this department. The reason was historical.

The first computer installed by Courtaulds Ltd., in 1958, was an NCR 405, programmed in machine code.

In view of the complexities of programming the decision was taken at the time that programming and systems analysis were to be separate functions. This is not to say that systems analysts were necessarily ignorant of programming, but programming courses in their case were intended to provide an "appreciation" of programming rather than to serve as a foundation on which to build programming skills. Broadly, this division had been maintained since, except for isolated projects where the systems analyst had previously been a programmer.

The application was, therefore, programmed by a team of Management Services programmers led by the Chief Programmer. The latter wrote the invoicing programs, and another senior programmer wrote the sales ledger and file update and transfer programs. Two more junior programmers also worked on the team, one writing all the sale statistical programs, while the other wrote all the input editing programs. Numerous minor alterations to the programs were requested by executives of Pinchin Johnson and Associates, Ltd., as programming proceeded. Thus, coordination of the project was again a major responsibility. A written specification had again been prepared, and all interested parties had a copy of this. All amendments were discussed and minuted, so that the specifications could be kept up to date. Even so, misunderstandings still arose, as they must when any communication of ideas takes place. However, it is not suggested that the whole task of programming should be undertaken by the systems analyst. In this case programming occupied four men for nine months (i.e. three man years). The work would not have been completed to this day if programming had been an additional responsibility of the systems analyst.

THE SECOND PARALLEL RUN

In one sense, the second parallel run presented a greater problem than the first in that the work had to be transferred as a whole. It was not possible to conduct a parallel run on a pilot basis. On the other hand, because the transfer was to be made between computers, reconciliation of output was easier. In fact, the parallel run proceeded smoothly, and after a month the decision was made to accept the accuracy of the new programs and "go live" on the new machine.

UPDATING OF STANDARD COSTS

Up to the present time no further changes have been made to this application. However, once confidence had been acquired by the Company in the capabilities of computers (following the original implementation of the application), other applications were designed, among them a cost accounting application. This would require an article in itself to describe, but the major feature is that the computer is used to calculate standard product costs. Master files are held for intermediate and final products, broken down into their material constituents. Standard material costs are stored in a look-up file, and regular runs are undertaken to cost new products. When standard material costs are changed, the master files are updated and new standard product costs calculated for all products. By passing the master final product cost file maintained for this application against the master product file maintained for the invoice application, it is possible to update the standard product costs stored in each record of the latter in a single run. Thus, real integration of data processing functions has been achieved.

QUESTIONS

1 How do the various steps described in this case compare with those discussed in the article by the Systems Analysis/Design Working Party (Selection 1)?

2 What are some examples of management-analyst interaction during the systems study for the invoicing application?

3 How would you prepare a system flowchart for the invoicing application?

4 What processing controls are introduced in the invoicing application?

IX. SYSTEMS MANAGEMENT: ORGANIZATIONAL CONSIDERATIONS

This article discusses some personnel-related issues in the management of computer work. Typical organization charts for small, medium, and large installations are illustrated; and the need for a clear statement of duties and procedures within the computer department is emphasized.

17 | DATA PROCESSING MANAGEMENT
DONALD L. ADAMS

Data processing is often the most poorly controlled and managed segment of a business. The cause of this situation appears to be twofold: management does not know how to evaluate data processing performance and results; and everyone has been so involved in developing the techniques of data processing that little attention has been devoted to data processing management. This article provides a checklist of effective techniques for the control of computer operations. Each topic is introduced by a question which tests for the presence or absence of an element of managerial control in the data processing function.

ORGANIZATION CHART

Does the data processing department have an organization chart?

Most business operations have a formal organization chart, but it is rare to find one in data processing. The need is obvious because lines of authority and responsibility must be clear and well defined. Some typical organization charts are presented—a small installation (Exhibit 1) corresponding to an equipment rental of less than $10,000 per month; a medium installation (Exhibit 2) in the $10,000 to $25,000 per month range; and a large installation (Exhibit 3) representing a monthly rental over $25,000.

SEPARATION OF DUTIES

Does the data processing department have an effective separation of duties?

One of the most essential internal controls in any business activity is a division of authority in order to provide a system of checks and balances. This

From *Management Controls*, July 1969. Copyright 1969, Peat, Marwick, Mitchell & Co.; used by permission. Donald L. Adams is a manager in the executive office of Peat, Marwick, Mitchell & Co., certified public accountants.

Exhibit 1
Typical organization chart—small computer installation

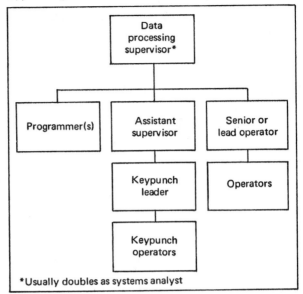

*Usually doubles as systems analyst

Exhibit 2
Typical organization chart—medium computer installation

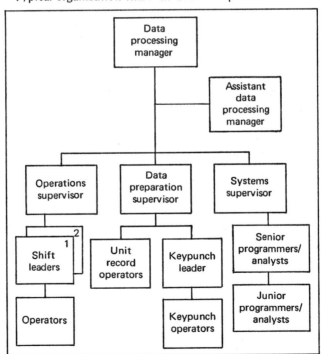

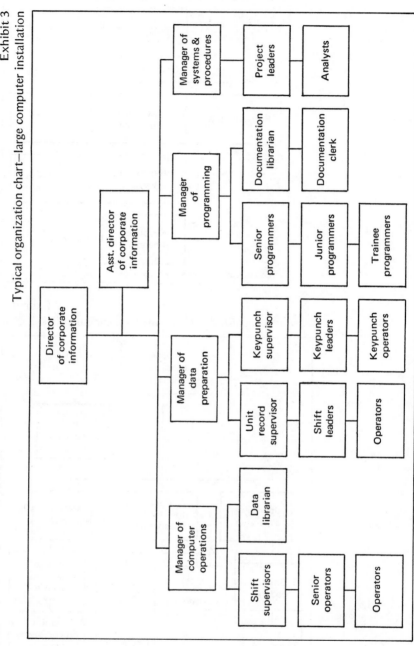

Exhibit 3

Typical organization chart—large computer installation

same principle must apply to the computer activity. Data processing consists of three basic functions—operations, programming, and systems. Within the limits of the number of personnel available, these three areas should be separate and distinct. If the functions overlap, control is weakened. As business information becomes more dependent upon computer processing, the possibilities for error and fraud are multiplied. Some overlap between programming and systems can be tolerated in small installations, but operations should be strictly segregated.

JOB DESCRIPTION

Have formal job descriptions been prepared for all positions?

Job descriptions are vital in any organization. They serve to define responsibility, guide new employees, and provide a basis for filling vacant jobs. Since data processing has evolved very quickly, jobs have developed in a haphazard manner, and in many cases they seem to defy description. Establishing detailed job descriptions should be one of the first steps in formalizing data processing operations.

CONTROL GROUP

Is there an independent control group that balances and evaluates data processing input/output?

The organization charts exhibited do not include a control group. This omission is deliberate. A control group must function independently of data processing operations. Almost all computer operations have such a group, but it is usually under the jurisdiction of the data processing manager. In such cases, the control function is being exercised but it is not an effective control. The group's responsibility under these circumstances is usually limited to balancing input and output with its related control. Such a control is designed to insure that no records are lost during processing. A control group's function should also include a quality control oriented review of the computer's output. This requires that the group be outside of data processing's control.

FORMALIZING PROCEDURES

Have machine operating procedures been formalized to present complete instructions covering each job?

In many installations there are certain jobs which are always run by one individual. He was the first man to run the particular job—a tricky one—and no one else has ever run it without a great deal of difficulty. This situation is usually created because no written instructions covering the job have ever been prepared. This need for complete write-ups is obvious on its face, but there are other important reasons. A large amount of the available computer time can be lost because of the time required to take down one job and set up another on the machine. Anything which reduces job transition time will make more time available for actual processing. By careful sequencing of the operator's instructions, it is possible to effect a significant reduction in the transition time. This is done by overlapping operations to allow for partial set up of one job while another job is being processed. Written job instructions are absolutely essential.

DOCUMENTATION PROCEDURES

Have effective documentation procedures been developed and are they enforced?

Documentation is one of the most neglected aspects of data processing management. Basically, it should involve the preparation of notes and working papers in support of the design, development, and implementation of each computer program within an installation. Everyone in data processing will acknowledge the need for documentation, but few can point with pride to the efforts they have made in this direction.

The reason is fairly simple to understand. When a computer is first installed there is a great deal of pressure on everyone involved. All efforts are focused on getting the computer running in order to justify its cost. At this stage, documentation is considered to be of very little immediate importance. The prevailing spirit is "We will catch up on that later." Human nature being what it is, the day for catching up never seems to come. For this reason, it is important to establish documentation standards early in the game and enforce them on a continuous basis. Generally, these standards should include: an outline of required documentation; standards to be employed in writing documentation; formal review and approval of all documentation; and procedures for correcting documentation to account for changes made in operating programs.

FLOWCHARTING

Has the organization adopted a standard flowchart convention?

Flowcharting is the basic component of any documentation system. To be of maximum benefit to all those who will use them, the charts should be prepared in a clear, concise, and uniform manner. These goals can be achieved by adopting an overall standard for the use of flowchart symbols and techniques. Use of the standards of the American National Standards Institute (ANSI) should be considered.

TESTING PROCEDURES

Does the installation use "open" or "closed shop" testing procedures for new programs?

Open shop testing permits the programmers to use the computer for program tests. In this case, the programmer serves as the operator and runs the new program. When and if the program develops problems, the programmer has a chance to manipulate the program through the console in an attempt to correct his program and get it running. This approach is quite popular with programmers but it can be fairly expensive because it eats up a large amount of computer time.

Closed shop testing bans the programmer from the computer room. Operating instructions must be prepared for each program and submitted with the new program for testing. Tests are run at regularly scheduled times during the day. When his test has been run, the programmer receives copies of all his output and copies of all console readings at points where the program halted or went into a loop. Based on this information, the programmer must prepare revisions to his program. This method forces the programmer to prepare written operating instructions, and reduces the amount of computer time devoted to program testing. Further, it allows testing to be carried out during regularly scheduled time periods each day. On the whole, closed shop testing is the most efficient method and should be the practice in most installations.

NEW PROGRAMS

Are testing procedures for new programs clearly defined?

Standards for such testing vary considerably from installation to installation. In many cases, programs are tested by running them against actual data and checking the resulting output. This is done because programmers do not want to spend the time required to prepare test transactions. Normally, a program will contain many instructions designed to handle data outside of the normal range of transactions. For example, a factory payroll program might be written so that no check may be issued for more than $250. Normal payroll data would not contain input for a check in excess of that amount, so it would not test this feature. Consequently, it would be necessary to create special data to test the program. It should be a requirement in every installation that all programs be tested by running them against special data created to test every decision within the program.

PERSONNEL EVALUATION

Is there an established, standard policy for the evaluation of data processing personnel? Are their salaries reviewed according to a regular schedule?

One of the limitations in the data processing function has been a lack of competent, imaginative employees. Data processing personnel are much in demand and have been able to obtain better jobs and pay by moving from company to company. It is essential to hire and retain good personnel. Since the market is competitive, personnel practices must be designed to reduce turnover. This can best be accomplished by compensating people on the basis of performance.

The methods used to evaluate employee performance should be formalized and spelled out in detail. Some techniques for developing and implementing employee work standards have been established and more can, with a little imagination, be created. For example, a time budget can be established for each job assigned to a programmer. The programmer would be required to report on job status each week. Such a system would prevent the rather common experience of having a new programmer report for work, assigning a project to him, and then having him leave a year later without having ever completed a program. Since data processing is so competitive, it is essential that salaries be offered in line with the competition.

LONG-TERM PLANNING

Are data processing requirements being planned on a five-year basis?

Rapid changes in data processing technology make it extremely difficult to prepare plans on a long-range basis. On the other hand, the investment in data processing requires the maximum use of planning to achieve an effective utilization of corporate investment. Orders for new equipment usually involve a fairly long lead time, so orders must be made well in advance. Without efficient planning, new equipment may be ordered and then received before the organization can place it into operation. Failure to plan in advance is probably the single most important reason for the relatively poor cost performance of many data processing installations.

This paper first reviews two common ways of assigning EDP responsibility within an organization. The results of a survey are then used to examine reasons for changes in location and to discuss problems occurring at various organizational locations. The gradual upward movement of EDP management in the organizational hierarchy is also noted.

THE PROPER PLACEMENT OF COMPUTERS | 18
PETER P. SCHODERBEK and JAMES D. BABCOCK |

Although many business-operated computers are not utilized to their full capabilities, their profit-making potential remains great. Having a computer does not automatically guarantee success since it is only one of the many requisites for the operation of a successful electronic data processing installation. One of the significant, if not the main, determinants is the organizational climate within which it must function. Some writers feel strongly about this:

> Nothing is more significant to the success of EDP operations than a strong, well-defined organization . . . . The organizational strength of the EDP group will be the single most important limitation on the extent to which EDP is effectively applied to the information processing needs of a company. The strong organization will successfully produce the sound application definitions, computer system design, effective operating procedures, and control-oriented programs which are essential to well-managed operations.[1]

> Perhaps top management's prime interest in the EDP installation program is getting it properly organized so that it has a reasonable chance for success.[2]

Failure to recognize the important organizational considerations can directly impair the efficiency and effectiveness of the computer's function. "Somewhere, somehow management must carve out a place in its organization chart for a major responsibility which has to do with the entire process of information gathering."[3] Where the responsibility for guiding and directing this function should lie is a matter of controversy. The two major arrangements mentioned most frequently are:

1. Locate the activity within the accounting or financial department

2. Establish an independent electronic data processing section

---

From *Business Horizons,* October 1969, pp. 35–42; used by permission. Peter P. Schoderbek is an Associate Professor of Management, University of Iowa; James D. Babcock is a graduate student at the University of Iowa.

1. Michael R. Moore, "A Management Audit of the EDP Center," *Management Accounting,* March 1968, p. 25.

2. Richard G. Canning, *Installing Electronic Data Processing Systems* (New York: John Wiley & Sons, Inc., 1957), p. 11.

3. Robert Beyer, "Management Services—Time for Decision," *Journal of Accountancy,* March 1965, p. 48.

EDP IN THE ACCOUNTING DEPARTMENT

When the computer was first introduced, the plausible course of action was to give the responsibility for computer systems to the controller or accounting department. This was done for a number of reasons:

1. The first interest in using computers arose among people in this area.

2. This is the traditional location of the punched card data processing equipment.

3. Many of the most easily mechanized data processing applications occur in the accounting areas.

4. The functions of the controller cut across all areas of the organization.[4]

5. The data flow is well-established and information needs are well known.[5]

One of the advantages of this location is that typically the controller is already experienced in the operation of management information systems and is also well qualified to become the manager of an electronic data processing system. Joplin notes some of these qualifications:

> The accountant, because of his experience with the only existing information system, has certain qualifications which should be considered when choosing the manager of information systems. Because of the length and nature of his association with top management, he is presumed to have their confidence, an important attribute in systems development. He has the knowledge of management's needs for information and the extent to which management relies upon such information for decision making. He is aware of the problems and limitations involved in supplying information for decision making.[6]

Another advantage of the accounting position would be a smoother transition to fully integrated computer systems. Since many accounting functions have already been mechanized by punched card applications, these can be easily converted without drastic changes in system and procedures.[7]

Locating the EDP system in the accounting department also has a number of disadvantages associated with it. The tendency of the accountant to place higher priority on his own work than on that of other user departments or of the company as a whole is scored big. Withington states that:

> The financial and accounting applications will always receive favored treat-

---

4. E. Wainright Martin, *Electronic Data Processing* (Homewood, Illinois: Richard D. Irwin, Inc., 1965), p. 484.

5. Bruce Joplin, "Can the Accountant Manage EDP?" *Management Accounting,* November 1967, p. 3.

6. "Can the Accountant Manage EDP?" p. 7.

7. William E. Reig, *Computer Technology and Management Organization* (Iowa City, Iowa: Bureau of Business and Economic Research, 1968), p. 33.

ment, and there may be a reluctance to start employing the computer in an operational or decision-making role which is foreign to personnel familiar only with accounting work . . . . It is difficult for the computer activity to provide important services for departments other than the one in which it is located, for however well intentioned they may be, the personnel dealing with the computer system's operation and the development of its future applications are naturally going to be most responsive to those who control their promotions and salary reviews. As a result, most or all of the organization's available resources for computer applications development will be channeled into the "parent" accounting department.[8]

Another drawback to this organizational set-up is the accountant's limited knowledge of new methods and techniques for handling information.[9] Often he will tend to slight these new approaches and concentrate more upon his functional area. Since he is usually judged on his performance in the accounting area rather than on his knowledge of computer techniques, any deficiencies in EDP may be rationalized by claiming insufficient time to accomplish both objectives.

EDP AS AN INDEPENDENT FUNCTION

An alternative to the above and one which finds acceptance in many companies is the operation of EDP as a separate activity reporting to one of the members of top management. The main advantage of this alignment is its neutrality and independence from pressures of particular groups in the organization.[10] Decisions will be made in the interest of the entire company rather than that of the department controlling the computer. The needs of the various departments will presumably be objectively evaluated, and service will be extended on the basis of priorities set by top management. Some departments will no doubt receive higher priorities for their applications, but this decision will be based on organizational requirements.

A second advantage is that the staff already has detailed knowledge of EDP equipment and techniques. They know how to utilize available information, how to derive information from new data, how best to secure data not in the system, and how to do all this at the lowest possible cost.[11]

A third benefit is that the computer department tends to take a broader view of systems problems. Operating managers too often take a narrower point of

---

8. Frederic G. Withington, *The Use of Computers in Business Organizations* (Reading, Mass.: Addison-Wesley Publishing Co., 1966), pp. 159–161.

9. Philip H. Thurston, "Who Should Control Information Systems?" *Harvard Business Review*, November–December 1962, pp. 137–138.

10. Rudolph Borchardt, "Computer Systems: How Now Their Effects on the Organization?" *Systems and Procedures Journal*, May–June 1967, p. 29.

11. C. I. Keelan, "Your Data Processing Organization 15 Years from Now," *Office*, June 1959, p. 140.

view and regard systems problems as separated by departmental lines. The staff does not confine its planning to existing organizational structures but looks at the firm in terms of overall flow of information.

This arrangement is, however, not without its shortcomings. One likely disadvantage is that operating managers may view the actions of this department as an intrusion into their areas, especially if the computer personnel try to by-pass management. Thurston notes this condition:

> Operating people resist planning in which they have no part; they resist the efforts of specialists to seek information or to install systems changes; and they delay accepting responsibility for new operating systems installed by specialists.[12]

Another possible disadvantage is the EDP staff's limited knowledge of the functional areas or departments of the company. The data processing personnel may have some difficulty in assembling the information necessary for systems decisions and in recognizing the changes needed to improve the operation. However, much of this can be alleviated by placing people knowledgeable in specific areas (accounting, production, and inventory control) into the EDP activity.

ANALYSIS OF LOCATION

Although the EDP function has traditionally been within the controller's domain, the decline of the accountant's control of the computer function has been such that his department no longer enjoys the dominant position it once held.

Were the computer to process only accounting work, there would be little reason to challenge the placement of this function within the accounting department.[13] However, increasing experience and greater confidence in the use of computers has provided a growing recognition of the computer's full potential. More and more companies are shifting to new and more sophisticated applications, and the percentage of computer time spent on routine accounting jobs is steadily decreasing.

Booz, Allen and Hamilton, in a 1966 study, determined that in many companies the finance and accounting applications comprised slightly less than half the computer effort. The 1968 study by the same firm indicated a continuance in the trend away from these applications. In three to five years, finance and accounting applications are estimated to decrease to only 29 percent of the total computer effort as against the 44 percent of the present time. Some of the results of these studies are presented in Exhibit 1.

---

12. "Who Should Control Information Systems?" p. 137.

13. Winford H. Guin, "EDP Systems in Organizational Structure," *Management Accounting*, October 1966, p. 45.

Exhibit 1

Computer applications at major computer installations

Application	Percent 1966	Percent 1968	Percent 1972*
Finance and accounting	47	44	29
Production	16	19	24
Marketing	12	13	15
Distribution	11	10	12
Research, development, and engineering	8	11	13
Planning and control	6	3	7

*Estimated.

SOURCES: James W. Taylor and Neal J. Dean, "Managing to Manage the Computer," *Harvard Business Review* (September-October, 1966), p. 102; and Neal J. Dean, "The Computer Comes of Age," *Harvard Business Review* (January-February, 1968), p. 89.

At least four facts play a major role in determining success in computer systems and have significant bearing on the location of responsibility. These factors are:[14]

1. Understanding of the objectives of an operation and knowledge of the existing operating patterns, coupled with ability to relate the information system to operating needs

2. Ability and organizational position to work with operating people to effect change

3. Competence in the designing of information systems

4. Motivation to make systems change

Because of the varying nature of the above factors, each company must decide for itself which organizational form can best fulfill these conditions for success. Placement of the EDP function will depend to a large extent upon the basic company philosophy and the capabilities of certain key personnel.[15] The obvious or presently convenient location may be inadequate for full utilization of computer facilities since conditions within the firm are continually changing and what is appropriate under present circumstances may be totally inadequate for future applications.

---

14. "Who Should Control Information Systems?" p. 138.

15. James E. Ewell, "The Total Systems Concept and How to Organize for It," *Computers and Automation*, September 1961, p. 10.

ORGANIZATIONAL LEVEL

Regardless of the locational preference of the EDP function, it is imperative that the individual in charge be afforded sufficient position in the organizational hierarchy to operate effectively. Many experts feel that the responsibility for the EDP function should be at a high level in the organization;[16] in fact, some recommended that the level be no more than one step below the president or operating head of the company.[17]

Locating this function at lower organizational levels can create difficulties for the person in charge. Since it is necessary for the EDP function to cut across company lines, it could easily fail if buried under several layers of uninformed management.[18]

Locating data processing at the lower organizational levels can cause its share of problems. The manager of data processing cannot easily discuss proposed systems changes with other functional vice-presidents; he must do his talking through his superior. Proposals tend to be "watered down" in the course of such a process. Also, the other executives, busy with the problems of their own functions and perhaps not confident about their knowledge of data processing, tend to procrastinate on data processing problems.[19]

RESULTS OF THE STUDY

The sample used for this investigation comprised 200 firms selected at random from *Fortune* magazine's listing of the top 500 industrial firms in the United States during 1967. A questionnaire was mailed to the EDP manager in these companies. A total of 109 usable responses (58 percent) were received and utilized in this study.

Organization Unit Responsible. The results of this study corroborate many of those reported in the literature. One of these findings is that the location of the computer activity in the organization is shifting away from the accounting department. Although 69.7 percent of the companies responding indicated that the original position of EDP was within the accounting department, at the present time only 45.0 percent have continued with this arrangement. A separate and independent electronic data processing function has been established in 49.5 percent of the firms, and miscellaneous departments comprise the remaining 5.5 percent. This information is summarized in Exhibit 2.

---

16. Lowell H. Hattery, "Organizing for Data Processing Systems," *Advanced Management*, March 1961, p. 25.

17. Marshall K. Evans, "Master Plan for Information Systems," *Harvard Business Review*, January–February 1962, p. 101.

18. W. C. Hume, "He Can Make the Difference Between Profit and Loss," *Iron Age*, January 2, 1964, p. 178.

19. Roger L. Sisson and Richard G. Canning, *A Manager's Guide to Computer Processing* (New York: John Wiley & Sons, Inc., 1967), p. 15.

Exhibit 2
Department responsible for EDP function (*n* = 109)

Department	Department Originally Responsible		Department Presently Responsible	
	Number	Percent	Number	Percent
Accounting	76	69.7	49	45.0
Data processing or systems	26	23.9	54	49.5
Administrative or management services	4	3.7	4	3.7
Information services	—	—	—	—
Functional department	2	1.8	1	0.9
Other	1	0.9	1	0.9
	109	100.0	109	100.0

A total of 45 companies (41.3 percent) have altered the organizational placement of the computer system from the original set-up. EDP was deemed important enough by 37 firms to give it a separate identity and organizational status, while in only five instances did the accounting department retain control; however, in these cases EDP was moved to a higher level within the department.

The reasons given for changing the location of the computer facility are listed in Exhibit 3. As indicated, the main inducement for change was the increased importance of the EDP function as a company-wide service for all departments, and not for only one or two as was past practice.

One of the more significant findings of this study is that 95.4 percent of the respondents believed that the EDP function should be independent of all operating departments. This weighty figure indicates that an independent

Exhibit 3

Reasons for changing original location
of EDP function (*n* = 45)

Reason	Number	Percent
Increased importance of EDP as an independent function	24	53.3
Need for better control	2	4.4
Organizational change	4	8.9
Increase efficiency	1	2.3
Need for more timely information	2	4.4
Other	12	26.7
	45	100.0

activity is judged to be more advantageous and efficient for realizing the computer's potential. What makes this even more meaningful is that only 49.5 percent of the businesses are presently organized in this manner. Even the companies with the computer located within the accounting department overwhelmingly favored functional independence.

The arguments advanced for this type of organizational design parallel those found in the literature. Most respondents (58.7 percent) felt that the computer activity should serve all departments equally and that the best way to accomplish this was to remove it from the jurisdiction of all functional areas, particularly that of the accounting department. Such action would tend to eliminate biases occurring when data processing personnel report to an operating manager. Over 12 percent concluded that independent status is also more conducive to management involvement while another 10.6 percent believed this arrangement gives more economical and efficient service to all users.

Two of the respondents who were accounting managers considered the accounting department the most appropriate location for EDP. No reasons were given for their viewpoint. Three respondents were of the opinion that the organizational location was of little consequence. According to them an effective computer system depends more on the individual in charge than on the organization. A competent and aggressive executive is the key ingredient without which even a well-organized system would fail.

Further support for the independent position can be found in an examination of the problems associated with EDP organizational location (see Exhibit 4). Most problematic situations are encountered in companies where the accounting department has responsibility for the computer; of the 49 firms (45.0 percent) with this design, only ten encountered no significant problems. On the other hand, an independent EDP service created fewer problems. Of the 54 respondents granting autonomy to their computer departments, 35 (64.8 percent) experienced no significant drawbacks related to the organizational design. The two main shortcomings that did occur were accounting bias and lack of management involvement. Although the weaknesses listed may not necessarily be a result of the structure of the data processing activity, there may be a relationship between computer location and the presence or lack of problems.

Organizational Level.   The results of this study indicate that the level of the EDP function in the managerial hierarchy has been moving upward. The survey conducted by Ernest Dale in 1960 showed that most of the EDP managers queried were members of middle management.[20] However, in the companies sampled, only 51.8 percent were originally in the middle management level or below, and the number presently at these levels has decreased even more (see Exhibit 5). Now middle management comprise 28.7 percent of the total, lower

---

20. Ernest Dale, *The Decision-Making Powers in the Commercial Use of High Speed Computers* (Ithaca, N. Y.: Cornell Studies in Policy and Administration, Graduate School of Business and Public Administration, Cornell University, 1964), p. 20.

Exhibit 4

Problems occurring at various organizational locations of EDP function

Department Responsible for EDP Function	No Significant Problems		Accounting Bias		No Management Involvement		Conflict Over Priorities		Poor Utilization		Poor Co-ordination		Other		Total	
	No.	%	No.	%	No.	%	No.	%	No.	%	No.	%	No.	%	No.	%
Accounting	10	9.2	17	15.6	8	7.3	4	3.7	4	3.7	4	3.7	2	1.8	49	45.0
Data processing	35	32.1	6	5.5	7	6.4	2	1.8	1	0.9	3	2.7	—	—	54	49.5
Administrative services	1	0.9	—	—	1	0.9	1	0.9	—	—	—	—	1	0.9	4	3.7
Information services	1	0.9	—	—	—	—	—	—	—	—	—	—	—	—	1	0.9
Other	1	0.9	—	—	—	—	—	—	—	—	—	—	—	—	1	0.9
	48	44.0	23	21.1	16	14.7	7	6.4	5	4.6	7	6.4	3	2.8	109	100.0

Exhibit 5
Level of EDP function in the managerial hierarchy (n = 108)

Level of Management	Previous Level of Management		Present Level of Management	
	No.	%	No.	%
President/vice-president	9	8.3	17	15.7
Upper management	43	39.8	58	53.7
Middle management	51	57.2	31	28.7
Lower management	5	4.6	2	1.9
	108	100.0	108	100.0

management 1.9 percent, while the majority (53.7 percent) are located at the *upper* management level.

Another indicator of the significance of EDP activity in the organization is the position of the executive in charge of the computer system (see Exhibit 6). This study also bears witness to the loss by the financial officer of his control of computer operations. While he still directs half of the installations, at one time he was responsible for over three-fourths of them. More responsibility has accrued at the vice-presidential level (an increase from 7.9 percent to 28.4 percent). It is interesting to note that the president or chief executive still has not taken direct responsibility as was suggested might happen.

From Exhibit 7 it can be seen that the higher the level of the computer location the more successful EDP appears to be. Of the 31 installations reporting to vice-presidents, 25 have experienced no significant problems. On the other

Exhibit 6
Executive responsible for EDP activity (n = 109)

Executive	Executive Previously Responsible		Executive Presently Responsible	
	No.	%	No.	%
President	3	2.8	2	1.8
Vice-president	8	7.3	31	28.4
Secretary/treasurer	3	2.8	4	3.7
Financial officer, controller	86	78.9	55	50.5
Director, management services	2	1.8	3	2.8
Director, data processing	4	3.7	10	9.2
Director, information	—	—	2	1.8
Functional department manager	2	1.8	—	—
No answer	1	0.9	2	1.8
	109	100.0	109	100.0

Exhibit 7

Problem occurrence and organizational location of EDP function (n = 109)

Executive to Whom Computer Activity Reports	No Significant Problems		Accounting Bias		No Management Involvement		Conflict Over Priorities		Poor Utilization		Poor Co-ordination		Other		Total	
	No.	%	No.	%	No.	%	No.	%	No.	%	No.	%	No.	%	No.	%
President	1	0.9	1	0.9	—	—	—	—	—	—	—	—	—	—	2	1.8
Vice-president	25	22.9	1	0.9	3	2.8	—	—	—	—	1	0.9	1	0.9	31	28.4
Secretary/treasurer	2	1.8	1	0.9	—	—	1	0.9	—	—	—	—	—	—	4	3.7
Financial officer, controller	10	9.2	19	17.4	11	10.1	6	5.5	4	3.7	3	2.8	2	1.8	55	50.5
Director of management services	—	—	—	—	1	0.9	—	—	—	—	—	—	2	1.8	3	2.8
Director of data processing	4	3.7	1	0.9	1	0.9	—	—	1	0.9	3	2.8	—	—	10	9.2
Director of information	2	1.8	—	—	—	—	—	—	—	—	—	—	—	—	2	1.8
No answer	1	0.9	—	—	—	—	—	—	—	—	—	—	1	0.9	2	1.8
	45	41.3	23	21.1	16	14.7	7	6.4	5	4.6	7	6.4	6	5.5	109	100.0

hand, 45 of the 55 departments reporting to the financial executive encountered organizational problems. In general, EDP activity appears to be most efficient when placed at a high level in the organization.

SUMMARY

The findings of this study indicate that the location of computer activity in the organization is shifting away from the accounting department. An independent EDP department was found in half of the firms participating in the survey, and nearly all the respondents stated that this function ought to be independent. The main reason given was that EDP serves many different departments in the firm and should not be subservient to any one function. Fewer problems were found to occur in organizations with functional independence for the computer activity.

The level of the EDP activity has been moving up in the managerial hierarchy. At the present time almost three-fourths of the EDP departments are located at the upper management level, indicating that companies were recognizing the importance of this function. Computer systems positioned at the higher levels were found to experience fewer problems than those located at the lower levels.

As is typical of other oil companies, this one operates through a group of highly autonomous subsidiary companies whose presidents report to top corporate management. The corporate organization of staff and operating functions is reproduced, for the most part, in the subsidiary companies; to some extent the same is true for the computer complex.

When corporate management decided, in 1965, to develop a consolidated information system, it established task groups in marketing, manufacturing, supply and transportation, and administration (largely accounting and control) to undertake the initial survey work in their respective areas. Computer applications related to personnel information were developed by the corporate employee relations staff.

A typical task force was composed of a director, a representative of the equipment manufacturer (who served as technical expert and design engineer), and representatives from various activities of the functional or operating units. Overall, some 500 senior, topflight people in the company participated in the task-force studies—and 200 of them were involved full time for six months. Subsequently, the task forces were replaced by permanent data systems development committees that decided on the applications needed in specific areas. This approach, coupled with a massive program of conversion to third-generation computers, was an attempt to involve operating people in the development of an information system that could serve the precise needs of user organizations. The one-time costs were high, but company management believes that the benefits have more than offset these costs.

The entire effort underscored the company's concern with moving ahead on several fronts simultaneously instead of building the information system piece by piece, as many companies have done.

As recently as 1964 the company had 40 computers at some 30 locations. Discussions with various equipment manufacturers convinced company management, however, that consolidation of computer equipment would result in at least a 30 percent saving on computer expenses; thus computer operations were consolidated in two of the subsidiary companies.

Progress was slow in reaping the benefits of this consolidation; finally, as the third generation computers were introduced, one person was designated as head, at the corporate level, of a data systems planning staff and was assigned responsibility for spearheading the development of a consolidated information system based on use of third-generation computers. The company's top management considered the appointment necessary in order to get the EDP effort off dead center.

Reprinted by permission of the publisher from AMA Research Study No. 96, *Organizing for Data Processing.* © 1968 by the American Management Association, Inc.

Each of the two major computer installations in the company serves the subsidiary in which it is located as well as other subsidiaries in the same geographical area. These installations offer hardware capability, programming services, and technical assistance to user organizations within the subsidiary companies they serve; systems development and design are carried out in various operating departments within the subsidiary companies. Since there is no computer facility at headquarters, one of the installations also serves corporate information needs. Both subsidiary facilities have IBM 360 equipment.

The two computer complexes are organized along similar lines. In one of the subsidiaries, however, the computer organization reports to the general manager of administration; in the other, to the vice president, administration. Exhibit 1 shows the structure of one of the complexes and its reporting relationships. The organization of the corporate data systems planning department is shown in Exhibit 2.

Working closely with the corporate EDP staff, each center has two primary objectives:

1. To attain standardization of computer input from the subsidiaries it serves and to work with these subsidiaries in determining the form of output

2. To develop applications to meet the needs of the subsidiary in which the computer center is located

Exhibit 1

Organization of an electronic data processing department

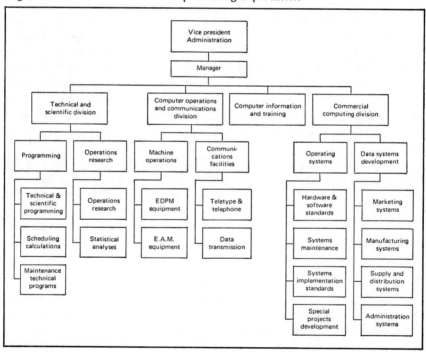

Exhibit 2
Organizational relationships and structure
of the corporate data systems planning department

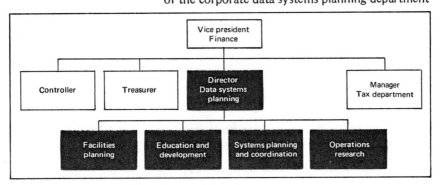

As noted, emphasis was placed at the outset on developing information systems in four areas: marketing, manufacturing, supply and transportation, and administration. In all the functional units in each of the subsidiary companies there are permanent data systems development groups. These groups evolved from the task forces that took part in the initial development efforts, and they are organized along the same lines. They design systems and the related applications. In some instances, the original task forces' ideas have had to be adapted to uses that can be made operational in a short time and that show an immediate benefit. In one subsidiary, for example, the marketing systems group, upon examining the 600-odd analyses and systems identified by the original task force, narrowed the list down to 15 proposed major applications and 119 subapplications.

The data systems planning staff at headquarters act as resident EDP experts for the subsidiary companies, which turn to it for counsel and advice in the development of their systems. In addition, the corporate group plays a direct role in the subsidiaries' EDP operations by:

1. Achieving compatibility among computer facilities and avoiding duplication in equipment and developmental efforts by (1) advising the subsidary computer centers and managements on all hardware proposed for installation, either in the centers or at terminal locations, and (2) coordinating and approving all software changes

2. Maintaining a manual of operating systems and application standards, and reviewing and approving additional standards developed by the centers

3. Consulting with subsidiaries regarding software

4. Reviewing the operation of the centers to ensure their efficient operation in meeting the needs of the subsidiaries

Also, the corporate data systems planning department is responsible for leadership and direction of the planning activities of the subsidiary data systems groups, for coordination of all computer and telecommunications systems operations, and for formulation of overall corporate policies and objectives governing both short- and long-term computer activities. The corporate group does not have authority over the subsidiary groups—each subsidiary, in developing its systems, is responsible for ensuring that the systems are compatible with others in the company.

Companywide coordination in systems development is accomplished in four ways:

1. Through the reviews and approvals described above

2. Through a number of coordinating groups headed by corporate EDP personnel and composed of representatives from the subsidiaries

3. Through two groups chaired by the corporate director of data systems planning and established expressly to exchange information on various elements of the information system

4. Through the assignment to each of the two computer centers of corporate data systems personnel who resolve systems anomalies and duplications, or if they cannot be resolved at the subsidiary level, call discrepancies to the attention of the corporate systems director

For some time, various subsidiaries within this corporation have been using operating models in making decisions. Under the present coordinated approach to EDP, a small corporate staff group is working with a committee of representatives from each of the subsidiaries to devise a consolidated model for short-term operations planning, as opposed to long-term capital or financial planning. With this model, operations planning will be related to profit-and-loss data from the subsidiary managements and departments can adapt their tactics to the overall strategy determined.

The corporate staff working on the consolidated operations planning model is intensely interested in the development of a corporate information system and in attaining uniformity in the subsidiaries' inputs into the system. The subsidiary models used in the corporate model are, in some cases, quite complex. One subsidiary, for example, has a model with 4,000 equations and 6,000 variables. Moreover, in some subsidiaries there are both tactical and strategic models, as well as combination models.

Another corporate department has responsibility for long-range (ten-year) financial and economic planning. While some simulation is done, the lack of internal feedback inhibits any modeling at the present time; but the department is in the process of converting to an IBM 360 program, which will enable it to engage in corporate simulation aimed at developing or revealing new relationships in data for use both in planning and in variance and probability analysis for control purposes.

In essence, the company has elected to implement a comprehensive information system all at once. Although its subsidiaries have used many fairly sophisticated information systems for some time, through headquarters guidance each has drastically revised its concept of an information system by examining minutely the needs of its major functional units. A significant proportion of the corporation's middle management has thus been involved in systems planning, which has been closely related to operating needs. This approach, in the opinion of company management, is providing data on which to build corporate models for advanced planning much sooner than if the company had adopted the function-by-function or subsidiary-by-subsidiary approach to systems development.

QUESTIONS

1 How is coordination achieved among various groups doing systems work?

2 How does the organization chart shown in Exhibit 1 compare with that discussed in the Adams article (Selection 17)?

3 How has the organizational location of Data System Planning affected the Company's systems work?

X. SYSTEMS MANAGEMENT: PERFORMANCE STANDARDS AND COST CONTROL

This paper explores some of the factors to be considered when setting performance standards for programmers: programming language, module size, logical complexity, input/output requirements, and programmer experience. The interaction of these factors when setting standards is then illustrated.

19 | SOME FACTORS INVOLVED IN THE ESTABLISHMENT OF PROGRAMMER PERFORMANCE STANDARDS

D. A. WATSON

The objective of this paper is not to develop a specific system for measuring programmer performance but to identify the factors required in such a system. As will be discussed later, performance standards are environment-dependent and therefore there can be no one system which is universally applicable. The implementation of performance standards should be treated similarly to the implementation of a computer system. The following stages are required: set the objectives; study the environment; identify factors and evaluate them, i.e. design the system; test them out in a pilot scheme; and implement.

This paper will try to establish the objectives, consider the effect of environment, decide what factors are important and then discuss a sample evaluation that has been used.

OBJECTIVES

There are two groups of people who will be concerned with any scheme for measuring programmer performance. Firstly, the managers will be looking for flexible control through it. Secondly, the programmers themselves will be looking to it to give them a fair deal. The system will not get off the ground unless it is fair, is seen to be fair, and does not require an excessive recording effort.

The manager's objectives, of control, should include

1. Scheduling—as is the standard workshop problem, involves the ability to estimate the future work load in relationship to the available capacity. The programming department is a workshop which produces running programs.

From *The Computer Bulletin*, (U.K.), June 1969, pp. 192–194; used by permission. D. A. Watson is Standards Manager for Computing and Data Processing at Rolls-Royce Limited.

264

2. Cost control—once a reliable schedule has been built up it can be converted to costs by the application of the appropriate rates. Typical rates which might be used could be: systems analysts £125 per week, programmer £100 per week.

3. Quality control—which requires a mixture of speed and accuracy combined with efficient use of computer time.

The programmers' objectives of getting a fair deal should include

1. Merit assessment—the performance standards must be designed to highlight the quality of performance. Where this is so, the co-operation of the programmers can be expected, particularly if the prospects of better pay and promotion are included. A bonus scheme could be incorporated into a sophisticated system but this would be dangerous unless carefully controlled.

2. Training—the system must highlight areas where programmer performance could be improved by training. This will encourage a more professional approach to the job.

3. Morale—since morale and productivity are closely allied, a department which has a plentiful but controlled workload will have a high morale.

ENVIRONMENT

It is the variations imposed by environmental considerations which make the design of a universal system of measuring programmer performance impossible. Some of the major considerations are

1. Management structure—a hierarchical management which allows specialization yields a higher productivity than a free form management. The free form situation, in which a project team made up of analysts, organization and method officers and programmers is seconded complete to a working area to implement a specific system, normally produces more effective systems but can lead to the under-utilization of programmers. The physically and organizationally tight-knit programming department is easier to control but problems remain in the assignment of individual programmers to the available jobs so as to give the correct balance of efficiency, career development and job interest.

2. Method—the nature and quality of the method standards affect performance. There can be no serious attempt to estimate and measure performance until a stable set of method standards exists. This can be illustrated by considering two similar programs which were tested differently. The non-desk-checked program required 14 test shots (10 on one day and four at one per day) involving a lapsed time of five days and a machine cost of £140. This should be compared with the program which had one day's desk-check and then required four test shots at one per day, so also taking a lapsed time of five days but at a reduced machine cost of £28.

3. Tools of the trade—if all programs have to be written from scratch, productivity will be lower than if an extensive library of properly designed modules, sub-routines and packages exists.

4. Program specification—this paper has assumed that the program specifications exist and that programmers are employed in converting them to working programs. A well written specification has two advantages: first, it enables the programmer to grasp the problems more readily; and secondly, it is less likely to be modified. The method by which the specification is produced will affect the approach to writing programs and hence to performance measurement, e.g. some installations will present the programmer with a complete specification while others will expect the programmer to write his own. In this latter case, performance will also be affected by whether the programmer writes and gets agreement to the specification before or after he has written the program.

FACTORS IN A PERFORMANCE MEASURING SYSTEM

The Programming Language.   Programming in a high-level language, like PL/1, is a different proposition from using an assembler language. In an installation where only one language is used this will not matter. It becomes significant if comparisons are to be made between programmers using different languages (e.g. FORTRAN, PL/1, and Assembler).

Module Size.   Programs are broken into modules so that modules can be written in parallel, to simplify testing and to ease the problems of modification. Large programs are often unwieldy but to segment by size alone (e.g. 150 executable statements) can produce unnatural modules. It is better to segment by logical steps but this can lead to modules of excessive size. The best approach is to segment by logical steps and also to apply a sensible size limit. If the program exceeds the size limit, consideration should then be given to changing the logic. Each module should be scheduled separately.

Logical Compexity.   A program which is small can nevertheless be logically very complex. It is necessary to rate complexity on some scale, e.g.

1 = easy

2 = moderate

3 = difficult

4 = complex

5 = highly complex

Other scales (say 1–10) can be used with more intermediate classifications but these are difficult to define and apply since they are largely a matter of judgment.

Regardless of complexity, the sheer size of a program affects certain activities, e.g. the number of lines of coding that have to be written and checked. In rating this factor it is useful to have a common base, e.g. 250 machine language statements. This has proved difficult to assess with high level languages.

Input/Output.   In commercial programs most of the programming effort is expended upon input/output requirements. To assess this, the number of record types (not the number of files) should be taken into account, since one record type can appear on two files (i.e. input and output) and one file can contain several record types. The degree of matching of record types must also be taken into account.

Programmer Experience.   So far we have dealt with factors which are independent of the programmer himself. These factors must therefore be weighted to account for the experience of the programmer. To rate experience we should take into account not only length of service but also aptitude and ability. An assessment based on service might be

Description	Experience	Output Rating
Trainee	0 - 1/2 years	0.50 (0.30)
Junior	1/2 - 1-1/2 years	0.75 (0.65)
Programmer	1-1/2 - 3 years	1.00 (0.90)
Senior Programmer	3 years	1.25 (1.00)

The figures in parentheses represent alternative ratings which some people consider more realistic. The rating for aptitude and ability will depend upon the grading methods used in each installation.

Machine and System Constraints.   The performance of the machine and its compilor together with the quality of the diagnostics available will affect the efficiency of testing. The measurement of this effect can only be done locally.

Machine Availability.   The number of test shots possible per day will also be a prime factor in estimating the time required to get a program running.

SAMPLE EVALUATION OF CERTAIN FACTORS

Systems have to be evolved which use those factors most relevant to the installation. Any system which used all the possible factors would be very complicated. For the purpose of presenting a sample evaluation, only three of the commonest factors have been used: Size (S), Complexity (C) and Number of record types (N). These factors have been evaluated to provide the number of man days required for each activity as follows:

Study specification	$C + N/4$
Block diagram	$S + 3C/2 + N/2$
Code	$1/4S (1 + C) + N/4$
Desk check	$S/4 + C/2 + 1$
Compile	$S/4 + 1$
Program test	$S/2 + N/2$
Document	1
System test	$C + 1$

This gives a total requirement of $\frac{S}{4}$(C + 9) + 4C + $\frac{3}{2}$N + 4 man days which can be simplified to give an approximate answer in the form $1/4SC + 2S + 4C + 2N$.

Instead of calculating individual activities according to the formulae, the total time can be calculated and then allocated as follows:

Study specification	10 percent
Block diagramming	25 percent
Coding and test data	25 percent
Desk checking	15 percent
Assembly, testing, etc.	25 percent

This will lead to approximately the same answers as by using the formulae.

CONCLUSION

The complexity of the formulae, even in a simplified system, only goes to show the difficulties involved in setting up and evaluating a system. The subject of establishing and applying standards for programmer performance is one about which very little is known still. There is therefore scope for research. Anyone who comes up with a viable system will have a very valuable asset.

The approach to the problem will be empirical. It involves the identification of the factors which are relevant in the environment. Data concerning these factors must be gathered and analyzed (probably in some form of regression analysis). Once this analysis has been completed the true weighting of the factors can be established. The gathering and analysis of data in this way is a long process. As an interim measure, an estimate of the weightings can be made and this can be refined by observation and reassessment. In small installations where control is strict and communication is no problem, this estimating method may give answers that are accurate enough to do away with the need for a more refined analysis.

Whatever system of estimating is eventually used some accurate data will be necessary. An installation could well begin now in collecting records of time spent on the five simple tasks shown above for each program under development. The length of time spent may well be found to be surprisingly large. This in itself should emphasize the need for realistic estimates of programmer performance.

Techniques found to be useful in collecting, reporting, and monitoring EDP performance and costs are reviewed in this article. Selected forms used in these processes are illustrated.

DATA PROCESSING *CAN* BE COST-CONTROLLED | 20
RUDOLPH E. HIRSCH |

Planning had seemed perfect for the new computerized production scheduling system. The system analysis staff had documented its designs exceptionally well, with inputs, outputs and computer file contents precisely organized. Approval by each of the plants to be affected was quickly obtained. Completion dates had been forecast by means of PERT techniques and included generous safety factors. The Data Processing Director had analyzed the specifications in detail and concluded that their complexity was such that his three best programmers would have to be assigned. On the basis of their past performance, he estimated that they would complete the required number of programs in approximately four months.

The new system became operational on August 15 instead of on the forecast date of the preceding January 2, due mainly to substantial programming time overruns. The plant managers expressed disappointment (some with considerable vigor, colorfully expressed), but were able to continue their conventional production scheduling procedures until the computerized system was finally able to take over. However, the Controller could not be supplied with the cost figures on the overrun that he had requested, since the Systems and Programming Department did not keep records on project costs.

This very typical incident illustrates a remaining deficiency in dealing with the difficulties of making predictions. By definition, predicting involves uncertainty, and refining of prediction techniques thus means reducing uncertainty to the lowest possible value. In the case of data processing costs and performance, the prediction techniques used are not yet as refined as possible under experience already on hand.

Present management practice in controlling data processing costs does not seem to have kept pace with progress in the other aspects of data processing. Thinking in regard to cost control generally appears more appropriate to the beginning days of computer use for commercial data processing in the early 1950's than to current requirements. Most computer-using organizations still seem to consider data processing largely as an overhead item; consequently, departments using data processing services are as a rule not charged for them. When data processing expense is charged out at all, charge-outs are usually limited to computer time required to produce output, while no charge is made

From *Price Waterhouse Review,* Summer 1970, pp. 65–72; used by permission. Rudolph E. Hirsch is Manager of Management Advisory Services in the Stamford/Bridgeport office of Price Waterhouse & Co., certified public accountants.

for the more costly items of system analysis, programming, computing time for program testing, and the invariable subsequent program changes. Present cost collection methods seem to be used primarily for accounting purposes and not for planning and control.

Further, in many enterprises, little or no justification seems to be required when a department requests data processing service. Even when justification is required, cost estimates are seldom developed and even more infrequently monitored. This casual approach may be a result of habit rather than oversight: after almost two decades of experience in commercial data processing, systems analysis and programming are still viewed by management as somewhat akin to research and hence allegedly beyond the scope of conventional cost administration techniques. This attitude was not without some justification initially, but a large body of experience has been gathered by now about commercial applications. Based on this experience, it is at present feasible to predict and control data processing costs just as effectively as, for example, manufacturing costs. Feasible, but seldom done.

As a result of this absence of effective data processing cost control, Parkinsonism has appeared in data processing as it has elsewhere. Data processing expense is steadily rising in proportion to total expense, and data processing headcounts in proportion to total employment. As I discussed in greater detail in an earlier article, computer output volume rises most rapidly in the absence of initial and continuing information justification and data processing cost charge-out. Much computer-produced information is requested for "political" reasons or because "it would be nice to have" as distinct from being needed; the discontinuance of a computer-produced report is seldom requested by its recipients once the report loses its importance, which all reports sooner or later do. Hence the importance of continuing information justification. However, in the usual absence of—and partially as a result of the lack of—justification requirements and cost charge-out procedures, an ever-increasing volume of computer-produced information is generated, and data processing expense is becoming an ever-larger proportion of total corporate and government budgets. Meanwhile, back in their sales offices, the computer manufacturers rub their hands in glee.

It would of course be inaccurate to say that cost control procedures and proper computer information do not exist. There are many excellent systems of this kind, particularly in some larger enterprises. Their procedures, however, are applicable at least in large part to all computer users. For example, the following costs charge-out method has worked well for a large corporate computer-user:

When a department requests computer service, the data processing department estimates the costs of that service and quotes a standard cost to the requesting department. If the latter accepts that cost, it will be charged that amount and none other, regardless of the costs actually incurred. This method has a double advantage: it not only permits "customer" departments to use data processing services with (budgetary) confidence, but also enables top management to monitor the efficiency of the data processing department simply by analyzing its "profitability." Under this method, highly technical data processing operations are being controlled effectively by nontechnical executives in the terms with which these executives are most familiar.

THE COMPONENTS OF COMPUTING COSTS

The total cost of electronic data processing includes far more than the actual cost of the "hardware" itself. At least all the following types of costs must be included:

1. Computer rental or other lease payments, or acquisition price amortization if the equipment was purchased. In the latter case, maintenance engineering costs are paid separately and must be included in this category.

2. Similar expenses for input data preparation equipment such as keypunches and verifiers, and output-handling devices such as form bursters and decollators.

3. Punched cards, printer forms and other kinds of expendable data processing supplies, including electricity attributable to the data processing equipment (and to its air conditioning!).

4. Data processing premises, including amortization of costs of special improvements, such as double flooring and air conditioning. (Virtually all computers require their own heavy-duty air conditioning or at least extensive modifications to existing central air-conditioning systems.) Office space for data processing management, programmers, systems analysts, control clerks, and the like must be included in these costs.

5. Salaries, including fringe benefits, for at least the following personnel:

    a. Data processing management
    b. Systems analysts
    c. Programmers
    d. Computer operators and other machine-room personnel
    e. Control clerks and tape/disk librarians
    f. Key punch operators and other data-preparation personnel
    g. Custodians, guards and other maintenance personnel

An obvious but often overlooked prerequisite for a cost control system is an appropriate provision in the chart of accounts for accumulation of each of the cost categories involved to facilitate subsequent charge-out. Assuming appropriate accounting facilities for the cost control system to have been established and "sold," the following points become relevant:

An effective data processing cost control system must account for all time spent by programmers and systems analysts, computer power-on time, expendable supplies and nonexpendable data storage such as magnetic tapes in use and disk space tied up. In a well-run computer installation, all time spent by programmers and systems analysts and computers, all supplies used and all data storage facilities preempted are attributable to particular projects or other legitimate uses. Thus if the reported sum of time, material, and data storage use amounts to less than the total available, the difference is a signal of inefficient or unauthorized usage of data processing resources.

"Overhead" items such as management salaries, premise charge-off and similar items are, of course, difficult to allocate directly to particular projects. However, since such items typically account for a substantial proportion of total data processing expense, it is important that these overhead items also be reflected in allocating data processing costs to particular projects. One useful and equitable method of assigning these fixed data processing expenses to particular projects is to assign to each project the same percentage of total fixed data processing costs as that project takes up of total variable data processing costs.

The computer itself can, and should be, used to collect, allocate and report on fixed and variable data processing expense. The description below of a data processing cost control system assumes that the computer will be used to do this.

AREAS OF COST CONTROL ATTENTION

Programming

The control and monitoring of programming effort and expense is a particularly critical item in a cost control system, since the methods (if any) of controlling this item have until now frequently been found spectacularly inadequate. An experienced data processing professional can estimate to within about 10 percent the number of statements or instructions a program will contain when finished. Despite this, the programming time (and thus programming expense) of a finished and properly functioning program frequently amounts to two or three times the initial estimate. I have been involved in cases of even larger overruns too painful to detail here; my experience has been that well over 90 percent of all programming projects ultimately exceed their original time and cost estimates. In part this discouraging experience is due to the absence of a generally available and acceptable rational programming time estimating system. Another common reason for programming time overruns is a frequent tendency by data processing management and programmers to begin the programming phase of a project before the program specifications have been completely defined; the resulting shortcomings become apparent quite late and then require time-consuming reprogramming and possible enlargement of scope. About as discouraging, however, is the general but unnecessary absence of a system for even reporting, let alone controlling or predicting, programming effort as a project proceeds.

At any one time, a programmer typically works on several different programs. As he completes writing a program or a major segment of it, he will send it to another department for keypunching and then to the computer for compiling or assembling (i.e. translating into computer code), followed by computer-testing to determine whether the program is in fact functioning correctly. Since at least several hours, and often days, elapse before the results of keypunching, compiling and testing are returned, programmers use this turnaround time lag to work on other programs. Therefore, a typical programmer may (and should) work on two or more programs simultaneously, and an essential feature of programming cost control is that each programmer will report the number of hours he has spent on each program.

It is always difficult to get people to describe accurately what they do, especially over any length of time. To overcome this problem, time-reporting must be formalized. Exhibit 1 represents a programmer time reporting form for use in a time and cost reporting system. Each system analyst or programmer may, despite his title, do work other than system analysis or programming; in fact, many computer users do not maintain a formal distinction between system analysts and programmers since their functions frequently overlap, especially at senior levels. Exhibit 1 therefore exemplifies a time reporting form covering all types of work each individual may be called upon to perform. An effective time reporting system must require that these time reports be turned in *daily*. If the reporting interval is weekly or longer, there will be a tendency to delay completion of time reports to the last possible moment, with a consequent reduction of recollections and hence of the accuracy of the information turned in.

The supervisor to whom these time reports are submitted should accumulate them and submit them on a weekly or other short interval basis for keypunching and computer processing, since the time information constitutes the basic data for all other control reports.

Time for Data Preparation and Computer Use

Exhibit 2 represents a computer time log, which should be produced daily for each computer used. Entries on such a report should be made manually by the computer operator or, if possible, automatically by the computer itself under control of its operating system or control program. The program identification, project or program type, chronological and actual computer running time, lost-time indication and operator identification must be entered for each program run. (If this log is completed manually, the information on it will be keypunched to produce by computer the Project Cost Analysis (Exhibit 3) and Programmer Performance Analysis (Exhibit 4).) It is obviously important that all computer time be accounted for on a computer log. Most computers are now equipped with elapsed-time meters and various programmable internal clocks; making sure that all time is actually being reported has become a relatively simple matter for management.

Once the information discussed has become available, it is possible to monitor and report on programmer and operator performance and project development,

Exhibit 1
Daily time sheet

NAME A. E. Neumann   EMPLOYEE NO. 39070   DATE 5/22/70

TIME CHARGED TO

TYPE OF WORK

PROJECT	PROGRAM	SYSTEM ANALYSIS	SYSTEM DESIGN	DETAIL DIAGRAMMING	PROGRAMMING	TESTING AND DEBUGGING	CONVERSION AND PARALLEL	DOCUMENTATION	TRAVEL	TRAINING	MEETING	OTHER*
1260	007				2							
8971	012			1								
6407	023			1								
6407	024				2	1		1				
0705	101											
TOTALS				2	4	1		1				

*For "Other" categories use the project code indicated below
90001 Vacation
90002 Holiday
90003 Personal Time
90004 Illness
90005 Professional or Technical Societies

Exhibit 2

Daily computer log

DATE 5/22/70

SYSTEM TYPE AND NUMBER S70/50-1

PROJECT PROGRAM IDENTIFICATION	PROGRAM CODE	OPERATION CODE	ELAPSED TIME			COMPUTER TIME			LOST TIME CODE	Trouble Report Number	OPERATOR	COMMENTS
			START	STOP	TOTAL	START	STOP	TOTAL				
0001/000		30	0801	0857	56	4625	4718	93			J.C.	
1214/004		10	0858	1004	66	4718	4828	110			J.C.	
0705/101	13	11	1005	1100	55	4828	4920	92			J.C.	
0041/012		10	1102	1240	98	4920	5083	163			J.C.	
1600/008		10	1241	1243	2	5083	5086	3	42	2-14	L.B.B.	
0705/101	13	12	1245	1314	29	5086	5134	48			L.B.B.	

OPERATION CODES:
10 – PRODUCTION
11 – DEBUGGING
12 – ASSEMBLY

20 – IDLE
21 – SPECIAL
22 – POWER OFF

30 – PREVENTIVE MAINTENANCE
31 – UNSCHEDULED MAINTENANCE

LOST TIME CODES:
40 – LOST TIME-COMPUTER
41 – LOST TIME-OPERATOR
42 – LOST TIME-INPUT DATA
43 – LOST TIME-PROGRAM
49 – LOST TIME-OTHER

Exhibit 3

Project and program time and cost analysis

PROJECT IDENTIFICATION 0702, CUSTOMER FILE PROCESSING

STATUS AS OF 7/31/70

PROGRAM	DESCRIPTION	TARGET DATE	SYSTEM ANALYSIS	SYSTEM DESIGN	DETAIL DIA-GRAMMING	PRO-GRAMMING	TESTING AND DEBUGGING	CONVERSION AND PARALLEL	DOCUMEN-TATION	TRAVEL	TRAINING	MEETINGS	COMPUTER TIME	KEYPUNCH AND DATA PREP.	COST
0000	GEN. PROJECT									8	1	4			$ 177
0001	INPUT EDIT	6/2/0						7	5			2	2		330
0003	CREATE FILE	7/9/0					4	6	8				4	1	541
0004	SELECT 01	8/4/0	1	2		30	13	4	9				3	1	962
0007	SELECT 02	8/6/0			2	15	11	1	6				1	2	510
0009	UPDATE	9/1/0				10	13	9	7				2	2	638
0015	RESTARTS	9/1/0	1	2	7	12	4		2			1	1	3	453
	TOTAL THIS PERIOD		2	4	9	67	45	27	37	8	1	7	13	9	$3,611
	TOTAL TO DATE		46	35	42	128	105	44	69	16	16	21	39	15	$9,771
	ESTIMATE		50	30	40	135	120	40	70	18	10	5	25	20	$8,607
	VARIANCE		-4	+5	+2	-7	-15	+4	-1	-2	+6	+16	+14	-5	+$1,164

Exhibit 4

Programmer performance analysis

NAME NORMAN, A.E.   REPORTING PERIOD 7/16-31/70

PROJECT AND PROGRAM	*IF COM-PLETE	DESCRIPTION	LANGUAGE	NO. OF INSTRUC-TIONS	PROGRAMMING HOURS				COMPUTER TEST HOURS			
					PERIOD	TO DATE ACTUAL	TO DATE ESTIMATED	VARIANCE	PERIOD	TO DATE ACTUAL	TO DATE ESTIMATE	VARIANCE
0041/012	::	TRAVEL EXPENSE DISTB.	COBOL	425	–	13	15	-2	–	2	2	0
0702/009	::	UPDATE CUSTOMER FILE	COBOL	650	–	64	50	+14	–	19	7	+12
0705/101		PRINT MAIL LABELS	COBOL	40	2	6	5	+1	1	2	1	1
1260/007	::	TIME CARD EDIT	COBOL	512	2	24	20	+4	–	4	5	1
6407/023		STORES ISSUE REGISTER	COBOL	375	1	9	7	+2	–	–	–	–
6407/024		STORES ISSUE TOTALS	COBOL	185	2	5	5	0	–	–	–	–
8971/012		OPTIMIZE MAINTENC.	COBOL	94	1	12	10	+2	–	2	2	0
TOTALS				2,281	8	133	112	+121	1	29	17	+12

progress, and expense. For this purpose, a Project Time and Cost Analysis such as Exhibit 3 should be produced at least semi-monthly. Note that with the information collected from the time reports and computer logs (Exhibits 1 and 2), plus the use of the time and cost estimates made at the beginning of each project and stored on computer files, producing the Project Control Report is a relatively simple matter. The Time and Cost Analysis will give management a clear picture of the development progress and expense of each project underway, and identify time and cost overruns for corrective action.

The information collected from the time reports and computer logs also enables management to analyze programmer performance, since this information also makes it possible to produce a Programmer Performance Analysis (Exhibit 4). This management report will be used to analyze programmer performance rather than project progress. Note that no attempt is being made to monitor systems analyst performance as closely, since overruns are far more frequent (and expensive) in programming than in system analysis.

This report, which will be produced for each programmer, will list on a cumulative basis all previous programs completed by him, in addition to those he is now developing. The report will make possible an accurate evaluation of each programmer's "growth rate" and present ability, since a programmer's ability is measured in terms of programming time and computer testing time required in relation to the length of his programs. Programming time and cost forecasts, not to mention the programmers' periodic counseling interviews, can thus become far more meaningful than is possible under conventional procedures. At present, few computer-using organizations collect or evaluate this information and therefore rely on more or less subjective factors.

Availability of this information is important because programmers must be controlled more carefully than is possible on the present subjective basis. Programming talent remains in short supply and accordingly is highly paid. The most costly resources should be the best-controlled. Until now programming has been an unfortunate exception to that rule.

Supplies

In most cases it is worthwhile to account for expendable data processing supplies. An exception might be made when no single application requires a disproportionate amount of supplies, or where total supplies expense is negligible, say less than 2 percent of total data processing expense. These conditions are rare, however, and therefore supplies expense must usually be controlled and allocated.

To do so it will be useful to distinguish between general-purpose and special-purpose supplies. General-purpose supplies are used by several applications; an example is blank or general-purpose forms, i.e. not prepared for a special installation but sold as a standard market item. General-purpose punched cards also fall into this category. It is usually not worthwhile to keep records on an application-by-application basis about the consumption of these general-purpose supplies. The total cost of such items is easy to ascertain and should be distributed to all applications using these supplies, in proportion to the total other costs of each application. Cases exist, of course, of all or most of a standard item being needed for a single application, such as a large supply of continuous-form gummed labels for computer-printing of mailing labels. In such cases the total cost of these supplies must be posted to the particular application, despite the fact that the supplies are general-purpose.

Special-purpose supplies are prepared for use exclusively by one or a few applications. Such supplies usually consist of preprinted punched cards or printer forms. The cost of such items should be charged to the application or applications making use of them, and should not be absorbed by all applications.

Data Storage

In any computer installation it is necessary to preserve information on computer-legible media from one processing cycle to the next. Such information will be kept on punched cards and/or magnetic storage media such as tapes, disks, drums and data strips. Of these, only punched cards are expendable, and their cost should be allocated as already described for supplies. Magnetic media, however, are reusable and their costs on a "rental" basis should be allocated among the applications using them. Allocation methods differ slightly between magnetic tapes and the other magnetic media.

In the case of magnetic tapes, rental for each reel of tape should be charged to the computer application using it for the period of the usage. Since the number of reels reserved by an application often increases with time, especially in the case of those applications that update transaction registers, it is useful for management periodically to audit the total number of tape reels reserved. Management should then make sure that the number of tape reels on rental is not growing unreasonably, and that the pool of unused reels, i.e. those not on rental, likewise is not too large.

Magnetic disks, drums and data strips should be charged to the respective applications using them, the charge to each application being calculated by the amount of data stored on those media by that application. The resulting rental will be charged to the application for as long as it preempts such data storage space.

Some of the magnetic storage facilities available will not be chargeable to individual applications. Control programs and other "utility" programs to facilitate such general functions as sorting must be stored for use by all programs. The actual data storage rate charged to individual applications should thus include an "overhead" amount for "amoritzation" of the storage required for these general-purpose programs.

CASE I | PROCTER & GAMBLE CO.

I shall begin my story with a touch of history. P&G created a Data Processing Department in 1954. We had no particular knowledge or deep conviction at that time about the subject. However, some guidelines were laid down early by top management:

1. The department was to be a corporate one, centralizing the study and application of computers, the installation and operation of systems.

2. Investment in Data Processing Systems was to be subject to the same Company approaches as were other investment of assets:

   a. justification procedures;
   b. rate of return criteria;
   c. audit of actual results;
   d. a stepwise, prove it as you go, test market approach to systems expansion.

Whether these guidelines were laid down out of inexperience in the field or profound wisdom, I will say that they have served us well. Today, 12 plus years later, we still operate under these basic policies and see no need to change them.

As you might imagine, with such a hardnosed cautious approach, it was a while before we were even ready to take a first step. Methodology for design and installation of systems had to be evolved, and much preliminary study of the Company's flow of data took place, looking for a solid place to begin.

The Company installed its first large-scale computer in 1957 (an IBM 705). We had concluded by that time that:

1. We did not know how to design and install any kind of a workable "total system"—it was too big and too tough a bite, certain to produce indigestion.

2. We should build from the bottom up with "subsystems" that could ultimately tie together into whatever kind of total system might be justified.

An analogy here is in the construction of the foundation and core of a building that can be added to later; perhaps some investment in extra footings; leaving reinforcing rods extended to tie to, future services stubbed in; but building no more square feet than can be justified at the moment.

Abridged from "Computers in Operational Planning, Analysis, and Control" by Donald I. Lowry, pp. 34–49, in *Computers and Management*, Boston, Harvard Business School, 1967. Reprinted by permission. Donald I. Lowry is Manager of Technical Staff Divisions, Proctor & Gamble Co.

I suspect that your primary interest is not in the design of systems, but in their use. Yet our experience leads me to conclude that your use of Data Processing Systems as a manager or a future manager will be shaped and *limited* by their design, and it is not a subject one can ignore or pass over lightly. Therefore, I shall continue with some illustrations of how P&G went about building and evolving what our "system" is today.

Our justification approach very early brought such obvious things as payroll, stock transfer, and dividend payments under study and design, where clerical savings were easy to document and calculate. However, we needed something more as the solid foundation block for a Company-wide network system.

One area of our business with much paper work was the daily transaction of receiving orders, translating these into various shipping papers and controls, and then preparing invoices and handling accounts receivable. This was chosen for detailed study.

By mid-1957 we were ready to go to test market with a resulting subsystem we called O.S.B. (Order, Shipping, Billing). We felt this was a sound foundation block, for the customers' order was one of the most basic pieces of data that could be built upon.

We tried it in one area of the country (not without some learning pains), got a satisfactory projection of payout, and then extended it in the P&G Company throughout the United States in steps that took several years to complete. This first block proved big enough to justify our investment in sufficient hardware and know-how to establish a network of regional data centers. These were scattered throughout the United States in strategical places, tied to a corporate center in our Cincinnati headquarters. Exhibit 1 pictures the network I have been talking about.

With the completion of this first major building block, and having a solid foundation of network operations, P&G turned its attention to adding other blocks. Exhibit 2 illustrates this. Obviously, once the O.S.B. block is laid down, if we can but incorporate daily production figures, we can project Finished Product Inventories, which gives another block. With inventories and sales recorded, an appropriate mathematical model can convert these into an optimum production schedule, giving yet another block.

The appropriate factors can expand these things into ordering of purchased materials, etc. Handling of commensurate systems such as Payment and Accounting Entries, Outbound Freight, also logically follow.

As you can see, our approach has been to build a structure, block by block, resting on basic source data and topped with some pieces of management information which can be split off of the blocks below. Both the walls and the roof of our total system still have many gaps and holes and the design of our house is subject to change as the requirements of the business change.

Now, if I have made the building of this house sound so easy you wonder why we have not finished it, allow me to pursue the point. These blocks do not come quickly or easily and in many cases cannot as yet be justified.

Exhibit 1
The P&G corporate data processing network

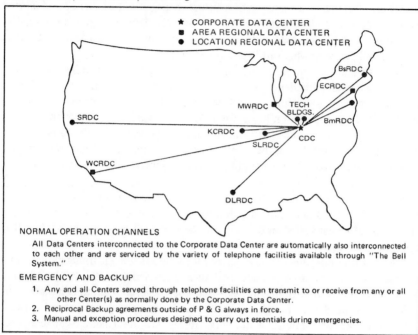

★ CORPORATE DATA CENTER
■ AREA REGIONAL DATA CENTER
● LOCATION REGIONAL DATA CENTER

NORMAL OPERATION CHANNELS

    All Data Centers interconnected to the Corporate Data Center are automatically also interconnected to each other and are serviced by the variety of telephone facilities available through "The Bell System."

EMERGENCY AND BACKUP

1. Any and all Centers served through telephone facilities can transmit to or receive from any or all other Center(s) as normally done by the Corporate Data Center.
2. Reciprocal Backup agreements outside of P & G always in force.
3. Manual and exception procedures designed to carry out essentials during emergencies.

Exhibit 2
Building blocks in the P&G system

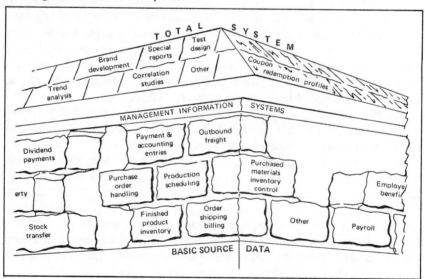

To illustrate, our outbound freight system is basically a costing (or a pricing) system. I am sure you can imagine adding a table of basic rate structures for various commodities to our source data, blending this with the flow of orders and shipments processed daily by the Order, Shipping, Billing Foundation system, and coming up with something that would:

1. give shipment planning advice for choosing the best carrier;

2. calculate the freight bill of the carrier;

3. prepare the bill for the carrier to reduce his cost or when his bill arrives, verify it as correct and approve for payment;

4. distribute the cost of freight to all commodities and brands in each shipment;

5. prepare various analyses and comparisons helpful in negotiating lower rates.

It might surprise you to know this simple logical extension of the system involves 23 different departments in our Company, requires many man years of skilled system analysis and programming time, and has an investment cost of perhaps a quarter million dollars—which, under our approach, must be carefully documented, justified, and approved by management before we proceed.

Someone once estimated that in the United States today, there are 13 trillion freight rates. Someone else counted them and corrected the figure to 1.44 septillion, or 144 followed by 24 zeros. Now of this "total U.S. file," P&G represents only a small fraction, but nevertheless a very significant number. Our system will eventually be required to handle over 2,000,000 individual rates. With all of the data associated with each rate, plus its pertinent control information, we are faced with a file that *could* consume upwards of 50 reels of tape. Obviously something had to be done to reduce the number of tapes so that the system would be operationally sound. A great part of our time was directed toward reaching this solution.

In our final design we could only justify including about 85% of our volume in the mechanized system. The rest is better handled in an old fashioned manual way.

To enlarge on this point of justification, it applies in our Company not only to bits and pieces of data systems, but to bits and pieces of hardware and communication systems. For example, shipping data which are processed in Cincinnati on a third generation 360–65 computer, transmitted in high speed (250 characters/second) sophisticated fashion via wire to Boston, printed out as a shipping paper and invoice on a high speed printer at several hundred lines/minute, are then taken to the warehouse by taxicab. Why? Certainly, an electronic transmission system would be technically feasible—but the taxi is cheaper and meets the time requirements. In the sense of complete mechanization, we do not ever expect to have a "total system."

Up to this point, I have painted a picture of a solid foundation of network operations encompassing most of the functional type data necessary to the transaction of the Company's daily business. In doing this, we designed in factors of flexibility which would let us, fairly economically, add to these data or extract from them for analytical purposes. We chose programming language and software so that we could maintain these systems in the face of a high rate of change.

To add one more pertinent factor: we, as a part of our fundamental policies of justification, established a full charge system to all users. Departments or Managers who request analytical or "Management Information" service are required to pay the full cost, including all programming and overhead charges. Again, as in other instances, the basic policy of the Company applies. If an individual Product Manager (or Brand Manager as we call them) elects to buy a service, be it P&G Data Processing or an outside information service, the price tag is quoted and he must justify this expenditure within the normal limits of budget control or profit commitment.

The key point is this—an individual manager is free to buy such management information service as he feels is helpful and justified. If a Brand Manager wants to buy (at a price) a trend analysis each month by brand size and by sales district, obviously such figures can be extracted from our functional O.S.B. system, which has the basic shipment figures in it.

And, of course, by adding population data to our source data (understand the up-to-date phrase is "data bank") this opens up many other combinations that a marketing manager might have interest in. The status of his brand development against the potential can be inexpensively calculated, for example, and used to guide his thinking in allocating spot TV spending or other promotions.

A question that may logically come to your mind is, under our approach of charging full costs to the customer, what brave manager first steps up and takes the development cost of a system against his budget? Doesn't this inhibit the growth of systems that might benefit many departments?

"Yes and No" is my answer, and I shall elaborate. Any corporate wide functional system such as the Order, Shipping, Billing I described earlier is justified and presented to Management as a total system, and the installation cost in each Department is borne by that Department regardless of local benefits or savings. Where a specific type of information report is requested by a Department or Brand on a price tag basis, the first fellow in pays the programming cost.

This does tend to screen out marginal projects and hold down indiscriminate use of the computer. If there is a problem in our approach, it is in the fact that later customers can ride the coattails and get great volumes of figures from existing programs at little added cost. The temptation to acquire more information than one has the capacity to use is not always resisted.

However, going back to the initial programming cost, the first man in may succeed in finding partners to share the cost if this seems to be limiting to him.

In practice this has not seemed limiting. Our various Divisions and Brands, while competitive and somewhat independent in their operations, are more than watchful of each other for good ideas. Also, in our Data Processing Systems Department and related Technical Staff budgets, P&G does allocate some funds (about 10%) to research on hardware, software, and systems techniques that are prorated on a basis of general overhead charge. This permits development of systems which a user might not yet be educated to want.

How do the staff groups charged with this responsibility then educate their users (or "sell" these opportunities) once they feel a worthwhile system with considerable potential has been developed? It is no harder or easier than selling any staff idea for improvement in any other area of the business—and it depends on what kind of charter and support the top management of a company gives its staff. Fortunately, in my biased opinion, our company makes good use of its staff and this is not an onerous task.

I was billed as discussing other areas of computer uses such as personnel. Here, too, we have taken the simple "what's justified" approach. Other than the routine of payroll and fringe benefit calculations, we do little. Perhaps it is because we are relatively a small company in personnel (about 36,000 employees worldwise for about 2¼ billion sales) that we do not feel the need for a computerized system to help decide which manager or employee is doing a good job and who is best suited for a new position. If we ever feel the need for more sophistication, we will price tag the cost and make our decision from that point.

In discussing other areas of use such as production, purchasing, financial, it is difficult to break these things out and talk about them separately. Our system design is based on a corporate wide approach and these "functions" are all wrapped together, as the name implies, into our "functional systems." You may recall, when I was illustrating systems design with a discussion of "Outbound Freight" that I mentioned 23 different departments were to some degree affected by this System. Scheduling of production, ordering of raw materials, choosing of carriers, payment of bills, and many other aspects so logically flow from basic shipment order data that they have been tied together in our design—and I shall not try to discuss "production" or "logistics" separately. I would stress again, however, that all pieces of systems are not computerized. For example, in some cases we have built inventory based production scheduling models but operate them via a manager's slide rule rather than a computer because it is cheaper.

To summarize, P&G has elected to invest in a corporate wide Data Processing Systems Department and to manage this investment (machines, people, skills) as it does any other type of investment so as to secure a rate of return. Our effective use of electronic data processing comes not so much from the equipment itself but from the special methods and systems we have developed to make it an integral productive part of our operations. Our basic approach has been to start with fundamental subsystems, carefully designing these and standardizing on machine language and other aspects of programming so that the systems could later tie together and data flow from one to the other. In the period 1954 to 1957 (between the creation of our DPS department and our first installation) much of our time was spent in evolving procedures and techniques to permit this integration. This has been a continuing evolution and even today we are working to help develop and test new languages such as PL/1 which will make the job even easier.

One of the early obstacles to integrating systems was in the hardware design itself. Both vendors of hardware and many of their customers seemed intent on highlighting the differences in commercial, scientific, and process control types of data processing rather than looking for the common elements and building on them. We were faced with a choice of scientific or commercial type computers as well as scientific and commercial oriented languages.

It was obvious to us early that there were many overlapping areas where these interests merged and both compatible hardware and software were needed to help design for integrated data processing. If Market Research people need to use Boolean algebra—if the best design in a production control system makes use of simulation for allocating product to the best warehouse location consistent with cost, use, turnover of stock for quality, etc.—if the proper statistical sample needs to be calculated in a process control operation—the line between "commercial" and "scientific" grows indistinct. For this reason we were one of the customers who for a number of years have pushed the vendors for more compatibility in hardware—and in our opinion the new "third generation" hardware has not only reduced the cost of integrating systems but has pushed back the frontier.

Another key point has been to build in standard blocks of programming so that systems can be easily maintained and kept up to date at a high rate of change. To build an elaborate, complex, sophisticated, ideal system that does everything is a poor investment if everything it is doing is out of date.

I cannot over-emphasize the practical importance of strong systems maintenance in a business environment such as ours—where customers' addresses, credit ratings, product mix in our warehouses, freight rates, base rates for labor, and so on, are changing by the hundreds each day. In fact, in the context of Exhibit 2, I would change the old adage, "Don't bite off more than you can chew" to "Don't build a bigger house than you can maintain."

Our approach has been conservative, perhaps—certainly not glamorous—but for our company, successful. To offer an overall evaluation, after our initial study and decision to go ahead on Data Processing Systems, we made a commitment to pay out the initial investment in a network system in four years—cross the line from red to black. We did that. As to the "price tag" services, such as control reports, management information to aid in decision making, the measurement here probably can only be reflected in the total record of the business and is difficult to split out from the other aspects of P&G's management approach. Our judgment says these services, too, have been a sound investment.

QUESTIONS

1 Does the Data Processing Systems Department have top-management endorsement?

2 In your opinion, how have the guidelines affected user participation? How have they affected the system's growth?

XI. SYSTEMS PROFESSION AND SYSTEMS-ANALYST EDUCATION

This selection discusses some of the issues facing the systems analyst. Results of a survey are considered in recommending actions that should be taken by computer manufacturers, users, data-processing practitioners, and faculty members.

21 | MANAGEMENT'S PROBLEMS IN THE 1970'S— SYSTEMS ANALYSTS
D. W. MOORE

Before considering the future it is important to reflect on what the professionals in commercial data processing have achieved to date, and whether they have justified the promises that they have made or that have been made on their behalf. Although blame for failures or credit for successes can be attributed to a number of causes, in the ultimate it is the people that have been involved who are responsible. Collectively these people are both senior management and the computer professionals. I propose to consider the problem of the computer professionals and in particular the small teams of individuals working on particular projects for identifiable managers.

ACHIEVEMENTS TO DATE

Data banks, management information systems and on-line interrogation are the current jargon of the informed journalist and of the computer salesman but, as you well know, these applications are not representative of the current platform of achievement. In order to obtain a better idea of the current situation my firm has recently undertaken a survey to obtain a clearer definition of the current situation and what existing users have planned for the future. In order to obtain the maximum response from the contributors the questions were kept simple and were directed towards the requirements of systems analysts.

I do not propose to go through the detail of the survey but a few statistics will indicate its strengths and its weaknesses. Although the sample is comparatively small the results indicate current trends and the need for serious thinking and urgent action if the potential of existing equipment is to be

From *Business Management and Computers* (London: *Accountancy,* the Journal of Institute of Chartered Accountants of England and Wales), pp. 31–47; used by permission. Copyright, D. W. Moore, Peat, Marwick, Mitchell & Co., Management Consultants, London, England. D. W. Moore is with Peat, Marwick, Mitchell & Co., chartered accountants.

realized. The message becomes even stronger with the realization that using computer power will not necessarily involve owning hardware in the future. It will however involve having staff available to design and implement systems.

The Sample. Questionnaires were sent, under personal cover, to 147 organizations who were known to have computer experience, but knowledge of whose experience was fairly limited. Completed questionnaires, or apologies for lack of cooperation for understandable reasons, were received in every case.

One hundred and two questionnaires were returned and it was necessary to discard two of these, so that we have 100 reports to analyze and no need to make calculations to establish percentages.

Fifteen organizations were users of bureau services, a feature that was deliberately included as, in the author's view, the bureau user should undertake his own systems work.

The classification of companies is shown in Exhibit 1. Exhibits 2 and 3 show when users installed their first machine and the year in which they took delivery of their current equipment.

Exhibit 1

Classification of companies contributing to the survey

Industrial group	Number in Sample
Engineering	30
Insurance, banking and finance	16
Food, drink and tobacco manufacture and distribution	14
Oil and chemicals, clay and cement, glass and other manufacture	12
Textiles, leather, wood and paper industries	10
Professional, scientific and other services	6
Public utilities	6
Extractive industries and metal refining	3
Local government administration	2
Transportation and communication	1
Total	100

Exhibit 2

First machines installed
(not necessarily still in use)

1960 or earlier	8
1962–64	19
1965	10
1966	14
1967	16
1968	14
1969	4
Total	85

Exhibit 3

Delivery dates
of current equipment

1963	2%
1964	1%
1965	5%
1966	19%
1967	25%
1968	31%
Due in 1969	17%

The drop in the figures for 1969 indicate that the questionnaires were only sent to future users who were already heavily committed. It does not indicate a drop in future deliveries to new users.

These various figures provide an assurance that the survey was reasonably representative of the computer population.

APPLICATIONS—TIME AND STAFF REQUIREMENTS

Operational Projects.   Exhibit 4 indicates the wide divergences in time and staff that has been required for the general range of applications. There is a clear indication from detailed figures that elapsed time and the man/month requirement of technical staff increases with the size of the machine. This confirms the generally accepted assumption that the opportunities provided by larger machines leads to fundamental changes of systems and of management information requirements and this in turn leads to a demand for larger technical teams and longer lead times.

No evidence was collected about the complexities of the systems, the amount of project planning and control, and experience of the staff or about manufacturers' software support. These items, in varying degrees, could have accounted for the significant differences.

Exhibit 4

Time and staff requirements for various applications

Applications	Opera-tional	Staff Employed —Project Team						Dev. Period in Months		
		Min.		Max.		Av.		Min.	Max.	Av.
		S.	P.	S.	P.	S.	P.			
1 General accounting	64	¼	1	10	12	2·3	4·1	3	32	13·1
2 Sales/order invoicing	12	1	3	5	10	2·3	5·2	15	36	23·8
3 Payroll	36	1	1	2	5	1·2	2·4	6	48	15·6
4 Marketing/ sales analysis	18	½	1	2	2	1·2	1·4	4	21	13·4
5 Stock control	29	½	1	2	6	1·5	2·9	4	36	13·1
6 Production control	23	1	1	4	4	1·5	2·4	4	15	8·8
7 Costing	14	1	1	3	1	1	1·7	3·2	24	11·7
8 Purchases/ ordering	8	1	1	2	4	1·2	2·2	4	18	9·6
9 Miscellaneous (commercial)	24	—	—	—	—	—	—	—	—	—
10 Scientific and engineering	8	—	—	—	—	—	—	—	—	—

Exhibit 5

Time and staff requirements for proposed applications

Applications	Planned	Staff Employed —Project Team						Dev. Period in Months		
		Min.		Max.		Av.		Min.	Max.	Av.
		S.	P.	S.	P.	S.	P.			
1 General accounting	37	1	1	11	24	2·4	4·3	5	32	16
2 Sales/order invoicing	12	1	1	3	5	1·5	3·0	3	30	14
3 Payroll	19	1	1	3	5	1·5	2·6	4	24	10·4
4 Marketing/ sales analysis	8	1	1	2	4	1·5	2·1	5	—	—
5 Stock control	23	1	½	3	5	1·8	2·6	4	24	13·3
6 Production control	31	1	1	6	4	2·1	2·8	9	32	17·7
7 Costing	14	1	1	3	2	1·5	2·0	6	34	15·5
8 Purchases/ ordering	4	1	1	3	5	1·8	3·0	9	20	12·6

Planned Projects. Figures were collected under the same classification for projects that users propose to undertake (Exhibit 5). A comparison of average staff and time requirements indicates a marked degree of optimism particularly in regard to the sales order invoicing operation.

Staffing. (See Exhibit 6.) The average staff of systems analysts and programmers for each installation is 4.8 and 7.8 respectively, a ratio of 1:1.6. This is distributed 4.0 and 5.2 respectively on new projects and 0.8 and 2.6 on maintenance.

Projection of the turnover of staff, based on experience over the past two years, indicates that the average installation will lose 2.2, or 46 percent, of the systems analysts and 4.5, or 58 percent, of the programmers during the next two years.

Exhibit 6

Systems analysts in an "average" installation

Strength at January 1, 19x1		4.8
Anticipated losses		2.2
Remaining experienced staff		2.6
Replacements	2.2	
Additional	3.1	
"New" staff		5.3
Strength at January 1, 19x3		7.9

Exhibit 7
Sources of new analysts

Intention	No. of Co.	No. of Analysts
External recruitment of experienced analysts	48	92
External recruitment of trainees or junior analysts	23	66
Internal transfer from Organization & Methods staff	10	12
Internal transfer from programming staff	49	114
Internal transfer from other departments	32	52

In addition to the replacement of losses, the average company will require 3.1 additional systems analysts to develop new projects and maintain existing ones over the next two years.

These significant changes will create major problems and retard progress and there can be no clearer indication for the need for good data processing management, project control and effective standards and documentation in every installation if the momentum to increase the use of computer equipment is to be maintained.

Exhibit 7 indicates the sources that existing users intend to tap for their replacements.

Training of New Analysts. When resources are limited it is essential that what there are should be used efficiently. Given the right environment and encouragement from management the efficiency and productivity of a systems analyst depends on clear objectives and professional communication standards of methods and documentation. In the author's view, a trained analyst working in a professional environment achieves more than twice the effective output of a person without normal training and for whom no clear objectives and standards exist.

The training experience and intentions of users was sought and the result is shown in Exhibit 8.

Exhibit 8
Forms of training

Form of Training	Companies— Past	Companies— Future
Mainly 'on the job'	59	48
Internal courses	23	32
Manufacturers' courses	42	34
Technical colleges	20	21
Consultants' courses	28	41
	172	176

The total of companies exceeds 100 as some have experience in more than one form of training, and intend to continue in this way. The form of training varies with the background and experience of the individual.

It is a matter of some satisfaction to see the "mainly on the job" coming down particularly as some companies have it as the only form of training.

Internal Training. Companies who have internal courses or use on the job training were asked why they considered external courses unsuitable and responded as follows:

	Yes	No
Cost?	15	14
Lengths of courses?	17	7
Content of course not geared to requirements?	28	9

They were not asked details of the courses on which they had formed these opinions.

It is disturbing to see cost expressed as a reason in so many cases. Organizations are prepared to pay upwards of $250,000 for a computer installation but regard the cost of training staff to get some benefits from it as an extravagance. It would be interesting to examine the cost excuse in greater detail. One wonders whether it is a sub-conscious justification of the data processing manager to stop his staff having the benefit of training that he has not had, or to have the staff exposed to alternative methods to those that he has built up.

It is equally disturbing to see the criticism of course content. The main point on which we received elaboration was that courses placed far too much emphasis on hardware and too little on the problems of a definition of the complete system, investigation, analysis and design. This is a view with which the author agrees and hopes to have overcome in his firm's systems analysis course.

The Lessons To Be Learned from the Survey. The demand for analysts is increasing for the following reasons:

1. more computers

2. more systems becoming live and requiring maintenance

3. updating of hardware leading to the restructuring and reprogramming of established systems

4. more projects starting and the projects of experienced users becoming more complex and requiring more systems work

5. computers becoming cheaper for the power they offer and first time users having the opportunity for more complex operations than their predecessors. One wonders whether they are aware of the additional staff demands that this imposes.

6. the power of computers, when associated with telecommunications, increases the range of computer users. No longer is it necessary for a small firm, subsidiary company, factory or depot to have a machine of its own. The hardware capital investment is comparatively small, but the requirement of analysts for such systems is no less because there is no computer in the building.

7. loss of experienced analysts to other countries

THE FUTURE

The number of computers in use will increase through the efforts of the computer manufacturers, if for no other reason. The part these machines will play, for well organized companies, will be considerable and the need for less well organized companies to become more efficient will necessitate their making better use of their computers.

To avoid the pitfalls and failures of the past and to ensure sensible balanced and imaginative progress in the future, action is required by the manufacturers, the users, computer professionals, consultants, the industry training boards and the universities.

Failure to take action could lead to further disillusionment, a lack of confidence when we look at the achievements of our national and domestic competitors and something for which our successors will have every justification to regret.

Action Required by Manufacturers. It should be a matter of some disappointment to a manufacturer to see the potential of their equipment being wasted through the absence of adequate staff. They must bear some responsibility. Perhaps it is asking too much for a manufacturer to replace a large machine with a smaller one because the full power is not being used or refuse to make a sale because the potential user is not prepared to invest in adequate staff.

For those who run courses for systems analysts, examine the contents and ascertain whether there is too much bias towards the hardware and insufficient towards the user's problems. The average systems analyst, in the author's view, spends no more than 20 percent of his time on hardware problems and the remainder organizing detailed data flow and contending with the problems of the people involved in the processing or of those who propose to make use of some of the output.

Action Required by Users. Management, get involved and remain involved with your computer staff and in particular with your data processing manager and systems analysts. Remember:

1. they are designing systems for your use which you can expect to have for a number of years

2. they cannot appreciate your requirements and problems unless you define and explain them

3. they appreciate your continuing advice and guidance in the same way as other staff. You are likely to get loyalty and a reduced staff turnover if the specialists recognize your involvement and they are encouraged to identify themselves with their company.

See that you are getting value for the money you have spent on the hardware. You will only do this by having good staff. Good staff are in short supply and the position is likely to deteriorate rather than improve. To overcome the problem you need to:

1. remember the only sources of analysts are other users and, subject to training, your own organization

2. identify good material in the organization, staff with real potential

3. allocate a portion of these to your data processing organization, have them properly trained

4. see that they are effectively employed after training. This will involve good data processing management, project control, well defined standards and good communications between your data processing department and other elements of the organization

5. study the career potential of every individual in the data processing organization. See that those who have management potential in data processing and outside of it get the opportunity to develop. Transfer inadequate staff out of the department. The only man who is more expensive than an inadequate systems analyst is the inadequate managing director. It is not only their salaries, but the cost of the hardware and computer staff that they are wasting. A badly designed system that is implemented could have long term effects on the future of the organization

You must be sympathetic to your young and ambitious staff. Had you been born 20 years later you might have been one of them. Remember the frustration you suffered due to non-communicative unsympathetic management when you were young. Are you any better than they were? Due to employment problems you may not have found it easy to change your job. The competent youngster of today has no such problem. He can afford to lose you; can your organization afford to lose him?

Management, through involvement, will recognize the complexity of the new systems that are being developed. They should realize that the range of knowledge and experience required to develop and implement these systems is beyond the capabilities of most of the staff, not because of ability, but through the time required for specialization and the continuing involvement needed to keep the specialist knowledge up-to-date. During the development of complex systems there will be a requirement for problem analysts and specialists in data base management, operating systems, telecommunications, mathematical techniques and all forms of related software in addition to application analysts and programmers. If management require complex systems they must recognize the need for specialist support and when it is required, know where it can be obtained and use it. It is unreasonable for the average data processing man to try and deal with these problems in addition to the standard ones, which are often difficult enough.

There is a real danger that the generalist will assume that he can and should master all aspects of the problems. You will be very lucky if he can and the probability is that he will not succeed but a great deal of time and sympathy will have expired before he admits it or you find out. The moral is "don't try and employ a good generalist on a specialist problem." You would not expect your general practitioner to do a heart transplant for you; but that does not mean that he is not a good doctor.

Action Required by the Data Processing Practitioner.   The first requirement of a data processing professional in a user organization is to identify himself with the organization as a whole and not just the computer department and its staff. He is paid, and well paid, to make his contribution to the success of the organization. He will do this by:

1. communicating with other members of the organization in a language they understand. If he must use professional jargon then he should explain its meaning. A patella may mean something to doctors, but I communicate more easily with my doctor if he calls it a kneecap.

2. acting in a thoroughly professional manner. This involves the use of standards, project control and continuing agreement with the user of the details of the systems he is designing. An architect checks his drawings and material specification with his client before commissioning the builders. The systems analyst should do the same.

If you do not have standards or your staff are not adequately trained, bring it to the notice of your manager and ask him to take corrective action. Failure to do so will reflect on you; conversely, it is far more satisfying to work as part of a well trained team who do things in a professional manner. You can then spend your intellectual capability on things that matter rather than on the time demanding trivia that arise in a slovenly team. Help to develop other people in your team. The more capable they are the more they can take over from you and collectively, the sooner you will get projects live. Each new project is a challenge, and it is the acceptance of this challenge that makes this profession so interesting and demanding.

Remember that you are paid at the equivalent rate of middle and the lower grades of senior management. You have, in many cases, reached this level at a very young age and much earlier than you would probably have done if the computer had not been invented or introduced into your company. Because of this you are probably rather less mature and experienced in management than your non-data-processing colleagues who are on the same level. Respect this difference and treat these colleagues with particular tact and respect. This achievement and place in the organization imposes responsibility in addition to privileges. The chairman and managing directors of the future are those who prove themselves with today's responsibilities. It is for you to identify and prove yourselves rather than expecting management to do it for you. It is you who are privileged to have opportunities to make progress at a rate not open to your fathers. Make the most of it, but remember companies employ computer professionals for the benefit of the company, not for any individual.

Action Required by the Universities. It is still very disturbing to learn from graduates coming into industry that unless they have been reading mathematics or sciences they have no awareness of the place and function of computers in industry. As a result practically all graduates think of computers as "number crunchers" and have the impression that unless they are to be engaged in scientific operations the equipment will serve no part in their lives.

The computer is a management tool for information processing and reporting and the more efficient managements are making increasing use of its power.

I would like the university staff to reflect on the ability of the computer to hold data and, provided the system is properly organized, to make such data rapidly available. The opportunity to study the structure of data banks and information retrieval is something that most students would welcome, irrespective of their subject. This experience would be invaluable to the graduate coming into industry as, subject apart, it would give him some idea of data structuring for decision making and provide him with an awareness of the capabilities of the machines that are likely to significantly affect industry and commerce during this working life.

CONCLUSIONS

I have covered some of the personnel problems that are facing management today. Problems that will increase rather than diminish unless those with responsibility take action to help themselves.

I have suggested what some of the steps to improve the situation might be.

The message that I would like to register with everybody involved with computers in any form is that it is not hardware that designs airline reservation systems, on-line management information systems, or even payroll applications or invoicing systems. It is the computer professionals and personnel, and this staff is only as good as the intelligence with which it was born, developed by education and appropriate training.

If a systems analyst is better than the selection procedure that identifies him, the training that was arranged for him and the standard of management thereafter, the employer can count himself very fortunate if the analyst stays once he becomes aware of alternative opportunities.

The effectiveness of the investment in computers eventually depends on the computer staff and this is a problem for every management. Competent data processing staffs are making a considerable contribution to the future of their companies. Inefficient staff, or an inadequate number of efficient staff, are often only another contribution to the cost of an expensive status symbol.

After reviewing steps in the life cycle of information processing systems, this paper identifies various positions concerned with information-processing technology. Appropriate college curricula and courses are then suggested.

22 | EDUCATION RELATED TO THE USE OF COMPUTERS IN ORGANIZATIONS
ACM CURRICULUM COMMITTEE ON
COMPUTER EDUCATION FOR MANAGEMENT

PURPOSES AND CONCLUSIONS

The purpose of this position paper is to provide a framework for the activities of the ACM Curriculum Committee on Computer Education for Management (hereafter referred to as the Committee), in order to help

1. Crystallize thinking about programs and courses, particularly management programs in business schools and elsewhere.

2. Define research areas for business schools, computer science departments, and industry.

3. Show the interrelationships between administrative information systems and other areas of computer applications.

4. Aid organizations in their planning for staffing and education of information processing department.

To fulfill these aims requires an analysis of the role of information systems in organizations and of the requirements this imposes on the organization staff; this is done in the following section. On the basis of this analysis proposals for educational programs and the curricula can be advanced, taking into account the existing characteristics of universities and other educational institutions and the possible role to be played by professional societies and major computer users; this is done in the third section.

The preliminary conclusions of the Committee are as follows:

1. Administrative information systems should be recognized as a function of vital importance to most organizations. There are needs for both qualitative and quantitative improvements in the educational preparation of those involved in administrative information systems. In some cases, improvement can be achieved through incorporation of known knowledge and techniques into existing curricula. In others, improvement must rest upon research into the design and implementation of large scale systems. In every case, the numbers educated must be increased to meet the future needs. Both those oriented toward general management and those oriented toward more specialized aspects

of computer systems technology and modeling techniques are needed. For the latter, a professional program in information systems analysis and design would organize and transmit the growing body of knowledge.

2. The most significant educational need at present seems to be for qualified teachers and researchers, both to train future practitioners, teachers, and researchers and to expand our base of knowledge. Resources should be devoted to meeting this need.

3. Opportunities for concentration and specialization in information processing systems should be available in management, computer science, and operations research curricula. Many graduates of these programs are now in, and in the future will enter, computer related positions.

4. Introductory material on information systems and their organizational impact should be in the program of all professional students in administration/ management programs. Effective organizational use of computers depends on knowledgeable managers as well as skilled information systems specialists. A critical need exists for management training leading to a systems oriented executive and emphasizing systems interrelationships, the role of information flow, and processing and technological aids to decision making. Meeting the need requires a new area in management schools—information systems—analogous to production, finance, marketing, organization, etc.

ORGANIZATIONS AND INFORMATION SYSTEMS—THE PROBLEM

How Organizations Use Computers in Information Processing

Organizations carry out varied activities. They bake and market bread, or provide medical care, or manufacture automobiles, or educate high school graduates, etc. Management of these ongoing activities requires information describing the status of resources in use and processes underway. Further, the overall administration of an organization needs information to carry out its functions of planning, development, and control.

The information processing required to meet these needs has always been present in organizations, in departments such as accounting or production control, and by the use of the "little black books" of important data kept by most managers. Computers offer the opportunity to formalize, systematize, and automate much of that processing. Hopefully, computerized information systems can provide reduced costs for information processing and/or information of greater value (for example, more timely or complete) and/or greater control of organizational activities.

Such formalized information processing systems have several organizational implications worth noting.

1. They may promote centralization, by removing much information production and dissemination from the control of decision makers and placing it within the automated system.

2. They provide the opportunity to automatic routine decision making activity; this raises a new genre of decisions—what to automate and what to leave to decision makers.

3. Automated decisions raise the need for explicit policy formulators which themselves require continuing attention.

4. They create another formalized activity, information processing, which must also be managed.

Thus, issues arising in the use of computerized information systems involve not only technological questions, but also questions of organizational structure, of authority and responsibility, and of the role of formal modeling and decision making techniques.

Nature of Administrative Information Systems

Administrative Information Systems (AIS) includes the functions commonly termed business data processing or commercial data processing, as well as the more exotic management information systems. All of these terms have been subject to a variety of interpretations in different contexts, and contain words which serve to perpetuate misunderstandings. The term data processing has to many the connotation of routine support functions, such as payroll preparation and transaction accounting, that are necessary for the operation of organizations but prosaic in character. By contrast, the term management information systems conjures up a vision of vice-presidents gathering information and transmitting decisions through individual, remote consoles, a vision which has caused the term to assume some disrepute among those concerned with the world as it is.

Administrative Information Systems are not restricted to businesses or commercial organizations in the sense of profit seeking enterprises, since similar functions are required in the operation of organizations such as hospitals, schools, libraries, research laboratories, and government agencies.

Many aspects of information systems suitable for supporting the internal administration of an organization are also appropriate to information systems supporting its external service activities. The key emphasis in our use of the phrase is on "systems," implying complex assemblages of subsystems designed for efficient continuing use. These require capabilities at a much higher level than those needed to support one-time information analysis.

The procedures used in early business data processing systems were very simple. Computerized systems duplicated existing manual and punch card systems and made little use of the power of computers. In recent years, these procedures have become much more complex, along with the parallel development of more complex information processing technology.

As an illustration of the evolution of information processing systems, consider inventory control. Most early computerized inventory control systems require one file with one record for each part containing data on quantity-on-hand, unit price, etc. Daily transactions consisted of orders requiring items to be removed from inventory and receipts resulting in items being added to inventory.

A second level of sophistication was reached when automatic reorder levels were added. Cost and usage data were added to the file and a procedure developed to determine when a reorder was necessary. The system produced an additional output—instructions to the purchasing department to acquire additional items.

A third level of sophistication resulted from adding automatic vendor selection, intended to reduce delays in manual production of purchase orders. This required that the inventory file show which vendors could supply each part. Since many parts could be purchased from several vendors and most vendors supplied several parts, a second file was added to the system containing constant information for each vendor. An efficient technique had to be developed for referencing and retrieving a particular vendor's record.

A fourth level of sophistication arose with requirements such as minimization of transportation costs. Since transportation costs frequently depend on shipping in carload lots, a model must be added to the system which determines what other parts could also be ordered at this time to fill the carload lot. The vendor-file reference must now indicate what parts each vendor can supply.

Furthur sophistication is introduced by the requirements for immediate status reports. This requires "on-line systems" whose design requires more complicated file structures and advanced queueing-theory models to predict performance measures such as average waiting time.

The above progression has required increasingly more complicated information processing techniques. It has also required the use of increasingly more complicated modeling techniques, both to implement the desired function and to design the information processing system itself. This simple example cannot adequately convey but can only suggest the enormous increase in complexity which may accompany an evolutionary development of the type described.

Administrative information systems typically involve a large body of hardware, software, and personnel resources. Numerous effects negligible in small systems become formidable as the size of the system grows and as the interrelationships of the parts must increasingly be considered in the operations of the whole. The "comprehension of complexity" is required in a way that has no counterpart in most traditional endeavors.

Some characteristics and major interrelationships in such systems are the following:

1. The system is to operate over a period of time so that a permanence of specifications must persist through changes of individual programs and individual programmers.

2. The system must process different types of inputs and outputs. The resources of the system (hardware, software, people, time) must be allocated to the various activities and actions scheduled dynamically.

3. The processing must be subdivided into a number of parts (programs) because the hardware/software is not capable of carrying out the entire operation at one time.

4. The programs operate on data which may have to be stored in data files for varying periods of time. Data organization is a major factor in the performance of the system. The programs themselves have to be stored as data and made available as needed.

5. The operational specifications are sufficiently complex that hardware configurations must be tailored so as to maximize the stated performance criterion. Considerable software usually must be developed for the specific system.

6. The complement of hardware and software involve enough one-time and recurring costs to justify considerable effort on "optimizing" the design of the system before construction is started.

7. The operation requirement and hardware/software capabilities change over time; hence the "optimum" design changes over time.

These characteristics indicate the education and skills necessary for successful implementation of such systems. The distinction between one-shot jobs or programs and "systems with permanence" is important. Although much of computer science has been concerned with problems a programmer faces in writing a program for a particular task, recently the discipline has begun to be concerned with the study of the nature of the interrelationships of a number of programs which must together satisfy a certain requirement. Constructing and operating computer centers is but a special case of implementing such systems.

Integration of Administrative Information Systems into Organizations

An administrative information system functions both to facilitate the operations of an organization and to provide information for management control.

Information systems evolve by going through evolutionary stages. Various authors divide these stages into different phases, but generally agree on the sequence. Each of these descriptions of the life cycle starts with a determination of what the system is to do; goes through a design phase, a programming and implementation phase, and operation of the system; and ends with the modification of the system. Exhibit 1 gives a comparison of the phases suggested by several authors and shows the phases covered by the positions in information processing technology used in this report.

The development of models and the implementation of their solution procedures enter into information systems design in several ways. Model formulation is important both for the design of information systems themselves and for the specification of certain information processing procedures within the system. Operations research, systems engineering, and accounting all provide viewpoints and techniques appropriate to such modeling.

Exhibit 1

Steps in the life cycle of information processing systems

Teichroew (a) 1968	Glans et al. 1968	British Computer Society Working Party 10 1967	Positions Used in This Report
Phase	Stage Phase		
(1) Perception of need	1 Study and Design	Information Analysis	Information analysis
(a) What should the requirements be?	1 Study present system	Appraisal of information needs	
(2) Statement of requirements	2 Determine system requirements	Outline, design, and justification of information system	
(a) Determination of requirements			
(b) Statement of requirements			
(3) Systems design	3 Design new system	Systems Design	Systems designer
(a) Generation of feasible design		Specification of processing requirements for system	
(b) Evaluation of feasible design			
(c) Selection of equipment			
(d) Improvement of feasible design		Procedure Design	
(e) Optimization		Planning and specifying noncomputer processing	
(4) Construction	2 Implementation	Programming	Programmer
(a) System		Planning and writing computer programs	
(b) Program			
(c) Files			
(5) Testing		Implementation	
		Implementation of system	
(6) Operation	3 Operation		IPD operation
(7) Modification			Programmer†

† Information analyst and systems designer will be involved if modifications are extensive.

Positions in Administrative Information Systems Development

There are a large number of positions in organizations which are related to information systems, and no standard list of job titles or job descriptions exists. For this paper we adopt a simplified classification which identifies major functions and permits discussion of educational requirements. This classification is only in part consistent with current practice, since it attempts to reflect structural trends accompanying the emergence of information systems as an identifiable organizational component.

Three different job specializations—information analyst, systems designer, and programmer—are identified and described; the analysis is summarized in Exhibit 2.

The distinction between these categories can be seen from the sequence in which problems become defined more and more specifically. The information analyst works with managers and specialists in modeling techniques to specify what functions the system will perform. The systems designer takes such specifications and, knowing the general capabilities of hardware and software, designs systems, subdividing the problem into parts. Each part is then given to a programmer, who develops and tests the individual programs. The programmer is oriented toward the tools he uses—hardware and software. The systems designer is technology oriented—the technology he uses is that of specifying a number of parts, both hardware and software, which together accomplish a set of requirements. The information analyst is user oriented; he must be able to articulate what managers want (or need) and to determine what proposed systems are feasible.

Information processing systems are tools constructed to serve some user or users, and the user must have the ultimate responsibility for what products he asks of the system. In large information processing systems the "user" is usually a number of individuals or even the organization itself. The determination of requirements is, therefore, not a simple matter and the actual collection involves discussion with the many users, and coordination and arbitration of competing requirements. The task is frequently given to ad hoc committees. The title information analyst, rather than systems analyst, is used to emphasize the collection and development of information processing concepts and requirements rather than the design of systems.

The systems designer receives a statement of requirements and then is concerned with how best to accomplish these requirements. (In practice, the systems designer may frequently be involved in the collection and recording of requirements, but as a liaison function, not by authority of position or knowledge.) The term systems designer is used to emphasize responsibility only for "how," not for "what."

In practice, the development of an information processing system is not the ideal linear process implied by Exhibit 1 and the above remarks. There are numerous feedback loops and iterations, with the several functions frequently overlapping with beneficial results. The task force or systems group may provide an effective environment for the fruitful interplay of the specialists. Also, the

Exhibit 2

Information processing technologists' positions

Title	Function	Knowledge	Communicates With	Orientation	Experience	Education Requirement for Entry
Programmer	Prepare, debug, and test programs according to specifications prepared by systems designer	Programing techniques, computer capability, software capability	Systems designer	Software and hardware oriented	With programming languages	Some college
Systems designer	Prepare specification for AIS and break it down into sufficient detail Perform feasibility studies	Systems design techniques, operations research	Information analyst and programmer	Concerned with overall system performance	Some programming experience desirable	Professional degree, master's level
Information analyst	Develop overall requirements concepts of AIS and how it will fit into the organization	Understanding of operation and goals of the organization and system design	Users, systems designer, and specialists in modeling techniques	User oriented	Some time in the organization	Master's level

development of information processing systems often requires the services of other specialists such as communications engineers, systems engineers, operations researchers, and accountants.

PROFESSIONAL DEGREE PROGRAMS
IN INFORMATION SYSTEMS DESIGN

A professional (master's degree) program in information analysis and systems design is needed. Positions exist in industry for which a body of prerequisite knowledge is required. More formal training than can be obtained in short courses or supplementary reading is needed. Such a program should be conceived as a new program at some institutions of higher education in the country today. The curriculum would consist of five major topic areas, with emphasis on applications and field study as well as theory.

Computer Science.   Particularly, this area would include topics in hardware and software systems. The systems analyst and designer needs to be familiar with this material but does not need the technical depth necessary for those who plan careers in academic computer science departments.

Information Systems.   This area would include general theory of systems, types of system organization, man-machine communication, and management and sociological aspects of systems. These topics would be covered in depth.

Management.   This would be a basic introduction to general management principles and functional areas. This area is necessary to enable systems designers to understand management practices and objectives and to apply management principles to management of information processing departments.

Operations Research.   This area would include techniques for model building and model solution both for deterministic and probabilistic models. These topics are necessary to permit systems designers to develop models and use appropriate optimization techniques.

Systems Design Techniques.   This area would include life cycle of information processing systems, planning and control of projects, documentation, formal techniques, use of generalized software packages.

Applications and field studies will examine implementation of systems design in such areas as computer center management, management information systems, and information retrieval systems.